Junio
2003

Con Aprecio y
admiración por su trabajo
espero que lo disfrute

Vanessa

ACCULTURATION
AND PSYCHOLOGICAL
ADAPTATION

Recent Titles in
Contributions in Psychology

ACCULTURATION AND PSYCHOLOGICAL ADAPTATION

Vanessa Smith Castro

Foreword by Ulrich Wagner and Thomas F. Pettigrew

Contributions in Psychology, Number 41
Paul Pedersen, Series Adviser

GREENWOOD PRESS
Westport, Connecticut • London

Library of Congress Cataloging-in-Publication Data

Castro, Vanessa Smith, 1969–
 Acculturation and psychological adaptation / Vanessa Smith Castro ; foreword by
 Ulrich Wagner and Thomas F. Pettigrew.
  p. cm. — (Contributions in psychology, ISSN 0736-2714 ; no. 41)
 Includes bibliographical references and index.
 ISBN 0–313–32327–5 (alk. paper)
  1. Acculturation. 2. Adaptation (Psychology). 3. Ethnicity. 4. Intergroup
 relations—Costa Rica. 5. Costa Rica—Ethnic relations. I. Title. II. Series.
 HM841.C37 2003
 305.8—dc21   2002070035

British Library Cataloguing in Publication Data is available.

Library of Congress Catalog Card Number: 2002070035
ISBN: 0–313–32327–5
ISSN: 0736-2714

First published in 2003

Greenwood Press, 88 Post Road West, Westport, CT 06881
An imprint of Greenwood Publishing Group, Inc.
www.greenwood.com

Printed in the United States of America

The paper used in this book complies with the
Permanent Paper Standard issued by the National
Information Standards Organization (Z39.48–1984).

10 9 8 7 6 5 4 3 2 1

This book was accepted as a dissertation at the University of Marburg. Zugl.: Marburg, Univ.
Diss.2001.

Contents

Tables and Figures

FIGURES

Foreword

Ulrich Wagner and Thomas F. Pettigrew

What can be said about ethnic intergroup relations in a country that up to now rarely has had the opportunity to analyze this topic empirically? This book contains an initial and ambitious analysis of intergroup relations in Costa Rica, the author's native land, which has witnessed little social psychological work.

Vanessa Smith Castro provides an excellent review of a range of social psychological theories that are woven together: theories of acculturation, ethnic identity, stereotypes, prejudice, intergroup contact, and self-esteem. The models' theoretical implications were tested on a data set of about 1,174 Costa Rican high school students who participated in the main study. With a variety of sophisticated methods, the analyses reveal that the theoretical predictions also hold for the Costa Rican cultural context. Thus, the book is an empirical cross-national validation of theories of North American and European origin.

This volume, then, is an important and groundbreaking work. It affords a valuable model for future research on intergroup relations in nations without an established body of work in the area. Its multifaceted point of view makes it highly useful for readers interested in intergroup relations theory and research as well as for professionals and scholars who specialize in intercultural comparisons.

Acknowledgments

As every researcher knows, any academic work is the product of teamwork. It simply could never have been written without the support and patience of one's family, friends, and colleagues. I would like to express my gratitude to them for sharing with me all the ups and downs during the process of completing this work.

I am grateful for the tireless effort that Debbie Carvalko at Greenwood Press devoted to this project. She has been a key source of support and a helpful guide for me as I began the enterprise to write a book. I am also grateful to Paul Pedersen, series editor, who offered indispensable insight and critique.

This research was funded by a grant of the Friedrich-Ebert-Stiftung. I would like to thank Mrs. Maria Holona from the section of foreign postgraduate students for her efforts and efficiency in all my requests and problems. She allowed me the trust and flexibility necessary to finish this work, although we have never met personally. I would also like to thank the faculty of psychology at the Philipps University, Germany. Any foreign student would envy me, knowing the way in which I was warmly integrated into the faculty.

I am privileged to have had the support of a marvelous supervision team, to which I am deeply grateful. Dr. Ulrich Wagner believed (perhaps more than I) in this project. I am indebted to him for his wisdom, help, advice, constructive criticism, and tireless enthusiasm. Dr. Thomas F. Pettigrew's contribution to this work was also decisive, intellectually and personally. It is an honor for me to receive the attention of one of the leading social psychologists in the world. Dr. Rolf van Dick carefully read every page in draft, and accompanied the process from the beginning. I am grateful for all his patience in answering every conceptual, methodological, and statistical question, but in particular for his constant encouragement.

The social psychology team at Philipps University provided me with the best emotional and intellectual environment one can imagine. Thanks to Dr. Andreas Homburg for teaching me how to organize my ideas and time, to Jost Stellmacher for his comprehension and emotional support, to Hinna Wolf for the "unofficial" supervision sessions, and especially to Oliver Christ for his patience and "good humor."

Many other colleagues and friends also played an important role in this work. I am especially grateful to Domingo Campos, principal of the Institute for Psychological Research at the University of Costa Rica, for his support in all phases of the project. Thanks also to Roxana Hidalgo, Daniel Rojas, Mariano Rosabal, Taly Dueñas, Leonardo Camacho, and Edgar Sánchez for their help in preparing the data collection, and to Marie-Pierre Aime for her decisive assistance in this phase of the study.

I thank my father, Carlos Smith, my mother, Melba Castro, my sister, Karla, and my brothers Daniel and Carlos, as well as my family-in-law, from whom I received continuous support and encouragement in spite of the long distance that divided us during my stay in Germany.

Most of all I would like to thank my husband, Rolando Pérez. I cannot thank him enough for his support, patience, and love during the hard time we both were completing our Ph.D. studies. This is for you.

Introduction

One of the most enduring ideas in social psychology is that social groups are important sources of self-definition (see Allport, 1954; Mead, 1934; Sherif & Sherif, 1979; Tajfel, 1981). Research in this field has shown that the way in which people relate to their social groups of reference as well as other relevant social groups in society has important repercussions for their psychological well-being and personal satisfaction (see Crocker & Major, 1989; Harter, 1996; Phinney, 1990; Wylie, 1979). Within acculturation research, these issues have been addressed in terms of the long-term psychological outcomes of interacting in culturally plural societies (see Berry, 1997; Bourhis, Moise, Perreault, & Senéca, 1997; Szapocznik, Kurtines, & Fernández, 1980). According to this line of research, living in ethnically plural settings implies a constant process of negotiation of the role that both ethnic ingroups and outgroups will play in the definition of the self. This has been conceptualized as decision-making processes regarding two central dimensions of acculturation: (1) the maintenance of cultural distinctiveness and (2) the maintenance of positive interethnic contact (Berry, 1997).

The well-known acculturation strategies of integration, separation, assimilation, and marginalization emerge from these decision-making processes. More specifically, those individuals who consider it of value to maintain their ethnic identity and, at the same time, to maintain relationships with members of other ethnic groups are considered to endorse an *integration* strategy. Those who posit an exclusive value on the maintenance of their cultural distinctiveness and do not cherish interethnic relations are assumed to adopt a *separation* strategy. By contrast, those individuals who are less concerned with the maintenance of their ethnic identity but value interethnic relations are seen to endorse *assimilation* strategies. Finally, those individuals who value neither the maintenance of their ethnic identity nor relationships with members of other ethnic groups are considered to be *marginalized*.

A great deal of research on interethnic contact and acculturation has shown that these strategies are also important factors affecting how individuals adapt to ethnically plural settings and, in turn, how satisfied they feel as individuals and as members of a subgroup within the larger society (Doná & Berry, 1994; Phinney, 1991; Ward & Rana-Deuba, 1999). Integration seems to afford the most positive psychological outcomes and marginalization the least, while assimilation and separation relate to intermediate levels of psychological adjustment.

The main goal of this book is to take a closer look to the process of acculturation among members of ethnic minorities and majorities in Latin American settings, focusing on the role of acculturation dimensions and strategies in shaping one important source of psychological adjustment; namely, self-esteem. This aim has at least three important challenges for empirical research on these issues. The first refers to the multiple causation of acculturation and psychological adaptation. The second involves the measurement of acculturation dimensions and strategies. The third relates to the inclusion of cultural variation in the analysis.

THE STUDY OF ACCULTURATION:
HEURISTIC AND METHODOLOGICAL CHALLENGES

Both research and theory have stressed the complexity of acculturation phenomena. Many studies have shown that there are several variables—other than acculturation dimensions and strategies—that might affect the way in which individuals came into contact and acculturate (see van Dick, Wagner, Adams, & Petzel, 1997; Doná & Berry, 1994; Lalonde & Cameron, 1993; Phinney, Chavira, & Williamson, 1992; Piontkowski, Florack, Hoelker, & Obdrzálek, 2000; van Oudenhoven & Eisses, 1998; Roccas, Horenczyk, & Schwartz, 2000). Factors range from the sociohistorical conditions that cause intercultural contact to specific individual differences in coping with these encounters. Thus, when studying acculturation processes researchers are faced with the task of taking into account other important determinants of the psychological outcomes of acculturation in order to detect the specific contribution of acculturation dimensions and strategies. The challenge consists in including those that are relevant.

Likewise, researchers are faced with the methodological challenge implicated in testing the independent effect of two dimensions and four strategies of acculturation on self-esteem. Clearly, this depends on the operationalization of the constructs. Traditionally, acculturation strategies have been measured with four (theoretically) independent measures of attitudes toward each of the acculturation modes (see Berry, Kim, Power, Young, & Bujaki, 1989). Although widely used, these scales have several shortcomings. One of their central limitations is that the more fundamental acculturation dimensions cannot be assessed with them, which implies considering other ways to measure acculturation dimensions and strategies.

In order to address the first challenge, a framework for research on ethnic groups is proposed here. As a possible heuristic, this framework selects several variables that have been found to affect how ethnic group members come into interethnic contact and acculturate, and articulates them in a model guiding the research summarized in this book. At the group level, perceived ethnic discrimination, perceived ingroup status, and the ethnic composition of the immediate environment appear to be consistent predictors of acculturation and psychological adaptation. At the individual level, individuals' experience of interethnic contact and demographic variables such as ethnicity, socioeconomic status, gender, and age have been found to be important determinants of acculturation outcomes. The first three variables represent group-level factors affecting acculturation. They refer to the objective features of the social context as well as the subjective experience of the intergroup context. The remaining variables are considered as individual-level factors affecting acculturation. These refer to the objective and subjective experiences that individuals bring into interethnic contact. Thus, while incorporating the potential effects of these variables in the analyses, this book provides a more differentiated picture of the multiple causation of adaptation in ethnically plural societies.

In order to address the second challenge, an alternative to the conventional measures of four acculturation strategies is proposed here. Two independent scales of ingroup identification and interethnic attitudes in combination with a dichotomization technique were employed to classify participants into four categories representing integration, separation, assimilation, and marginalization. Hence, this book highlights methodological issues exploring the advantages and limitations of this alternative approach and examining the cross-cultural applicability of the measures involved in this procedure.

THE STUDY OF ACCULTURATION: INCLUDING CULTURAL DIVERSITY

Most research on acculturation has focused on the processes of adaptation to North American and European settings. Yet very little is known about these issues in African, Asian, or Latin American contexts, in which perhaps most acculturation takes place. The study of acculturation in settings other than Western industrialized countries not only represents a further challenge for cross-cultural psychologists, but also a promising avenue for increasing our knowledge about the psychological consequences of cultural contact and acculturation.

Latin America represents an outstanding case of intercultural contact and acculturation. Because Latin America emerges as the convergence of indigenous, European, and African cultural systems, the people of Latin America show a variety of ethnic heritages without comparison in any other region that deserve more attention than they have received before.

Thus, in order to respond to the third challenge, this book is devoted to the analysis of acculturation and psychological adaptation in Costa Rican settings. The Costa Rican society reflects the cultural diversification that characterizes Latin American countries in many ways.

As most countries in Latin America and Caribbean regions, Costa Rica is made up of a variety of ethnic and cultural groups. Most of them (approximately 95%) are of European heritage, principally of mixed Spanish and Native American ancestry, or "Mestizos." The principal ethnic minorities of Costa Rica are the native community, or "Indígenas," comprising approximately 1% percent of the population, the Chinese community, also constituting 1% of the total population, and the Black or Afro-Caribbean community—the focus of this book—which represents the largest ethnic minority of the country, comprising about 2% of the Costa Rican population.

The African immigration to Latin America began with the European "conquista." After emancipation, there were also important emigration flows of African descendants within Latin American countries. Most Blacks in Costa Rica are descendants of this second immigration flow, which began in 1872 with the arrival of the first groups of "guest workers" from Kingston, recruited to build the Atlantic Railroad (Meléndez & Duncan, 1981). The social situation of Blacks in Costa Rica during the late nineteenth and early twentieth centuries was not very different from their situation in other Latin America countries. The Black community was the target of racist immigration and residence laws that restricted them to the Caribbean coast for many decades. Only as late as 1949 the new constitution abrogated the apartheid on the Atlantic Railroad, providing citizenship and full guarantees for all nationals regardless of their ethnic background (Fernández, 1977). Currently the integration policy has gradually shifted away from the negation to the recognition of the ethnic diversity of the country (see Dobles, Fournier, & Pérez, 1996). However, this is not to say that interethnic relations are completely harmonious. Issues such as discrimination and prejudice toward ethnic minorities are ubiquitous in Costa Rican society (see Duncan & Powel, 1988; Ruiz, 1988).

Finally, as in several Latin American countries, the Black community has maintained a particular cultural background that certainly shapes their economic, politic, social, and cultural integration. The cultural heritage of the Black community is a syncretism of English, African, and Spanish practices, while the cultural background of the White majority is strongly influenced by the Spanish Catholic tradition (Sawyers & Perry, 1996).

Thus, while including both ethnic majority and minority members, this book addresses the particular experiences of group members who differ in terms of their histories, cultural backgrounds, and relative social statuses. It is assumed that the effects of acculturation can be observed among members of all groups involved in intercultural contact, but at the same time it is expected that these effects vary across groups according to their specific characteristics (Berry & Sam, 1997).

In summary, this book attempts to offer a comprehensive view of acculturation and adaptation in a region largely neglected by cross-cultural psychologists. At the same time it represents a value opportunity to test the cross-cultural applicability of theoretical models and empirical methods derived from research on acculturation to North American and European settings.

A NOTE ON ORGANIZATION

This book begins with an account of relevant theoretical and empirical literature on interethnic contact and acculturation. Chapter 1 focuses on recent developments in acculturation research. Two distinct approaches have guided research on these issues: the linear–bipolar approach and the two-dimensional perspective. The former assumes that acculturation is a process of absorption into the dominant culture, while the latter suggests that individuals can maintain positive ties with the mainstream culture without losing the cultural distinctiveness provided by their ethnic group of reference. Special attention is paid here on the second approach. One of the most cited works within this perspective involve Berry's acculturation model. In fact, Berry (1980) was one of the first writers to propose that the dimensions of acculturation can be thought as independent factors. However, Berry's model is one of several orthogonal approaches reviewed here (e.g., Bourhis et al., 1997; Sayegh & Lasry, 1993; Szapocznik et al., 1980). While incorporating the extensive literature of social identity and intergroup relations in their conceptualizations, these new perspectives are especially appropriate to understand the complexities of acculturation in modern national states.

Chapter 2 deals with the first dimension of acculturation, defined here as the level of identification with the ethnic groups of reference or ethnic identity. Using the social identity theory (Tajfel & Turner, 1979) as the conceptual basis for the analysis of this dimension, this chapter examines relevant correlates and determinants of ethnic identity. The social identity approach provides a comprehensive view of the meaning and consequences of ethnic group memberships in ethnically plural societies by addressing cognitive mechanisms, motivational processes, and the specific features of intergroup relations as central determinants of ethnic identity.

In Chapter 3 the extensive literature on intergroup relations is examined in order to address the processes underlying the second dimension of acculturation, contact, and participation. Amazingly, many researchers on acculturation have neglected the specific issue of intergroup relations in their analyses. This chapter provides valuable insights from this literature to understand more deeply how people came into contact and acculturate.

Chapter 4 integrates both theory and empirical findings reported in previous chapters in order to describe, explain, and predict the specific outcomes of the two dimensions and four strategies of acculturation for individuals' personal adjustment to ethnically plural societies.

In Chapter 5 the discussion turns to methodological issues. Because one important concern of this book is to provide data suitable for cross-cultural comparison, most measures used here were derived from scales successfully used in other cultural settings. Hence, this chapter pays special attention to the assessment of acculturation dimensions and strategies and the processes of scale adaptation, including the results of a preliminary study conducted to test the psychometric properties of the measures.

Chapter 6 is a detailed description of the empirical test of the central research hypotheses. Data show that the process of acculturation is highly complex, revealing the existence of both general aspects of the acculturation processes that apply across ethnic groups and specific outcomes depending on the particular characteristics of the ethnic groups and their relative status in the society. Although complex, the pattern of relationship among the variables is highly concordant with predictions derived from research on acculturation, social identity, and intergroup relations. Furthermore, the present results show an amazing concordance with data from research carried out in diverse cultural settings in countries such as the United States, Canada, Germany, Switzerland, Slovakia, Australia, and New Zealand, suggesting that we are perhaps faced with universal patterns, at least in Western societies. This is discussed with more detail in Chapter 7, which address both empirical and methodological issues and provides some suggestions for future research.

1

Cultural Contact
and Acculturation

Traditionally, cross-cultural psychology has been concerned with variation on human behavior across cultures. Since opportunities for intercultural contact in the world are increasing and societies are becoming more ethnically diverse, some cross-cultural psychologists have focused on the cultural and psychological changes resulting from intercultural interactions within larger national frameworks. The field, which deals with processes and outcomes of intercultural contact in plural societies, is known as acculturation research (Berry, Portinga, Segall, & Dasen, 1992). In this chapter the more recent developments of this field will be examined.

The first section presents some basic definitions that are shared by most authors. However, since the concept of acculturation has become widely used not only by cross-cultural psychologists but also by the public, some conceptual distinctions and specifications are necessary. The second part summarizes the principal theoretical models proposed to describe the process and outcomes of acculturation. The literature offers various theoretical models to address these issues. The approaches are in part overlapping and interrelated; nevertheless, it is worth reviewing their contributions separately before examining commonalities. The third part systematizes the main factors underlying the process of psychological acculturation. Based on previous conceptualizations (Berry et al., 1992), this section presents a framework for research on acculturation involving ethnic groups with a long experience of intercultural contact. The major aim of this framework is to provide a conceptual guide for the present research by stressing those variables assumed to be central in the study of acculturation and adaptation among these types of acculturating groups. The chapter ends with an overview of the central hypotheses advanced from the proposed framework.

ACCULTURATION

The term *acculturation* was introduced by anthropologists to refer to cultural changes that emerge from intercultural contact. Redfield, Linton, and Herskovits (1936) proposed the following definition: "Acculturation comprehends those phenomena, which result when groups of individuals having different cultures come into continuous first-hand contact with subsequent changes in the original culture patterns of either or both groups" (p. 149). A more specific conceptualization was proposed by the Social Sciences Research Council (SSRC) in 1954:

Acculturation may be defined as cultural change that is initiated by the conjunction of two or more autonomous cultural systems. Acculturative change may be the consequence of direct cultural transmission: it may be derived from noncultural causes, such as ecological or demographic modifications induced by an impinging culture; it may be delayed, as with internal adjustments following upon the acceptance of alien traits or patterns; or it may be a reactive adaptation of traditional modes of life. Its dynamics can be seen as the selective adaptation of value systems, the process of integration and differentiation, the generation of developmental sequences, and the operation of role determinants and personality factors. (p. 974)

In spite of the apparent consensus around this definition in cross-cultural psychology, acculturation must be distinguished from other terms widely used in social sciences to refer to related but different phenomena. One of them is the term *enculturation*. Enculturation refers to the process by which the developing individual learns the culture (language, norms, values, etc.) of his or her group (Berry et al., 1992). Together with socialization, enculturation forms part of the mechanism of cultural transmission within a culture. In contrast, acculturation refers to second-culture acquisition through contact with different cultures.

Acculturation is also to be differentiated from *cultural change*. Cultural change is used to describe the process that leads to changes at the population level when the sources of change are internal events such as invention, discoveries, and innovation within a culture. By contrast, acculturation refers to the process that leads to changes at the population level when the source of change is contact with other cultures (Berry, 1995). Furthermore, contact or interaction between cultural groups is supposed to be continuous and firsthand. Thus, although acculturation research deals with individual reactions to cultural change whatever its origins, there are some types of contact that are not directly included in the current definition, such as short-term accidental encounters or diffusion of ideas, values, and artifacts over long distances (e.g., through mass media).

A further distinction has been introduced by Graves (1967) concerning the level of analysis involved in the concept. He points out that acculturation at the population level should be distinguished from individual acculturation experiences. According to this, acculturation is employed to refer to changes in social structure, economic base, and political organization of the groups involved in the acculturation process, while *psychological acculturation* is used to refer to changes in behaviors, attitudes, values, and identities of the individuals whose referent groups are experiencing acculturation. Thus, while keeping levels of analysis straight (Pettigrew, 1996), acculturation research is able to account not only for individual differences on acculturation within a cultural group, but also for the systematic relationships between group-level and individual-level phenomena.

While psychological acculturation refers to the changes resulting from intercultural encounters at the individual level, the term *psychological adaptation* is used to describe the personal long-term outcomes of these processes. Adaptation has been commonly referred to as the level of "fit" between the acculturating individual and the mainstream cultural context (Berry, 1997). Positive adaptation comprises a clear sense of personal and cultural identity, good mental health, high self-esteem, and the achievement of efficient cultural and social competencies, while negative outcomes are reflected in anxiety, depression, feelings of anomie, psychosomatic symptoms, and identity confusion (Berry & Sam, 1997; LaFromboise, Coleman, & Gerton, 1993; Phinney, 1991; Willams & Berry, 1991). Although psychological acculturation and adaptation seem to be intrinsically related to each other, it seems important to distinguish the psychological changes underlying acculturation from the specific psychological outcomes of acculturation. In this chapter the focus will be on the former; the specific consequences of acculturation for individuals' well-being will be discussed in more detail in Chapter 4.

Finally, the term acculturation has been used by some authors as virtually synonymous with *assimilation*, while other scholars define assimilation as only one possible outcome of acculturation (see Berry, 1997). These differences are related to how the acculturation process has been conceptualized by the different theoretical models. These will be discussed in the next section. For the moment, the central idea is that acculturation refers to both the general process (that takes place over time) and the results (that are both cultural and psychological) of cultural contact (Berry & Sam, 1997).

In summary, while attempting to understand psychological responses to intercultural contact, cross-cultural psychologists use the term acculturation to describe cultural changes that occur when two more or less autonomous cultural systems come into continuous contact. The concept of psychological acculturation is employed to refer to changes on individuals' behaviors, attitudes, and values resulting from such encounters, and the term psychological adaptation refers to the psychological outcomes of acculturation.

Since the core of the concept is the idea that acculturation results from cultural interactions, it is necessary to recognize that in most cases cultural groups in plural societies have unequal access to socially valued resources (wealth, income, property, and cultural products). Likewise, it should be noted that cultural groups vary in the ways in which they come into contact (colonial expansion, international trade, invasion, or migration).

The consequences of these issues for the research on acculturation involving ethnic groups will be discussed in the third section of this chapter. For the present conceptualization, structural inequalities and the nature of contact imply that in practice the acculturation process mostly has a greater impact on and is more evident among immigrants and ethnic minorities than among members of the host or dominant culture. Because of this, it is not surprising that most research on acculturation has been conducted with the former acculturating groups. Nevertheless, it is argued here that both cultural and psychological changes take place in all groups involved in the contact. Cultures are viewed here as changing contexts, and acculturation as a special case of mutual influence between cultures.

MODELS OF ACCULTURATION

Much of the research on acculturation in recent decades has been guided by two distinct sets of models: linear–bipolar models (e.g., Gordon, 1978) and two-dimensional or multicultural models (e.g., Berry, 1980). Linear models assume that acculturation is a process of absorption into the dominant culture implying a loss of identification with the culture of origin (or ethnic group). By contrast, the basic premise of bidimensional models is that individuals can develop positive ties with both the referent ethnic group and the new or mainstream culture. The next section focuses on the central assumptions of these models and offers some research examples.

Linear–Bipolar Models

Among early theorists the process of immigrants' and ethnic minority members' adaptation to the host or larger society was described as a unidirectional process involving a change in their values, attitudes, and behaviors and a decrease in their identification with their groups of reference. Thus, it is not surprising that acculturation phenomena were commonly studied under the term of assimilation.

Assimilation Model

Based in the analysis of the social structures underlying American interethnic relations, Gordon (1978) proposed a model that describes the adjustment of immigrants and ethnic minority members to the larger society. According to Gordon, when immigrants settle in the new nation, several changes occur in their social structures, cultural patterns, and psychological features from one generation to another. He employed the term assimilation to describe these changes and proposed the following subprocesses or stages of assimilation: (1) cultural assimilation or acculturation, defined as the gradual acquisition of cultural patterns of the host society; (2) structural assimilation (i.e., the entrance into the societal network of groups and institutions of the society); (3) marital assimilation or amalgamation, indicated by large-scale interethnic marriages; (4) identificational assimilation, which referred to the self-identification as a member of the host society; (5) attitude receptional assimilation; (6) behavioral receptional assimilation; and (7) civic assimilation. The last three referred to the condition in which interethnic relations are free of prejudice, discrimination, and intergroup conflict, respectively (see Table 1.1).

As the definition suggests, assimilation is a gradual process of absorption into the host society at both the group and individual levels. According to the model, cultural assimilation represents the first stage of the process. It may

Table 1.1
Gordon's Model of Assimilation

TYPE OF ASSIMILATION	SUBPROCESS
Cultural assimilation or acculturation	Change of cultural patterns to those of host society.
Structural assimilation	Large-scale entrance into institutions of host society.
Marital assimilation or amalgamation	Large-scale intermarriage.
Identificational assimilation	Development of sense of peoplehood based exclusively on the host society.
Attitude assimilation	Absence of prejudice.
Behavioral assimilation	Absence of discrimination.
Civic assimilation	Absence of valued and power conflict.

Source: Modified from Table 1 in Gordon (1978, p. 16).

take place in the absence of other types of assimilation and may continue indefinitely. However, acculturation does not represent a prerequisite or guarantee for structural assimilation and reduction of intergroup conflict. This is particularly evident in the unique experience of those groups faced with forced spatial isolation and segregation (as in the case of Native Americans) or blatant discrimination and racism (as in the case of African Americans). Gordon (1978) points out that structural assimilation, rather than acculturation, is the central process of assimilation: "Once structural assimilation has occurred, either simultaneously with or subsequent to acculturation, all of the other types of assimilation will naturally follow. . . . Acculturation, as we have emphasized above, does not necessarily lead to structural assimilation, structural assimilation inevitably produces acculturation" (p. 178).

The logic of this generalization is that structural assimilation involves primary (intimate or family-oriented) interethnic relationships that will lead to a substantial increase of interethnic marriages. Once marital assimilation fully takes place, the minority group loses its ethnic identity, while strong ties with the host society emerge gradually; since descendants of intermarriages become ethnically indistinguishable, prejudice and discrimination should no longer be a problem. Thus, the result of assimilation is a situation in which the minority ethnic group becomes an indissoluble part of the mainstream culture (Gordon, 1978).

Theoretically, assimilation could have different outcomes according to what kind of intergroup relation is desirable in a society (e.g., melting pot or cultural pluralism). The central assumption of the model is, however, that contact with the host society leads to a loss of the original cultural patterns and identity as groups and individuals move through the assimilation stages. The best way to describe this assumption is conceiving assimilation as a continuum, with strong ties to the ethnic group of reference and high cultural and social distinctiveness at one extreme and strong ties to the host society, low identification with the referent ethnic group, and low cultural distinctiveness at the other extreme. Even *biculturalism* was seen as the midpoint of the continuum, representing a transitional phase on the way to complete assimilation (Bourhis, Moise, Perreault, & Senéca, 1997).

A substantial amount of empirical research has been guided by the assimilation model (see Buriel, 1987; Padilla, 1980; Polat, 1998; Portera, 1985; Szapocznik, Scopetta, Kurtines, & Aranalde, 1978). Acculturation has been inferred using generational status or length of residence in the host country or assessed using ethnic self-labeling, attitudes toward both the referent ethnic group and the mainstream culture, and familiarity with traditional and mainstream cultural patterns. The major goal of these studies has been to test the hypothesis that the more time people have been interacting with the dominant society, the higher their engagement into the dominant cultural values and the lower their ethnic group identification will be.

In a study of Italian immigrants in Germany, Portera (1985) found a relationship between preferred ethnic label ("Italian" or "German") and age at immigration. "German" was used significantly more among those who were born in Germany or arrived at a younger age. Expecting to find a similar tendency, Polat (1998) conducted a study with 306 Turkish immigrants in Hamburg. However, the results revealed no such relationship. Instead, Polat found an association between age at immigration and self-report of mastery, exposure, and use of German language as an index of involvement with the host society. Forty-four percent of those who were born in Germany ($N = 129$) and 40.6% of those who arrived at preschool age ($N = 64$) reported good knowledge of German, while only 11% of those who arrived at adolescence ($N = 45$) evaluated their German proficiency as good. A similar pattern was found when respondents reported the use of German language with friends, brothers, and sisters. On the other hand, the self-report of Turkish language proficiency and usage shows a reverse pattern. In contrast to 62.2% of those who immigrated at adolescence, only 3.1% of German-born participants report good Turkish knowledge. Phinney (1990) suggests that the use of labels varies across ethnic groups. This is related to the fact that the use of an ethnic label among those who are racially and ethnically distinct is at least partly imposed, while members of other ethnic groups can see the usage of ethnic labels as an option. Thus, because of their distinctive appearance Turkish immigrants may be pressed to continue expressing a Turkish identity despite their relatively poor involvement with their ethnic group.

The work of Buriel and colleagues (see Buriel, 1987; Buriel & Vasquez, 1982) provides more examples of research within the assimilation model of acculturation. The aim of their studies was to explore the association between generational status, preferred ethnic labels ("Mexican," "Mexican American," "Chicano," "Latino," "Spanish American," or "Anglo American") and several indices of involvement with Mexican culture (e.g., Spanish language proficiency, ethnic behaviors) among Mexican-American children and adolescents. The first study (Buriel & Vasquez, 1982) was conducted with ninety Mexican-origin youths equally distributed in three generational categories: first generation (respondent and both parents born in Mexico), second generation (at least one parent born in Mexico), and third generation (respondent and both parents born in the United States). Results revealed a preference for the label "Mexican" in the first generation, followed by a decrease in its use in the second and third generation, as well as a decrease of Spanish language mastery from the first to the third generations. Similar results were obtained in a further study reported by Buriel (1987) with Mexican Americans and (as a control group) Anglo-Americans ($N = 96$, age fifteen to seventeen years). Here the data showed that the use of "Mexican" virtually disappeared in the second and third generations.

As part of the first study, Buriel and Vasquez (1982) explored the relationship between Spanish proficiency and preferred label. It was shown that even though respondents of the first generation preferred the label "Mexican," they were not more Spanish proficient than the second-generation respondents. Moreover, third-generation respondents continued to call themselves "Mexican American" despite the fact that their Spanish mastery was relatively poor compared to first- and second-generation participants. A further study reported by Buriel (1987) was conducted with eighty Mexican-American and Anglo-American children between seven and nine years old who participated in a bilingual–bicultural Follow Through Program designed to promote sensitivity to both Mexican- and Anglo-American traditions. Children were rated for identification with Mexican-American or Anglo-American culture by their teachers. It was shown that identification with Anglo-American culture increases from the first to the third generation (i.e., third-generation children did not differ from Anglo-American children in their identification with Mexican-American traditions). However, there was no support for the hypothesis that children lose their Mexican identity when acculturating to Anglo-American cultural patterns.

Similar results were found by Rosenthal and Feldman (1992) among Chinese descendants. Exploring ethnic identity of first- and second-generation Chinese-Australian ($N = 96$) and Chinese-American ($N = 141$) adolescents (mean age sixteen years) revealed that some aspects of ethnic identity such as ethnic identification and behaviors decline over time, but evaluative components of ethnic identity (such as importance) remain stable. Thus, these findings provide virtually no support for the idea of a mutual exclusion between ethnic and mainstream identification. On the other hand, research on social or ethnic identity suggests that such results can be discussed in terms of the relationship between what people say they are (ethnic self-labeling) and what they actually do (ethnic behavioral patterns) or feel (e.g., ethnic pride), and the need to assess these components of ethnic identity separately (see Phinney, 1990).

Linear Model

Focusing precisely on the distinction between self-labeling and behaviors, Szapocznik and his colleagues (Szapocznik et al., 1978) developed a model of acculturation within the assimilation framework (see Figure 1.1). According to their unidimensional model, acculturation is a linear function of the amount of time a person interacts with the host culture, while the "rate" of acculturation varies across the age and sex of the individual. Furthermore, the model distinguishes between behavioral and value acculturation. The former includes the gradual acquisition of the more overt aspects of the host culture, such as customs, habits, and lifestyle; the latter involves the adoption of the basic cultural values of the larger society.

The model was tested in a study involving Cuban-Americans ($N = 265$) and Anglo-Americans ($N = 201$) from the Miami area. Self-report of both behaviors and value orientations (e.g., preference for Spanish or English) were em-

Figure 1.1
Linear Model of Acculturation

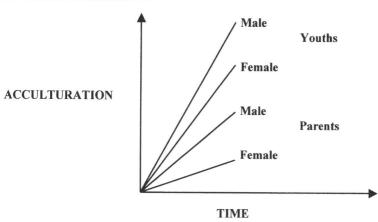

Source: Modified from Figure 1 in Szapocznik, J., Scopetta, M., Kurtines, W., & Aranalde, M. (1978). Theory and measurement of acculturation. *Interamerican Journal of Psychology, 12*, 115. Used by permission of the Interamerican Journal of Psychology.

ployed to assess acculturation level. Consistent with the model, results showed that both behavioral and value acculturation were related linearly and positively with time of exposure to the host culture. The rate of acculturation was related negatively with age, but only along the behavioral dimension. Finally, it was found that males tended to acculturate more quickly than females, but once more, only at the level of behavioral acculturation. Thus, the results support the linearity assumption only partially. According to Szapocznik, individuals might learn the behaviors required to function in the new cultural environment before they assimilate the values of the mainstream culture. In addition, central elements of the culture (e.g., values) might be more resistant to change than peripheral aspects (see Phinney & Rosenthal, 1992; Triandis, Kashima, Shimada, & Villareal, 1986).

In her study on acculturation and family structure among Mexican Americans, Keefe (1980) found that while they lose awareness of and contact with their Mexican cultural heritage from one generation to another, the traditional extended family structure remains intact.[1] Using a similar line of reasoning, Keefe argued that values and behaviors related to the family are more resistant to change, not only because of their central position within the Mexican tradition, but also because the traditional extended family may have a buffering function against prejudice and discrimination.

In summary, studies of generational differences provide some support for the linear model, showing a fairly consistent increase in identification with the mainstream culture with each successive generation. Research within this model clearly shows that acculturation varies as a function of the time a person has been in contact with other cultural groups. However, it also shows that many characteristics of the ethnic groups in question (such as structure, cohesiveness, distinctiveness, and status within the society) and individuals' demographic characteristics (e.g., gender, age) are important as well. In addition, researchers have shown the complexity of the acculturation process in that behaviors, values, and identity are often differentially related to acculturation. However, the assumption that increments of involvement with the larger society are inevitably accompanied by decrements of identification with the ethnic groups of reference remains highly questionable.

Two-Dimensional Models

Contrary to linear–bipolar models, several researchers suggest that individuals can maintain ethnic distinctiveness while they simultaneously develop a positive identification with the larger society by engaging in social networks (e.g., Berry, 1997; Bourhis et al., 1997; Rogler, Cortes, & Malgady, 1991; Sayegh & Lasry, 1993; Szapocznik, Kurtines, & Fernández, 1980). Accordingly, a number of multidimensional conceptualizations have been proposed in recent years.

Acculturation–Biculturalism Model

Szapocznik and colleagues (1980) point out that their unidimensional model can be applied only in monocultural contexts. However, in those instances in which immigrants or ethnic minority members interact with other cultural communities, they need to develop skills that are necessary to participate in both the host and original cultures. The authors suggest that two distinct processes emerge when the cultural context is bicultural: adaptation to the host culture and retention (or loss) of original cultural characteristics. The former is conceptualized as a linear function of the time a person has been in contact to the host culture, while the latter depends on characteristics of the cultural community of reference, such as degree or availability of community support. Individuals' demographic characteristics, such as gender and age, influence the amount of change in both processes. Figure 1.2 shows the relationship between biculturalism and cultural involvement proposed by Szapocznik and colleagues for the specific case of Cuban Americans.

To test the model, Szapocznik's group (1980) developed a measure that assesses two separate dimensions: biculturalism and cultural involvement. Computation of the scores for each dimension is based on two scales measuring involvement with both the Cuban and American cultures. The scores for cultural involvement are obtained by adding the scores on both subscales; the scores for biculturalism are computed by subtracting them from each other. Thus, under the assumption that the two scales are equivalent measures of the degree of involvement in the two cultures, scores close to zero should represent biculturalism, scores less than zero "Americanism," and scores above zero "Cubanism."

Figure 1.2
Acculturation–Biculturalism Model

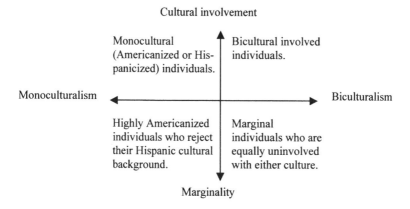

Source: Reprinted with modifications from *International Journal of Intercultural Relations,*
vol. 4, Szapocznik, J., Kurtines, W. M., & Fernández, T., Bicultural involvement and adjustment in Hispanic-American youths, Figure 2, p. 362, Copyright 1980, with permission from
Elsevier Science.

More recently, Rivera-Sinclair (1997) tested the acculturation–biculturalism
model in a cross-sectional study with 254 Cubans (age eighteen to ninety) of
several residence statuses (immigrants, refugees, students, and residents). Using the biculturalism–involvement scale described earlier, Rivera-Sinclair found
some support for the basic assumptions of the acculturation–biculturalism
model: The longer the participants had been exposed to American culture, the
more bicultural they were. Subjects who reported having two support communities were more bicultural than those who perceived the presence of only one
support group. Younger Cubans tended to be more bicultural than older.
   One of the major contributions of this model consists in showing that the
adaptation to a new cultural context does not imply the loss of ties with the original cultural community. Acculturation is viewed here as a two-dimensional
process that varies according to cultural contexts. Moreover, the model makes
clear the need for separate measures of both processes. However, the zero-
sum assumption behind the methodological procedure has been widely criticized (see Doná & Berry, 1994; Rogler et al., 1991; Sayegh & Lasry, 1993).
While the model conceptually supposes the independence of two dimensions
(adaptation to the host culture and culture retention), methodologically it fails
to overcome the assumption of polarity of acculturative involvement. Note
that with the proposed method for computing scores an individual who is
equally noninvolved in either the Cuban or the American culture would have
identical scores on biculturalism as an individual who is equally highly involved in both cultures. The dimension of involvement was introduced by

Szapocznik and his coworkers (1980) actually "to distinguish the true bicultural individual from the 'mock bicultural' individual" (p. 361), but the bipolar dimension of monoculturalism, on one extreme, and biculturalism, on the other, still remains as the basic assumption of the model.

Quadri-Modal Acculturation Model

A further (and perhaps the most influential) two-dimensional model has been developed by Berry and colleagues (Berry, 1980, 1984; Berry, Kim, Power, Young, & Bujaki, 1989). Focusing on the process of adaptation to ethnically plural contexts, Berry and colleagues argue that during the process of acculturation individuals and groups are confronted with two basic issues: (1) cultural maintenance and (2) contact and participation. The former involves the decision to maintain one's cultural identity and patterns, the latter to engage in positive intergroup contact. Four possible outcomes or forms of adaptation emerge when evaluative responses to these dimensions are dichotomized: integration, assimilation, separation, and marginalization (see Figure 1.3).

Since these forms of adaptation imply decision-making processes, the term *acculturation strategies* has been employed to describe them. More specifically, when individuals hold positive relations with the larger society or other ethnic groups and this is accompanied by maintenance of the ethnic identity and traditions, the *integration strategy* is defined (quadrant I in Figure 1.3). The *assimilation strategy* emerges when individuals do not wish to maintain their cultural identity and seek or prefer interaction with the mainstream culture (quadrant II). The *separation strategy* is defined when individuals have a

Figure 1.3
Acculturation Strategies

ISSUE 2: Is it considered to be of value to maintain relationships with other ethnic groups?	ISSUE 1: Is it considered to be of value to maintain cultural identity and characteristics?	
	YES	NO
YES	I INTEGRATION	II ASSIMILATION
NO	III SEPARATION	IV MARGINALIZATION

Source: Modified from Berry (1984, p. 12).

Note: As pointed out in several publications, evaluative responses to these issues can be measured through a continuous scale from "totally disagree" to "totally agree." However, for the present conceptualization they are taken as dichotomous "yes" and "no" responses (see Berry, 1984, 1995, 1997).

strong identification with their own culture and avoid contact with other groups (quadrant III). Finally, *marginalization* results when individuals lose cultural and psychological contact with both their own ethnic group and the larger society (quadrant IV).

According to Berry (1997), these strategies can be observed both at individual and group levels of analysis. That is, within a particular acculturating group some individuals may adopt the assimilation strategy, whereas the majority of their coethnics support the integration strategy. Similarly, it is possible that a particular acculturating group overwhelmingly endorses the assimilation strategy while other groups from other cultural backgrounds adopt the separation strategy. Furthermore, these strategies could be adopted by members of nondominant groups and by members of the dominant society. However, Berry suggests other terms to refer to these acculturation modes when they are pursued by the dominant society regarding how nondominant groups should acculturate. Specifically, he suggests the notion of *melting pot* to describe voluntary assimilation, *pressure cooker* to address forced assimilation, and *segregation* when separation is imposed by the dominant group (Berry, 1980, 1997).

While distinguishing who is making the decision about acculturation, these terms provide a more differentiated approach, recognizing the relative power of the groups involved in the acculturation process. The major problem with these concepts is, however, that they reflect not only attitudes and practices of members of the dominant groups, but also current ideologies or long-term policies in the larger society. The terms segregation, melting pot, and pressure cooker are also broadly used in political discussions, have become part of daily discourse, and have multiple meanings. Using them indiscriminately could lead to a confused level of analysis. Hence, the term "acculturation strategies" will be used here for individuals' and groups' attitudes toward these four ways of acculturating, and their actual behaviors that might vary according to the attitudes (Berry, 1997). Other terms, such as "modes of acculturation," "acculturation orientations," or "acculturation types" are used here synonymously with acculturation strategies.

In order to validate their model, Berry and his colleagues (1989) conducted several empirical studies across a variety of acculturating groups in Canada, including native peoples, immigrants, and ethnic groups. This research program produced four scales representing independent measures of attitudes toward each of the four acculturation modes in important life domains, such as friends, customs, Canadian society, and so on. Each scale includes a number of statements that are responded to on a Likert scale. For instance, integration is measured through items like, "While living in Canada we can retain our Korean cultural heritage and lifestyle and yet participate fully in various aspects of Canada society." A typical item to tap separation is, "Most of my friends are Koreans because I feel comfortable around them, but I don't feel as comfortable around Canadians." The typical statement for assimilation is,

"We're living in Canada and that means giving up our traditional way of life and adopting a Canadian lifestyle, thinking and acting like Canadians." Finally, marginalization is measured through items like, "These days it's hard to find someone you can really relate to and share your inner feelings and thoughts." Higher scores indicate stronger endorsement or preference for the acculturation mode in question.

Within Berry's research program, psychometric analyses have shown some support for the reliability and validity of the scales. Cronbachs's alphas range from 0.68 to 0.90, and the scales behave in a predictable way when checked against several acculturation indexes (e.g., ethnic identity, newspaper readership, club membership, and language proficiency and preference). However, most of the further research within this model rarely employed the same instruments. Differing numbers of items were employed, and in some studies not all strategies were assessed (e.g., Phinney, Chavira, & Williamson, 1992). Internal consistency of these new versions range from 0.55 to 0.89, and test–retest reliability evidence is virtually absent. These and other problems related to the measurement of acculturation will be examined in more detail in the methodological section. The relevant point for the current discussion is that in spite of these measurement insufficiencies, empirical data provide certain support for the quadri-modal conceptualization.

Empirical research shows that integration is the most preferred strategy among respondents from different acculturating groups in various cultural settings. It was found to be overwhelmingly endorsed by adults (Berry et al., 1989) and adolescents (Phinney et al., 1992), by members of dominant and nondominant ethnic groups in Western and Eastern Europe (Piontkowski, Florack, Hoelker, & Obdrzálek, 2000), and by immigrants in societies that profess to promote multiculturalism, such as Canada (Doná & Berry, 1994), but also in societies that favor assimilation policies, such as Israel (Roccas, Horenczyk, & Schwartz, 2000). Typically, this relatively high endorsement of integration is followed by a preference for separation over assimilation, while marginalization seems to be the least preferred strategy. In addition, the literature suggests that integration represents the most adaptive strategy and marginalization the least. Assimilation and separation are linked with intermediate levels of adjustment (see Berry, 1997; Doná & Berry, 1994; Phinney, 1991; Ward & Rana-Deuba, 1999). As pointed out before, the specific psychological outcomes of acculturation strategies will be discussed in more detail in Chapter 4. For the present discussion it is important to note that empirical evidence is consistent with this pattern; however, it should be considered carefully, since the endorsement of a specific strategy and its potential outcomes varies greatly depending on numerous group-level and individual-level factors.

Several studies have sought to identify the principal variables underlying the adoption of a specific acculturation mode. In their work on acculturation attitudes, Berry and his coworkers (1989) found that both psychological variables (e.g., ethnic identity and language preference) and demographic factors (such as socioeconomic status, education, age, and length of residence) were associated with the way in which individuals acculturated. The correlational pattern depended, however, on the acculturating group in question. Among Australian Aborigines ($N = 110$), those who identified themselves primarily as Australians favored the assimilation strategy, while those who saw themselves as Aborigines endorsed the integration mode (see Sommerland & Berry, 1970). Among French Canadians ($N = 49$), education and socioeconomic status correlated positively with the endorsement of integration and separation. Within the Portuguese-Canadians sample ($N = 117$), age and length of residence in Canada were positively correlated with assimilation among parents, while among children these variables were negatively correlated with integration and marginalization. Among Korean Canadians ($N = 150$), having a "Korean" ethnic identity was associated with the separation strategy but also with the marginalization mode. Finally, among Hungarian Canadians ($N = 50$), the knowledge and use of English as well the preference for English was related to assimilation (see Berry et al., 1989).

Similarly, in a study on acculturation strategies among high school and college students in the United States, Phinney and colleagues (1992) found that the relationships between these factors and acculturation strategies vary across groups. Participants in this study were 417 high school students (mean age 16.5 years) and 223 college students (mean age 20.2 years) from different ethnic groups, including Asian, Black, and Hispanic Americans. Within the high school sample, the support of integration was stronger among those who identified themselves as bicultural than those who considered themselves as primarily ethnic (e.g., primarily Hispanic) or primarily American. The support for the assimilation strategy was higher among college students from Asian and mixed backgrounds than among Blacks and Hispanics. Finally, within the high school sample, Black males endorsed the separation strategy more than Black females. This strategy was also more favored by foreign-born college students as well as by foreign-born Asian high school students than by their American-born peers.

Research in Europe provides a similar picture. In a recent study, Piontkowski and colleagues (2000) examined the predictive power of typical intergroup variables (i.e., intergroup attitudes and behaviors) on the adoption of acculturation strategies among such dominant groups as Slovaks ($N = 153$), Germans ($N = 300$), and Swiss ($N = 193$), and such nondominant groups as Turks ($N = 110$), former Yugoslavs ($N = 303$), and Hungarians ($N = 135$). On the basis of the social identity theory (see Tajfel & Turner 1979), Piontkowski and colleagues considered in-group bias, in-group identification, perceived similarity, interethnic contact, perceived outcomes from interethnic contact, and perceived permeability of group boundaries as predictors of acculturation strategies.

Their results show, once more, that the set of variables predicting acculturation strategies varies sharply across ethnic groups. However, some general patterns could be identified. Among the dominant groups, the integration strategy was strongly associated with anticipation of positive outcomes from interethnic contact, perception of similarity between the own group and the acculturating group, less pride in being a member of the dominant group, and less in-group bias. In contrast, assimilation, separation, and marginalization were associated with expected negative outcomes, perceived dissimilarity, and strong in-group bias. With regard to the members of nondominant groups, when they perceived the group boundaries as impermeable they tend to adopt either the separation or the marginalization mode. The specific endorsement depends on the ethnic identification: Those who favored the separation strategy showed high levels of ethnic pride. Ethnic identification was also found to be an important predictor for assimilation. In this case, individuals who wanted to assimilate showed low levels of in-group identification.

The relationship between acculturation modes and intergroup variables was also demonstrated earlier by van Dick, Wagner, Adams, & Petzel (1997). Within a research program to validate a German version of the acculturation scales with six different samples from East and West Germany (total N = 856), they show that positive attitudes to a multicultural society (integration modus) correlate highly and negatively with blatant and subtle prejudice (Pearson's correlation coefficients ranged from $-.41$ to $-.66$) and national pride ($r = -.33$ to $-.55$).

Thus, evidence suggests that the variables associated with the support of acculturation strategies may vary according to the characteristics of each acculturating group and their experiences with regard to the mainstream culture (Berry et al., 1989; Pettigrew, 1988; Phinney et al., 1992). Specifically, while assimilation seems to be a viable option for many Americans of European heritage, this strategy may be unlikely for other groups in specific situations. Among Australian Aborigines, Canadian Indians, Black Americans, or Turks in Germany, assimilation may be virtually impossible because of cultural distance, racial distinctiveness, and structural barriers.

Berry's model is not exempt from criticism. For instance, Sayegh and Lasry (1993) draw attention to some conceptual and methodological inconsistencies, arguing that the first dimension of his model assesses attitudes (identification with the reference ethnic group) while the second is a measure of behaviors (intended interethnic contact). The authors proposed an operationalization based exclusively on ethnic identification toward the heritage and host cultures, which elicits four adaptation strategies (integration, assimilation, ethnocentrism, and marginalization).

Similarly, Ward and colleagues (Ward & Kennedy, 1994; Ward & Rana-Deuba, 1999) point out that use of four independent measures of acculturation strategies restricts the possibility of studying the more fundamental components of acculturation; namely, cultural maintenance and interethnic contact. These writers propose an alternative method to assess acculturation strategies using two independent measures of in-group identification and interethnic attitudes. On the basis of responses to each measure, individuals are classified on one of the four acculturation modes.

Finally, Bourhis and coworkers (1997) proposed further conceptual improvements regarding the marginalization mode. Contrary to Berry—who sees this orientation as characterized by a loss of identity, acculturative stress, and feelings of anomie—Bourhis and colleagues argue that psychological distance from the "own" ethnic group does not necessarily imply cultural alienation. It depends largely on the importance that individuals attribute to their ascribed categories in their lives. Thus, using individualism–collectivism terminology, "marginalization" is not the appropriate term to describe this acculturation strategy among idiocentric individuals (Triandis, Bontempo, Villareal, Asai, & Lucca, 1988). In their reformulation, Bourhis and colleagues distinguish two variants of marginalization: "anomie" and "individualism." In addition, they criticize the lack of attention paid on how the characteristics of intergroup relations within the host society determine the acculturation strategies of immigrants and ethnic minority members. In effect, even though Berry developed his model based on individuals' and groups' responses to changes in Canadian immigration policy, this issue has been neglected in his research program.

While the first two problems have been resolved by introducing changes in the nature of the measures (Bourhis et al., 1997; van Dick et al., 1997; Mielke, 1996; Sayegh & Lasry, 1993; Ward & Kennedy, 1994; Ward & Rana-Deuba, 1999), the latter have led to the development of a further model, which is known as the Interactive Acculturation Model (IAM). With this model, Bourhis and coworkers more explicitly incorporate the interplay between host community members' and immigrants' acculturation strategies.

Interactive Acculturation Model

The IAM was developed on the basis of three elements: (1) immigrants' or ethnic minority members' acculturation strategies according to their cultural identification, (2) majority members' attitudes toward immigrants' acculturation, and (3) the relational outcomes derived by combining these sets of orientations. According to Bourhis and coworkers (1997), three different relational outcomes emerge depending on the concordance or discordance between immigrants' strategies and host community members' orientations: consensual, problematic, or conflictual. These outcomes include communication patterns, interethnic attitudes, and psychological well-being. Figure 1.4 outlines a simplified version of the model.

As can be seen, consensual outcomes are predicted to emerge in three cells of the model; namely, when both dominant community members' and immigrants' orientations match regarding to integration, assimilation, and individualism. In those cases, harmonious intergroup relations are expected, including positive interethnic attitudes, effective intercultural communications, and low psychological distress. Discordance between the acculturation strategies elicits problematic and conflictual relational outcomes. Problematic outcomes are

Figure 1.4
IAM Model

HOST or MAJORITY COMMUNITY	IMMIGRANT or MINORITY COMMUNITY				
	Integration	Assimilation	Segregation	Anomie	Individualism
Integration	Consensual	Problematic	Conflictual	Problematic	Problematic
Assimilation	Problematic	Consensual	Conflictual	Problematic	Problematic
Segregation	Conflictual	Conflictual	Conflictual	Conflictual	Conflictual
Exclusion	Conflictual	Conflictual	Conflictual	Conflictual	Conflictual
Individualism	Problematic	Problematic	Problematic	Problematic	Consensual

Source: Modified from Figure 4 in Bourhis et al. (1997, p. 382).

likely to emerge in ten cells of the model; for example, when immigrants adopt the integration strategy while host community members prefer them to assimilate. Conflictual relational outcomes emerge systematically related to segregation and exclusion orientations in twelve cells of the model. The specific outcomes of discordance range from communication breakdowns, negative intergroup stereotypes, and moderate levels of psychological distress to intergroup conflict, direct discrimination, blatant prejudice, and high levels of psychological distress.

According to the IAM, the specific endorsement of an acculturation strategy and the relational outcomes depend greatly on two macrolevel factors. The first concerns the specific integration ideologies pursued by the state, which may range from a "pluralism ideology" to an "ethnist ideology" (see Bourhis et al., 1997). Integration policies are expected to shape the acculturation orientations attenuating or accentuating the patterns of relational outcomes described here. The second factor is related to the characteristics of the immigrant groups and their relative position within the larger society. To address these issues, Bourhis and colleagues incorporate the concept of group vitality to refer to the relative strength or weakness of a group in a society, which depends on its status (e.g., social prestige and acceptance), demographics (e.g., size, ethnic density), and available institutional support (e.g., churches, businesses, government agencies). It is expected that the greater the vitality of a group, the more likely this group will be to adopt orientations according to its priorities and needs. In those cases, immigrants' acculturation strategies may directly influence the acculturation orientations of host-community members and integration policies. In contrast, low-vitality groups are expected to be more vulnerable to the negative impact of such dominant group orientations as exclusion.

Perhaps the major limitation of this model is the lack of empirical evidence of its validity. Empirical research within this framework is "under way" (Bourhis et al., 1997, p. 384). However, there are some studies that have addressed particular predictions of the IAM. Roccas, Horenczyk, and Schwartz (2000) examined the relationship between acculturation discrepancies (resulting by subtracting participants' acculturation strategy from the strategy perceived as expected by members of the dominant community) and well-being among immigrants from the former Soviet Union in Israel ($N = 100$). In general terms, participants perceived that members of the host community expected them to relinquish their ethnic identity and to assimilate to the mainstream culture more than they actually wished to do. Furthermore, these discrepancies were related to well-being among those participants who attributed high importance to conformity (the tendency to restrain actions and inclinations that might violate social norms).

A different design was employed by van Oudenhoven and Eisses (1998) to examine the outcomes of the interplay between immigrants' and host-community members' acculturation orientations. Participants were Moroccans in Israel ($N = 94$) and The Netherlands ($N = 97$), as well as majority members in both countries ($N = 86$ in The Netherlands, $N = 78$ in Israel). Measuring both acculturation strategies among Moroccans and majority members' attitudes toward Moroccans and their acculturation orientations, van Oudenhoven and Eisses found that in both societies (but particularly in The Netherlands) majority members showed more sympathy toward those Moroccans who assimilated than toward those who integrated, and that Moroccans who endorsed the integration strategy experienced more prejudice than Moroccans who chose the assimilation strategy.

With specific regard to the vitality of acculturating groups, Lalonde and Cameron (1993) demonstrated that the adoption of a particular strategy depends on the perceived social status of the referent ethnic group. In their study, those participants from "stigmatized" groups (Afro-Caribbean Canadians, $N = 43$, and Chinese Canadians, $N = 41$) were more supportive of a collective acculturation orientation (equated with integration strategy) than those from "less" stigmatized groups (Italian Canadians, $N = 118$, and Greek Canadians, $N = 47$).

In sum, research guided by two-dimensional models has shown that conceptualization of acculturation as a multidimensional process is especially helpful to understand cultural change and interethnic relations in ethnically plural contexts. Researchers have identified a number of important factors influencing the way in which individuals tend to acculturate. At the group level, nature of the intergroup contact, attitudes in the dominant society toward immigration and toward specific ethnic groups, as well as specific characteristics of acculturating groups such as status and distribution appear to be consistent predictors of acculturation strategies. At the individual level, socioeconomic status, gender, age, and experience of previous interethnic contact seem to have great impact. In particular, those variables that are important predictors of intergroup relations are also relevant determinants of acculturation strategies.

A FRAMEWORK FOR RESEARCH ON
ACCULTURATION WITH ETHNIC GROUPS

The study of the acculturation process has shifted from an anthropological focus on changes in cultural systems to an intergroup perspective of the psychological process and outcomes of intercultural encounters. Currently, important insights about acculturation derive not only from cross-cultural psychology, but also largely from research on intergroup relations. Thus, substantial research on psychological acculturation has been amassed over recent decades within both research traditions. The result of this concern is a new psychology of acculturation that has produced a complex literature, characterized to some extent by a lack of agreement around key concepts and variables affecting individuals' adaptation in modern plural societies.

Recently, there have been attempts to integrate the field's large and diverse literature (Berry, 1997; Rogler, 1991; Ward & Rana-Deuba, 1999). Based on this work and empirical data derived from the acculturation models already described, Table 1.2 summarizes several factors that have been found to affect the acculturation process and provides some concrete examples.

According to this schema, the principal factors affecting the acculturation process can be classified into group-level (including both societal and situational variables) and individual-level or person variables. At the group level of analysis, majority members' acculturation orientations, citizenship laws, or education policies could be taken as indicators of group-level factors affecting acculturation. Another way to address these issues is to employ self-report measures of perceived discrimination (e.g., Ethier & Deux, 1994). The use of such measures allows one to address how the objective characteristics of intergroup relations are subjectively perceived to affect individuals' adaptation. Within situational factors, the ethnic composition of the immediate environment (ethnic density) represents a further factor affecting acculturation. With specific regard to acculturating groups, objective and subjective (perceived) status have been shown to have a substantial relationship with acculturation and adaptation.

Within individual variables, this schema distinguishes between those factors that exist prior to intercultural contact and those that arise during the process of acculturation. Together with other demographic variables, age at immigration is a consistent predictor of adaptation of immigrants; thus, the acculturation process is especially "smooth" when it starts at a younger age. However, among refugees and asylum seekers, the most important preacculturation factor seems to be the posttraumatic stress, related in most cases to the reasons for migrating (Berry, 1997). Within the factors arising during the acculturation process, frequency and quality of contact, acculturation dimensions, and strategies are important predictors of adaptation.

This conceptualization is based on the universalistic assumption that the psychological process underlying acculturation can be observed in all accul-

Table 1.2
Factors Affecting the Process of Acculturation

FACTORS	FEATURES	EXAMPLES
Group level		
Society of origin	Political context	Civil war, repression
	Economic situation	Poverty
	Demographic factors	Population explosion
Host society	Immigration policy	From a pluralist to an ethnist
	Attitudes toward immigration	ideology
	Attitudes toward specific	Mainstream acculturation strategies
	groups	Stereotypes, prejudice,
		discrimination
Acculturating	Vitality	Status, distribution (ethnic density)
group	Changes in economic, social	Structural barriers cultural changes
	and cultural features	(e.g., language, religion, food)
Individual level		
Factors prior to	Demographics	Age, gender, education,
acculturation	Cultural	Socioeconomic status
	Personal	Language, religion, cultural
	Migration motivation	distance
		Health, coping strategies
Factors arising	Acculturation strategies	
during	Contact/participation	
acculturation	Cultural maintenance	
	Prejudice and discrimination	

Source: Modified from Table 8-1 in Berry & Sam (1997, p. 301).

turating groups, indicating the central variables that should be taken into account when carrying out studies on this area (see Berry, 1997). Empirical research shows, however, that the relative contribution of these factors varies greatly across cultural groups and contexts. Thus, although this point does not diminish the validity of the universalistic argument, it is worth attempting to distinguish between general aspects that apply across groups and specific factors that contribute to understanding the unique experience of particular acculturating groups.

The literature distinguishes five different acculturating groups on the basis of their "voluntariness" of intercultural contact, their mobility and permanence.

These are refugees, asylum seekers, sojourners, immigrants, indigenous peoples, and ethnic groups (see Berry, 1997). Sojourners and immigrants are characterized by high voluntariness of contact, while indigenous peoples and refugees have entered into contact involuntarily. On the other hand, indigenous peoples are sedentary, while immigrants, sojourners, and refugees are defined as migrant. Finally, within the latter groups, immigrants are relatively permanently involved in contact, while sojourners and asylum seekers are in temporary contact.

Long-established ethnic groups with secure status of residence (e.g., French Canadians or Black Costa Ricans) represent those types of acculturating groups in (more or less) voluntary and permanent contact with other groups within the same national framework, representing a further subgroup of the society. Members of these groups grow up dealing with two cultures. One might say they have been acculturating every day since they were born. Thus, those factors existing "prior" to acculturation—which might deeply affect acculturation processes among refugees or sojourners—are largely irrelevant when working with ethnic groups. In these cases, factors related to the specific intergroup relations within the larger society might be more important for the acculturation process (see Berry & Sam, 1997). On the basis of the literature reviewed here, Figure 1.5 depicts a possible way to systematize the key factors affecting acculturation of ethnic groups attending to their particular experience of acculturation.

This framework selects several variables assumed to affect the psychological adjustment to ethnically plural societies among ethnic group members. At the group level, three different factors have been included: (1) perception of discrimination, which provides information on how attitudes toward their own group prevailing in the broader society are perceived; (2) perceived in-group status, which is the subjective reflection of the position of a ethnic group in the social hierarchy; and (3) the ethnic distribution of ethnic groups or ethnic density, which allows one to examine the potential effects of the ethnic composition of the immediate environment on psychological adaptation. At the individual level, the framework focus is on (4) individuals' experience of interethnic contact, and their demographic features, such as (5) ethnicity, (6) socioeconomic status, (7) gender, and (8) age, as well as the (9) acculturation dimensions, and (10) acculturation strategies. The major goal of the present research is to examine the specific effect of acculturation dimensions and strategies on psychological adaptation (focal variables) while controlling for the remaining eight variables (control variables).

Psychological adaptation represents the outcomes of the processes of acculturation in terms of individuals' level of psychological adjustment. Adaptation is expected to be deeply shaped by evaluative preferences of one of the four acculturation modes. These, in turn, are assumed to emerge from two orthogonal dimensions of acculturation, which comprise in-group and intergroup attitudes, respectively (Berry, 1997). It has often been argued that the

Figure 1.5
A Framework for Research on Acculturation with Ethnic Groups

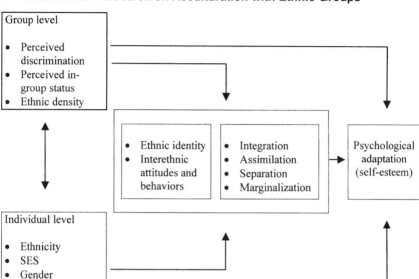

separate consideration of the dimensions might be especially helpful to understand psychological adaptation (e.g., Berry, 1997; Bourhis et al., 1997; Rogler et al., 1991; Sayegh & Lasry, 1993; Szapocznik et al., 1980). However, while focusing on the strategies, researchers have often neglected the specific effect of the two underlying dimensions. The present research, by contrast, seeks to provide more information about the relative contribution of each dimension on psychological adaptation.

As can be seen in Figure 1.5, the dimension of cultural maintenance is redefined here in terms of ethnic identity (i.e., the identification with one's own ethnic group as a subgroup of the larger society). Similarly, contact and participation is referred to here in terms of interethnic attitudes and behaviors. In original formulations, cultural maintenance and contact and participation were approached within a framework of modernization focused on the retention and practice of "traditional" values, and customs versus the adoption of "modern," "alien," or "new" cultural patterns (see Segall, Dasen, Berry, & Portinga, 1990). In this framework, the focus is on the attitudinal response to the ethnic group of reference and other relevant ethnic groups (see also Sayegh & Lasry, 1993).

The rationale for these specifications is found, among other places, in the particular nature and quality of the intercultural contact of ethnic groups. As pointed out before, long-established ethnic groups have a long experience of intercultural contact and represent structured ethnic subcommunities that form an integral part of the larger national state. Clearly, minority and majority members differ in their social status within the larger society. However, there are no "new" or "modern" cultural patterns to be acquired. Similarly, there is no "host" culture to which members of these ethnic groups must adapt; they simply belong to it.

Yet these groups have maintained distinct cultures over time while interacting with each other within the national framework. In effect, members of ethnic groups are seen (and see themselves) as culturally distinct from other groups in a society on the basis of their "ethnicity"; that is, their specific cultural practices and outlooks that distinguish them from other groups (Giddens, 1993). In addition, many ethnic groups constitute ethnic minorities in a sociological sense. They experience social disadvantage as a result of direct (intentionally generated) and indirect (reproduced and perpetuated) discrimination (Pettigrew, 1991); they are subject to prejudice and racism, and in some cases they are physically and socially isolated from the larger community.

Thus, since ethnic groups are characterized by high cultural distinctiveness and (in the case of ethnic minorities) by low social status, ethnic identity and interethnic attitudes should represent central variables in the acculturation process among members of these groups. In effect, ethnic identity has been found to be a topic of great concern among members of clearly identifiable ethnic minorities affecting both the self-perception and the psychological relation to outgroups (Phinney, 1990; Berry, 1997). Hence, it is essential to understand what leads individuals to identify with specific social categories, and whether a strong sense of identification with the ethnic culture of reference has a positive impact on psychological adaptation or, conversely, promotes internalization of negative stereotypes (Phinney, 1991).

Similarly, in ethnically plural societies ethnic group members are faced with the demand to develop cultural and social competencies to interact with both the ethnic group of reference and other ethnic groups within the larger society (LaFromboise et al., 1993). In this sense, attitudes toward out-groups might represent a further central source of psychological adaptation. Thus, it is also necessary to understand why and when individuals engage in positive interethnic contact, and the specific contribution of this acculturation dimension to psychological adaptation.

In order to provide some answers to these questions, recent literature on social identity, intergroup relations, and psychological adaptation will be reviewed in the next chapters. For the present, some general predictions can be advanced from the literature reviewed here. It is suggested here that maintenance of cultural distinctiveness accompanied by positive attitudes toward other groups (integration) affords the best psychological outcomes. By contrast, the loss of cultural contact with both the ethnic group of reference and the larger society (marginalization) is the least adaptive strategy. The options of rejecting the own culture (assimilation) and avoiding intergroup contact (separation) are associated with an intermediate level of adjustment (see also Berry, 1997; Doná & Berry, 1994; Phinney, 1991; Ward & Rana-Deuba, 1999).

The present research examines these predictions among members of two different ethnic groups. However, in order to analyze the specific contribution of the acculturation strategies on psychological adaptation, it is necessary to recognize the potential effects of other factors that might influence the predicted effects by virtue of their relations with the focal variables. While controlling for ethnicity, socioeconomic status, gender, age, ethnic composition of the immediate environment, and measures of perceived ethnic discrimination, perceived in-group status, and interethnic contact, this research also attempts to provide a more differentiated picture of the multiple causation of adaptation in ethnically plural societies.

SUMMARY

This chapter has focused on recent developments in acculturation research, defined as the field of cross-cultural psychology that deals with processes and outcomes of intercultural contact in ethnically plural societies (Berry et al., 1992). Two distinct approaches have guided research on these issues: the linear–bipolar approach and the two-dimensional perspective. The former assumes that acculturation is a process of absorption into the dominant culture, implying a loss of identification with the culture of origin (or ethnic group), while the latter suggests that individuals can maintain positive ties with the mainstream culture without losing the cultural distinctiveness provided by the ethnic group of reference. Special attention has been paid here to the second approach. While incorporating the extensive literature of social identity and intergroup relations in its conceptualization, the two-dimensional perspective seems to be especially appropriate to understanding acculturation within modern national states.

According to this perspective, the adjustment to ethnically plural contexts is highly determined by how individuals relate to (1) their ethnic groups of reference and (2) other relevant outgroups. Four strategies of acculturation emerge from the evaluative responses to the in-group and out-groups: integration, assimilation, separation, and marginalization. These strategies are assumed to relate in a predictable fashion to psychological adjustment. Integration is expected to provide the best psychological outcomes compared with the other three modes. The major goal of this research is to test this proposition in two ethnic groups that have a long experience of contact.

Research has also detected a number of important factors that might moderate or even explain these effects. Factors range from the specific economic and political conditions that cause intercultural contact to specific personality traits influencing individuals' responses to these encounters. Therefore, several attempts have been made to systematize the vast and complex literature produced by years of research on these issues. On the basis of previous models (Berry, 1997), a simplified framework for research on acculturation with ethnic groups has been outlined in this chapter in order to guide the present research (see Figure 1.5).

The framework selects several variables assumed to deeply shape acculturation processes. These are perceived ethnic discrimination, perceived ingroup status, ethnic distribution of the ethnic groups or ethnic density, individuals' ethnicity, socioeconomic status, gender, age, and interethnic contact. The selection of these control variables responds to the need to explore more deeply the relative contribution of the dimensions and strategies of acculturation on psychological adaptation. The next chapters provide a more detailed picture of each component, its determinants, and its correlates.

NOTE

1. Extended family is defined as "a localized kin group consisting of a number of related households whose members interact together frequently and exchange mutual aid" (Keefe, 1980, p. 89). The kin group includes all consanguinal kin on both the mother's and the father's sides, as well as all relatives who have married consanguines.

2

Ethnic Identity

This chapter considers the first dimension of acculturation, called *cultural maintenance*. Cultural maintenance was analyzed originally within the framework of modernization rooted in sociological and anthropological traditions of thinking. Focusing on the influence of Western industrialized societies on persons and groups from nonindustrial countries, the special concern of this research field was the transition from "traditional" to "modern" attitudinal and behavioral patterns (see Segall, Dasen, Berry, & Portinga, 1990). More recently, with increasing interest in acculturation processes in modern plural societies, cultural maintenance has referred to the extent to which individuals desire to retain cultural distinctiveness, deciding whether to preserve their cultural identity, customs, and traditions or relinquish their cultural backgrounds in order to become part of a larger society (Berry & Sam, 1997). As pointed out in Chapter 1, the issue of cultural maintenance among long-established ethnic groups within modern national states can be discussed with a focus on their ethnic identity.

The major aim of this chapter is to examine important social psychological processes underlying the subjective relation to the in-group. The first part deals with the conceptualization and operationalization of ethnic identity and its components. The second part addresses relevant social psychological mechanisms underlying ethnic identity formation. Because of its important contributions in understanding ethnic identity process, this section focuses on formulations derived from the social identity approach (Hogg & Abrams, 1988; Tajfel, 1981; Tajfel & Turner, 1979; Turner, Hogg, Oaks, Reicher, & Wetherell, 1987). The third section presents a review of relevant empirical literature on ethnic identity.

ETHNIC IDENTITY AS A MULTIDIMENSIONAL CONSTRUCT

In her review of the empirical literature from 1972 to 1989, Phinney (1990) criticizes the absence of a widely agreed-on definition of ethnic identity as indicative of conceptual confusion among researchers. Ten years later, the literature still shows a great diversity of conceptualizations.[1] Probably this is due not only to the lack of conceptual clarity, but also to the fact that ethnic identity has been (and is still) considered from a diversity of perspectives within anthropology, sociology, and psychology. In addition, most researchers have acknowledged the multidimensional character of ethnic identity, focusing frequently on different aspects of the construct. Finally, the literature offers a wide range of ethnic identity measures, which in turn make it problematic to compare not only notions but also empirical results. Nevertheless, there is general consensus on conceptualizing ethnic identity as the ethnic specification of social identity as defined by the social identity theory, namely as "*that* part of individual's self-concept which derives from his knowledge of his membership of a social group (or groups) together with the value and emotional significance attached to that membership" (Tajfel, 1981, p. 255, italics in original).

Within this general understanding of ethnic identity, several authors have devoted their attention to the multidimensional nature of the construct, taking a closer look at the components that may contribute to individuals' sense of membership in a social group (see Luhtanen & Crocker, 1992; van Dick & Wagner, 2001; Ellemers, Kortekaas, & Ouwerkerk, 1999; Klink, Mummendey, Mielke, & Blanz, 1997; Phinney, 1990; Verkuyten & Lay, 1998).

Three major components have been distinguished from Tajfel's (1981) definition of social identity: "a cognitive component, in the sense of the knowledge that one belongs to a group; an evaluative one in the sense that the notion of the group and/or of one's membership of it *may* have a positive or negative value connotation; and an emotional component in the sense that the cognitive and evaluative aspects of the group and one's membership of it *may* be accompanied by emotions (such as love or hatred, like or dislike) directed toward one's own group" (p. 229, italics in original). A fourth component has been identified by other authors as the behavioral (Phinney, 1990) or conative aspect (van Dick & Wagner, 2001).

Cognitive Component

Ethnic identity has been conceptualized by some researchers with a focus on the cognitive aspect of the construct as ethnic self-labeling, self-identification, and self-categorization or self-stereotyping. For example, in their study on ethnic identity among various ethnic minority members in the United States, Lorenzo-Hernández and Ouellette (1998) define ethnic identity as "the perception and awareness of being a member of any national, cultural or ethnic category" (p. 2007). In a similar vein, Deux, Reid, Mizrahi, and Ethier (1995) define social identities in terms of those constructions of self that locate a person in a certain social category (e.g., ethnicity). Thus, ethnic self-identification refers to the usage of an ethnic label to describe oneself. By using an ethnic label, individuals express that they define themselves in terms of their shared similarities with members of specific ethnic categories or in-groups in opposition to other ethnic categories or out-groups (Turner, Oakes, Haslam, & McGarty, 1994).

With regard to operationalization, ethnic self-identification has been assessed in a variety of ways: by asking participants about their ethnicity and parents' ethnicity, employing open-ended questions or multiple-choice items to assess participants' ethnic self-labels (Phinney, 1992), or presenting items such as "I think and act like other members of my group" (van Dick & Wagner, 2001), "I am like other members of my group" (Ellemers et al., 1999), or "I consider myself as belonging to my group" (Klink et al., 1997), where the words "my group" are replaced for the social category under study. In most cases, however, ethnic self-identification has been inferred from participants' ethnicity without knowing if a person considers himself or herself a member of the specific ethnic groups in the study (e.g., Martinez & Dukes, 1991). The result is a notable amount of confusion in the interpretation of data.

Affective Component

Most writers focus on the feelings of attachment with the ethnic in-group or sense of belonging to it. Thus, with specific regard to African Americans, Brookins, Anyabwille, and Nacoste (1996) define group identification as psychological "closeness" to the Black community. Similarly, Sellers, Smith, Shelton, Rowley, and Chavous (1998) define it as the significance that individuals attribute to their membership within the Black racial group. The operationalization of the component includes items such as "I feel an overwhelming attachment to Black people" (Helms, 1990), "I have a strong sense of belonging to Black people" (Sellers et al., 1998), or "Overall, my group memberships have very little to do with how I feel about my self" (Luhtanen & Crocker, 1992).

One may argue that mere self-categorization into a social category automatically elicits certain emotions and evaluations associated with that category that are difficult to distinguish empirically. Based on a similar assumption, researchers have interpreted misidentification among children of stigmatized ethnic groups (that is, choosing a label distinct from the ethnicity of the parents) as a sign of poor self-concept (see Cross, 1991, for a critical review of this assumption). In addition, it has been found among adults that descriptions of group identities contain more statements of values and emotions than descriptions of personal identities, which include more traits and attributes (Bettencourt & Hume, 1999).

Other authors, however, argue for conceptual and empirical specification. The conceptual point has been addressed by van Dick (2001) and Wagner (1994), who draw attention to the semantic distinction between identification as a member of a social category (cognitive component) and identification with the category (affective component). In other words, when individuals identify themselves as members of a social category they do not necessarily express that this fact is relevant for their self-concept; the importance and affective attachment is given only when they identify with the social category. On the measurement level, principal components and confirmatory factor analysis support the conceptual distinction between cognitive and emotional facets of group identification (van Dick & Wagner, 2001; Ellemers et al., 1999; Klink et al., 1997). On the empirical level, it has been shown that individuals belonging to the same group show differential responses on in-group-favoring bias according to their affective commitment to the group (Ellemers, van Rijswijk, Roefs, & Simons, 1997).

Evaluative Component

Several researchers focus on positive or negative value connotations of ethnic membership. Aboud and Doyle (1995) define the development of ethnic "in-group pride" in terms of evaluative preference for the own ethnic group, while Ichiyama, McQuarrie, and Ching (1996) define ethnic identity as the attitudes that individuals exhibit toward their own ethnic group. Based in the notions of "reflected appraisals" or "looking-glass self" rooted in the symbolic interactionist tradition (Cooley, 1956; Mead, 1934), several researchers (e.g., Luhtanen & Crocker, 1992; Sellers et al., 1998) include in the operationalization not only individuals' judgments about how good or worthy their in-groups are (private collective self-esteem or private group regard), but also their judgments about how others evaluate their groups (public collective self-esteem or public group regard). The core assumption here is Mead's (1934) idea that the self as object is only experienced "indirectly, from the particular standpoints of other individual members of the same social group, or from the generalized standpoint of the social group as a whole to which he belongs" (p. 138). In other words, individuals' self-concepts are shaped by how they believe others and "generalized others" see them.

The evaluative component has been assessed in different ways. In research with children, the classical technique (see Clark & Clark, 1939) is an indirect measure of attitudes and preferences that consists of having subjects make evaluative choices of ethnic stimuli such as dolls, line drawings, or photographs (e.g., Aboud & Doyle, 1995). In studies involving adolescents and adults, questionnaires have been used more frequently. Attitudes are assessed by having participants rate themselves in relation to negative and positive adjectives (e.g., Ichiyama et al., 1996), by questions such as "If you could choose, would you like to be a Turk or not?" (Verkuyten, 1990), or by items such as "I think my group has little to be proud of" (Ellemers et al., 1999), "I feel that Black community has made valuable contributions to this society" (Sellers et al., 1998), or "I am proud to be Chinese" (Rosenthal & Feldman, 1992).

The question remains whether the evaluative component can be clearly distinguished from the affective dimension. Since affective commitment to a group is more likely to be expressed when the group is positive evaluated—by virtue of its positive contribution to individuals' social identity—these components are expected to be highly interrelated (see Tajfel & Turner, 1979).[2] In addition, both exploratory and confirmatory factor analysis show discrepant results: While some researchers were able to disentangle the two components (e.g., van Dick & Wagner, 2001; Ellemers et al., 1999; Luhtanen & Crocker, 1992), other authors have found no hints of a conceptual distinction (Klink et al., 1997; Phinney, 1992).

However, this distinction is helpful (at least theoretically) in understanding ethnic identity and its outcomes among members of ethnic minorities. Because ethnicity is an ascribed rather than an achieved social category, and because of issues such as prejudice, racism, and discrimination, both components may contribute differently to the ethnic identity of members of minority ethnic groups.[3] In fact, Crocker, Luhtanen, Blaine, and Broadnax (1994) found that compared with Asian and White Americans, Black American subjects show the lowest levels of public collective self-esteem (evaluative component), but there was no evidence that identification with their ethnic group was affected by these reflected appraisals. Similarly, Mlicki and Ellemers (1996) found in a series of studies with Polish and Dutch students that while Polish students evaluated their national traits more negatively than Dutch students, they also showed a stronger sense of national identity. Moreover, Polish students did not engage in self-protective strategies to improve their national self-image when the opportunity was given.

Behavioral Component

Critics hold that most social psychological approaches focus exclusively on the minority aspect of ethnic minorities, ignoring the ethnic aspect of the groups (Sellers et al., 1998; Verkuyten, 1997a). Ethnic group members are not only defined (appreciated or rejected) by others because of cultural distinctions, but also define themselves as distinct by virtue of their common ancestry, religion, language, customs, and values. Such involvement in cultural practices is to some extent responsible for the maintenance and reproduction of the group, which in turn shapes the self-perception of its members. Usually, cultural involvement has been assessed through specific cultural practices such as language, religious affiliation, artistic expressions, knowledge about culture or history of the ethnic ingroup, and so on. Since measures of this aspect are based on self-reported behaviors, it can be defined as the behavioral component (Phinney, 1990). A slightly different connotation has been introduced by other authors with the term *conative identification* (van Dick & Wagner, 2001; Klink et al., 1997), which is used to address the intention to participate in relevant group practices and to remain a member of the group. The behavioral component has been assessed mostly by direct questions about the extent to which participants engage in particular ethnic behaviors or by items such as "I often participate in cultural practices of my group, such as special food, music, customs" (Phinney, 1992).

In sum, modern conceptualizations of ethnic identity emphasize the multidimensional character of the construct, distinguishing between cognitive, affective, evaluative, and behavioral aspects. These aspects are expected to contribute differently to an individual's sense of belonging to an ethnic group (Luhtanen & Crocker, 1992). Research has provided some support for these assumptions, but empirical evidence is still inconclusive. It is expected that the salience and interrelationship of the components of ethnic identity vary across ethnic groups depending on their particular history, culture, and structural features. This has raised a controversy about the distinction between general aspects that apply across groups and specific elements of ethnic identity that are only shared by members of a particular ethnic group.

For instance, Sellers and colleagues (1998) include in their operationalization of racial identity among Black Americans a dimension labeled "ideology," which refers to individuals' beliefs, opinions, and attitudes about how in-group members should act (in political terms) toward the larger society. This dimension is operationalized through items such as "Black people should not marry interracially" (nationalistic subscale), "Black people should treat other oppressed people as allies" (oppressed minority subscale), "Blacks should strive to be full members of the American political system" (assimilation subscale), or "Black values should not be inconsistent with human values" (humanistic subscale). According to the authors, these subscales are based specifically on the unique ideological profiles of African Americans, which limit their applicability to other ethnic groups. From a more universalistic perspective, other writers argue for the development of measurements applicable across groups to allow data comparison. Phinney's (1992) Multigroup Ethnic Identity Measure and Luhtanen and Crocker's (1992) Collective Self-Esteem Scale are examples of such instruments. One possible way to deal with both universality and specificity is to supplement general measures with items directed to assess specific aspects of the ethnic groups under study.

Attempts to address ethnic identity more analytically have produced, at the same time, a great divergence in conceptualizations and operationalizations. However, most researchers seem to share a general understanding of ethnic identity based in the European tradition of research initiated by Tajfel (Tajfel & Turner, 1979; Turner et al., 1987). Because of the relevance of this approach for the understanding of ethnic identity, it does merit further scrutiny on its conceptual grounds.

UNDERSTANDING ETHNIC IDENTITY FROM THE SOCIAL IDENTITY APPROACH

The social identity approach is used here as a generic term involving two (closely) related but (strictly speaking) distinct theories of the social psychological phenomena underlying group behavior. The first, social identity theory, refers to the body of ideas developed by Henri Tajfel and his students at the university of Bristol since the beginning of the 1970s (see Tajfel, 1978; Tajfel & Turner, 1979). The second, self-categorization theory, represents John Turner and colleagues' work since the early 1980s (Turner et al., 1987).[4] The former is a theory of intergroup conflict and social change that integrates the social categorization process, individuals' need to maintain and enhance a positive social identity via positive in-group distinctiveness, and subjective beliefs of the "nature" of social structures (Tajfel & Turner, 1979). The latter represents a theory of psychological group formation focused on self-categorization processes. Its central argumentation is that a salient social identity changes (more precisely, depersonalizes) individuals' self-perception and behavioral patterns (Turner et al., 1987; Turner et al., 1994). The fundamental assumption shared by both theories is that group-based self-categorization has a central role in the emergence of collective phenomena, including social stereotyping, social influence, crowding behavior, social movement participation, prejudice and intergroup conflict, social cooperation, and (as assumed here) acculturation-related processes.

Social Categorization and Social Identity

The role of social groups in regulating individuals' social behavior has been explicitly addressed by both the social identity theory and the self-categorization theory as part of their central assumptions. Tajfel and Turner (1979) posit that social groups provide individuals with a framework of reference for orientation in the social world and self-definition: "They [the social groups] create and define the individuals place in society" (p. 40). This argument is clearly reflected in their definition of social identity as the part of individuals' self-concepts derived from their group memberships. In concordance, social groups are defined as cognitive entities; that is, as collections of persons who perceive themselves as members of the same social category, share an emotional attachment to it, and evaluate it similarly (Tajfel, 1981; Tajfel & Turner, 1979). In addition, it is assumed that individuals are motivated to identify themselves in terms of social categories in order to fulfill two basic needs: the need for simplification, predictability, and structure, and the need for a positive and coherent self-image. Hence, *uncertainty reduction* and *self-esteem enhancement* are assumed to contribute decisively to the emergence of group phenomena (Hogg & Mullin, 1999).[5] It is with these assumptions in mind that the specific theoretical pieces of the approach can be outlined. Tajfel and Turner (1979) distinguish three basic processes underlying group formation: social categorization, social identification, and social comparison.

Social categorization refers to individuals' tendency to organize their social environment by forming relevant groups or categories. According to the social identity theory, the mere categorization produces a perceptual overestimation of intracategory similarities (e.g., "Costa Ricans are all the same" or "Germans are all the same"), as well an overestimation of intercategory differences (e.g., "Costa Ricans and Germans are strongly different from each other"). In addition, accentuation effects are assumed to be more pronounced when they are relevant, useful, or salient to individuals in a given moment, and particularly on those dimensions that are subjectively related to the categorization (Tajfel, 1981). Thus, if the dimensions of comparison were "sense of rhythm" or "vivacity," it is quite probably that the categorization Costa Rican–German becomes salient, but if the dimension of comparison were "nurturance," it is likely that other category differences (e.g., gender) will be accentuated (see Hogg & Abrams, 1988).

The process of social identification refers to the extent to which individuals perceive and define themselves as members of a specific social category. In the self-categorization theory this process is addressed under the term of *self-categorizations*, defined as cognitive groupings of the self in terms of accentuated similarities between oneself and other in-group members and accentuated differences between oneself and out-group members (Turner et al., 1987). Like social categorizations, group-based self-definitions are regulated by the accentuation principle already described. Furthermore, social identifications are not only relational (how similar or distinct "we" are from "they"), but also evaluative (e.g., "we" are better than "them"), and are determined by the need for positive self-esteem (see Hogg & Abrams, 1988; Tajfel & Turner, 1979).

The social identity theory specifies that social categories provide a relevant framework of self-reference only when they are compared with other social categories subjectively available to individuals when making concrete judgments, that is, via social comparison. Tajfel's (1981) argumentation was that "a group becomes a group in the sense of being perceived as having common characteristics or a common fate mainly because other groups are present in the environment" (p. 258). The notion of social comparison used in the social identity theory represents a reformulation of Festinger's (1954) social comparison theory. In concordance with Festinger, the social identity theory acknowledges individuals' tendency to evaluate their abilities and opinions by comparison with others. Contrary to Festinger, who assumed that social comparison takes place only when objective reality checks are not available, the social identity theory argues that all knowledge is socially produced via social comparisons (Tajfel, 1981). In addition, since individuals obtain self-esteem benefits through favorable social comparisons, it is assumed that there is a general tendency to perceive in-groups as positively distinct from other relevant out-groups (Tajfel & Turner, 1979).

Proceeding from these premises, the central hypothesis of the social identity theory is that in intergroup situations individuals tend to differentiate their social group from others in a way that positive outcomes of the comparisons contribute to maintain a positive social identity. When social comparison, however, leads to negative outcomes (social identity is unsatisfactory) individuals tend to (re)establish a positive social identity by restoring positive intergroup distinctiveness. This produces a "shift" in individuals' self-perceptions and actions from a point near to the interpersonal extreme of social behavior, in which individuals act guided by their idiosyncratic characteristics, to a point near to the intergroup extreme, in which individuals act in terms of their shared membership in social categories, behave similarly, treat out-group members similarly, and perceive them as stereotypically homogeneous (Tajfel, 1981; Tajfel & Turner, 1979).

One of the major goals of the self-categorization theory is to address under which conditions the categorization process affects the self-definition and in turn regulates the shift from interpersonal to intergroup behavior (Oaks, 1996; Oaks, Haslam, & Reynolds, 1999; Turner et al., 1987; Turner et al., 1994). Turner and coworkers (1987) assume that the categorizations used to define oneself exist at least at three different levels of abstraction related by class inclusion: self-categorization as human being (the superordinate level), self-categorization as a interchangeable member of a social group (intermediate or social-identity level), and self-categorization as a unique person (subordinate or personal-identity level).

According to Turner and colleagues (1987), the level of abstraction of a self-categorization varies depending on individuals' readiness in using self-categories (*relative accessibility*) and the "match" between stimuli and categories being perceived in a given moment (*comparative fit*). Relative accessibility reflects perceivers' past experiences, current motives, and goals that favor or limit the use of a specific self-category, while the comparative fit depends on the comparison process itself, which is governed by the accentuation principle described earlier.

In order to detect the rules underlying the categories' fit to the perceived reality more precisely, Turner and colleagues (1987) introduced the concept of the *meta-contrast ratio*, which is defined as "the ratio of the average difference perceived between members of the category and the other stimuli (the mean inter-category difference) over the average difference perceived between members within the category (the mean intra-category difference)" (p. 47). According to this, the probability that the self and other persons will be categorized as an entity is higher when the intragroup differences are perceived as smaller than the intergroup differences (Turner et al., 1994). Oaks (1996) points out that the meta-contrast ratio provides only a partial explanation for the use of categories. The perceived differences and similarities are not only defined by the comparative fit but also by the *normative fit*, which refers to the match between the normative content of the category and the stimulus persons. For example, "differences" between Costa Ricans and Germans will tend to be high when they are perceived to behave in the expected way; that is, confirming perceivers' normative beliefs, theories, and stereotypes about how Germans and Costa Ricans should behave.

Assuming a functional antagonism between the different levels of self-categorization, the central hypothesis of the self-categorization theory is that as a group-based self-categorization becomes salient (in virtue of its accessibility and fit), individuals' self-categorization becomes depersonalized; that is, individuals' cognitions, feelings, and behaviors are governed more by their self-perceptions as interchangeable members of their in-group than by their self-definitions as unique personalities (Turner et al., 1987).

Sociostructural Variables and Social Identity Management Strategies

The psychological process described here represents only a part of the explanation. Social interaction does not occur in a social vacuum; it takes places in a specific sociohistorical context, characterized by structural inequalities that determine the emergence of intergroup behavior. In this sense, the need for positive social identity itself is not an alternative to explain conflictual group interests, social stratification, or the large-scale effects of structural processes (Turner, 1996). The theory does not pretend to reduce the macrolevel phenomena to psychological process, but to provide certain knowledge about the psychological mechanisms that might contribute to reproduce or change the macrosocial dynamics of societies.

This point is of special relevance for studies involving ethnic minorities in societies stratified by power, wealth, and status, in which members of ethnic minority groups are often disadvantaged on several dimensions. The social identity theory argues that subordinate group membership potentially confers on its members a negative or threatened social identity. It will produce an unsatisfactory state, which mobilizes individuals to (re)establish a positive social identity. Consistent with this idea, it can be assumed that lower-status groups have (1) a lower self-esteem and (2) a stronger need for favorable group distinctiveness. However, research shows an inconsistent picture. Members of stigmatized groups do not necessarily exhibit lower levels of self-esteem than members of other groups (Crocker & Major, 1989). In addition, there is evidence that members of ethnic minorities who identify strongly with their ethnic groups also show positive attitudes toward other relevant out-groups (Phinney, Ferguson, & Tate, 1997). Finally, it has been found that low-status group members tend to perceive in-group and out-group homogeneities uniformly, and in specific situations they perceive the in-group as more homogenous than the out-group (Lorenzi-Cioldi, 1998).

These findings show that phenomena such as in-group favoritism, out-group derogation, and out-group homogeneity are by no means universal. Individuals act and react differentially to a threatened social identity. It can be argued that in specific occasions individuals seek solutions on the basis of their particular characteristics, but in other situations they act as interchangeable members of their group. In order to specify how people manage the problem of a low-status group membership, the social identity theory introduces the notion of *subjective belief structures*, defined as individuals' beliefs about the features of the intergroup relations in their societies (Tajfel, 1978; Tajfel & Turner, 1979). Within the social identity theory, individuals' belief structures have been analyzed with regard to the supposed legitimacy of the group positions, the assumed stability of status hierarchy, and the perceived permeability of the boundaries between the groups (Ellemers, 1993; Tajfel & Turner, 1979; van Knippenberg & Ellemers, 1990).

Perceived legitimacy and stability define how "secure" or "insecure" the position of a group within the status hierarchy is, and consequently how secure or insecure the social identity of its members is. A secure intergroup comparison context is based on the absence of cognitive alternatives to the status quo (Tajfel & Turner, 1979). For instance, when no cognitive alternatives are subjectively available, group members may accept their low-status position and might not feel motivated to engage in social comparison processes. On the other hand, insecure comparison contexts are those in which the relationship between the groups is perceived as unstable and illegitimate. In these situations, there are active comparisons between the groups involved (even if they are of different status). Consequently, individuals perceive a threat to their social identity and seek to change that state by restoring positive distinctiveness (Tajfel & Turner, 1979).

However, it is the perceived permeability of the group boundaries that is assumed to define the specific strategies that may be used to manage the unfavorable situation. Tajfel (1978) identified two types of beliefs with regard to the permeability of groups: social mobility and social change. The former refers to the belief that the social structure of a society is flexible and permeable, so that individuals can "pass" from low-status groups to high-status groups. The latter refers to the belief that the boundaries between groups are rigid and impermeable, making it impossible for individuals to "leave" their groups.

On the basis of social mobility and change, Tajfel and Turner (1986) distinguish three strategies to improve the outcomes of intergroup comparisons: *individual mobility, social creativity*, and *social competition*.

Individual mobility refers to the strategy of social identity improvement by leaving the low-status group and joining the high-status group. It is basically an individualistic strategy rooted in the belief that personal characteristics (e.g., abilities, effort) will provide a solution for a threatened social identity. As the name suggests, individual mobility implies that group members react to threats at the interpersonal level of interaction; namely, as unique personalities exhibiting low in-group identification (Tajfel & Turner, 1979).

Social creativity represents a strategy to enhance social identity by improving the "comparativeness" of the in-group. It is a "creative" strategy to the extent that it implies a redefinition or alteration of the intergroup comparative terms and represents a collective strategy since it is based primarily on social comparisons, but it does not imply an immediate change in the actual intergroup hierarchy (Tajfel & Turner, 1979). The social identity theory distinguishes three variants of social creativity: (1) comparing the in-group to the (relevant) out-group on a new (more favorable) dimension, (2) changing the values attributed to the features of the group, and (3) selecting other relevant out-groups for comparison.

Finally, social competition represents attempts to change actual positions in the status hierarchy via direct competition with the relevant dominant out-group. It involves a wide range of possibilities, including civil rights movements (e.g., the Black civil rights movement in the 1960s), armed movements (e.g., the Zapatista army of national liberation in Chiapas), and the extreme use of violence (e.g., the terrorist actions of ETA in Spain).

Empirical evidence from research within the social identity approach is relatively consistent with its theoretical premises. Research shows that group members accentuate similarities between themselves and other in-group members and exaggerate differences between the in-group and out-groups (Krueger, 1992). It has been also shown that group members tend to ascribe more homogeneity to out-groups than to the in-group (see Simon, 1992, for a review). Group members tend also to ascribe (more) positive characteristics to in-group members and evaluate their performance or products more positively than out-group members (Ellemers et al., 1997; Wagner, 1994). In conditions of threatened social identity, group members show lower levels of self-esteem (Wagner, Lampen, & Syllwasschy, 1986), express less satisfaction with their in-group (Spears, Doojse, & Ellemers, 1997), and exhibit lower levels of in-group identification (Ellemers, van Knippenberg, de Vries, & Wilke, 1988). Members of "threatened" groups also tend to display more out-group derogation (Branscombe & Wann, 1994) and/or to devalue or reduce the importance of the dimension on which the outcomes of intergroup comparisons are negative (Major & Schmader, 1998).

Research also shows that the effects described depend on the following:

1. the degree of identification with the relevant in-group.
2. the salience of the categorization in the setting.
3. the relevance of the comparative dimension.
4. the extent to which the groups could be compared (e.g., ambiguous similarities).
5. the perception of intergroup competition or threat to the in-group.
6. the numerical relation of the groups.
7. the relative status between groups.
8. the presence of possibilities for status improvement, such as perceived (im)permeability of the groups, (il)legitimacy, and (in)stability of their relations.

Although research within the social identity approach has provided supportive data, some evidence remains inconclusive. Perhaps the most controversial findings are related to the motivational assumption of the theory. The relation between self-enhancement motives and group behavior has been addressed systematically via the self-esteem hypothesis, which states that successful intergroup discrimination enhances self-esteem (corollary 1), but also that a threatened self-esteem promotes intergroup discrimination bias (corollary 2) (Hogg & Abrams, 1990). Recent reviews and meta analyses (Aberson, Healy, & Romero, 2000; Rubin & Hewstone, 1998) show that empirical evidence supports corollary 1 more than corollary 2, and that both high- and low-self-esteem individuals exhibit in-group bias. Conceptualization and measurement problems have been included as possible explanations of the inconsistent results. Several authors call attention to the distinction between individual and collective self-esteem, the existence of different dimensions of self-regard and different areas from which it is derived, as well as to the potential differences between results obtained in laboratory settings and those in field studies (see Branscombe & Wann, 1994; Crocker, Blaine, & Luhtanen 1993; Rubin & Hewstone, 1998; Aberson et al., 2000).

In summary, research within the social identity approach has shown that group-based identity, such as ethnic identity, is the result of the interaction of cognitive self-definition processes, individuals' needs for finding a place in the society, and macrostructural determinants of groups' relations. Research has identified several variables influencing self-definition as a member of a social category, which in turn regulates social behavior toward the in-group and out-groups. For the purpose of this research, the focus has been on factors affecting how members of low-status or stigmatized groups manage the negative outcomes of intergroup comparisons, as in the case of many ethnic minorities in modern societies.[6] Three structural variables have been identified as pivotal in the analysis of identity management strategies: the relative permeability of the group boundaries, the stability of group status, and the legitimacy of the status hierarchy. Clearly, more research (especially outside the laboratory) is needed in order to detect the specific interaction patterns between these variables.

The reason for the special interest in the social identity approach to group behavior here is that these theories provide important insights to understand the social psychological processes underlying the dimension of cultural maintenance among ethnic groups. In effect, when ethnic-group members make decisions about how to acculturate, they are immersed in a context in which the ethnic categories are most likely to be salient and relevant. After all, individuals are making decisions about their place in society. This is especially true for clearly identifiable ethnic minority members faced with issues of prejudice and discrimination.

Attempts to incorporate several predictions of the social identity approach into acculturation research have already been done, especially within bidimensional acculturation models (e.g., Bourhis et al., 1997; Lalonde & Cameron, 1993; Piontkowski et al., 2000). Recall, for example, Lalonde and Cameron's (1993) study on the relationship between perceived status and acculturation strategies, showing that members from (more) stigmatized groups are more likely to endorse collective strategies such as integration. Remember also Piontkowski and colleagues' (2000) work, in which members of nondominant groups were found to adopt the separation or the marginalization mode when they perceived group boundaries as impermeable. In concordance with the framework for research proposed in Chapter 1, these results corroborate the importance of these factors for understanding the dimension of cultural maintenance itself, the specific acculturation modes that emerge from it, and their effect on psychological adjustment.

In order to detect further variables affecting cultural maintenance, several empirical studies on ethnic identity will be reviewed in the following section. It deals with those studies that explicitly address ethnic identity and have been carried out in natural settings (with some noted exceptions from laboratory research) or with "natural" groups as opposed to artificially created group memberships.

ANTECEDENTS OF ETHNIC IDENTITY: EMPIRICAL EVIDENCE

Research on antecedents of ethnic identity has focused on three central issues: the impact of context variables such as relative size or status of the ingroup (cf. Ichiyama, McQuarrie, & Ching, 1996), the role of individuals' demographic features (cf. Broman, Neighbors, & Jackson, 1988), and/or the psychological process underlying the development of ethnic identity (cf. Cross, 1991; Phinney, 1989).

Contextual Factors

Contextual factors have been investigated through a wide range of highly interrelated but distinct variables, including nature and structure of intergroup relations (e.g., perceived discrimination or low in-group status), the characteristics of the immediate context (e.g., numerical relation of the ethnic groups within the neighborhood, in school, or at work), and several features of the groups, such as their structure, organization, and cohesiveness. From the perspective of the social identity approach, these aspects reflect those intergroup situations in which ethnic identity is exposed to threat (e.g., through perception of stigma) and/or becomes salient (e.g., through the numerical relation of the groups).

With regard to perceived attitudes toward the in-group, Ichiyama and colleagues (1996) found in a study on ethnic identity among Hawaiian students in California ($N = 119$) that the more favorable the perceived attitudes toward the in-group, the more positive the students evaluate their ethnic group, and, in turn, the more likely they were to interact with in-group members. However, the expected effect of perceived attitudes toward the in-group on cognitive aspects of Hawaiian identification did not reach statistical significance, indicating (as mentioned) that the reflected appraisals might affect some but not all components of ethnic identity or at least influence them differentially. Similar findings were reported by Verkuyten and Lay (1998) in their study on ethnic identity among Chinese adolescents in The Netherlands ($N = 98$). Using Luhtanen and Crocker's (1992) collective self-esteem scale, they found that the perceived social status of the in-group affected the evaluative (public subscale) but not the affective (private subscale) components of ethnic identity.

Another way to address the effect of reflected appraisals is to examine the impact of perceived discrimination or prejudice on ethnic identity management strategies. In order to address these issues, Ethier and Deux (1994) conducted a longitudinal study with Hispanic students ($N_{time\ 1} = 45$, $N_{time\ 2} = 39$, $N_{time\ 3} = 36$) during their first year at universities attended predominantly by Anglo-American students. Findings show that in the new context students reacted in two different ways: Those who were highly involved with their ethnic background before college were less likely to perceive threats to their ethnicity, became more involved in Hispanic activities at the college, and showed an increase of their identification with the in-group compared to those who reported weak previous group involvement. The latter perceived more threat to their ethnicity, evaluated their ethnic group more negatively, and showed a decrease in their (in any case low) ethnic identification.

In laboratory settings, Phinney, Chavira, and Tate (1993) exposed Hispanic high school students ($N = 109$) to negative or neutral information about their ethnic group. Compared to those who received neutral information, students in the threat condition evaluated their ethnic group more negatively. However, in concordance with other findings (e.g., Crocker et al., 1994), the threat condition did not affect students' ethnic self-concept assessed through Luhtanen and Crocker's (1992) private collective self-esteem scale. In this study, baseline ethnic identity (affective, evaluative, and behavioral components) did not significantly influence participants' responses to threat. However, the within-condition correlations indicated that subjects who were strongly identified with their ethnic group were more likely to affirm a positive view of their group when exposed to threats than low identifiers.

In a similar line of research, Rosenthal, Whittle, and Bell (1989) exposed Greek-Australian adolescents ($N = 119$) to positive, negative, or neutral information about their ethnic memberships. Consistent with the findings described earlier, respondents in the negative condition exhibited less positive attitudes toward the in-group than participants in the positive and neutral conditions. Furthermore, Rosenthal and colleagues showed that exposure to both negative and positive information about ethnic membership makes participants' ethnic identity salient, resulting in a stronger accentuation of cultural differences between Greeks and Australians.

Taken together, these results provide important insights into the way ethnic group members manage threats to their social identity. At the same time, these results uncover the complexity of the issues. Attempts to systematize the relationship between threat, social context, and responses to unsatisfactory social identity have recently been done by Branscombe, Ellemers, Spears, and Doosje (1999). They developed a taxonomy of threats and their effects on social identity management strategies among high and low identifiers. The model predicts, for example, that out-group derogation is likely to be elicited by high identifiers when exposed to negative social comparisons with relevant out-groups, while low identifiers are expected to react to these kinds of threats with disidentification. When individuals are exposed to another type of threat, response patterns among high and low identifiers are assumed to be different. For example, low identifiers (but not high identifiers) will react defensively to categorization threat (being assigned to a social category against one's will), exhibiting further disidentification and accentuation of in-group heterogeneity. Both threat and response are expected to vary according to context-dependent variables such as frame of reference (intragroup versus intergroup comparisons), kind of groups (e.g., face-to-face groups versus large social categories), and nature of the self-categorization (imposed versus self-selected group memberships). Clearly, much research is needed, especially outside of the laboratory, in order to validate these predictions. In natural settings, variables such as the ethnic composition of the immediate context and the specific structural features of the ethnic groups are also important determinants of ethnic identity.

With regard to the effects of ethnic composition of the immediate environment on ethnic identity, Hutnik and Sapru (1996) found among Indian college students ($N = 50$) that the salience of their ethnicity on self-descriptions increased as the number of coethnics in the immediate context increased. Similarly, in their study on ethnic self-identification among Dutch ($N = 291$) and Turkish ($N = 199$) children, Kinket and Verkuyten (1997) showed that the spontaneous use of an ethnic category for self-description depend on the percentage of coethnics in the classroom. However, the relational pattern varied across groups. While Turkish children were more likely to use an ethnic category and evaluate their ethnic group more positively when the percentage of Turkish classmates was higher, Dutch children used an ethnic category more frequently when the coethnics density was lower; that is, when ethnicity was salient in virtue of numerical distinctiveness. Furthermore, there was no evidence for effects of ethnic composition of the classroom on the affective component of ethnic identity. Finally, Broman, Jackson, and Neighbors (1989) reported data from a large national sample of Black Americans ($N = 2,107$), indicating that ethnic identity (defined as feelings of closeness with the in-group) was positively related to reports of being raised in predominantly Black contexts.

Stigmatized ethnic minorities are usually characterized by both low social status and high salience. However, regardless of these features, ethnic minorities differ from each other in terms of their cultural background, structure, organization, and cohesiveness. Thus, examining the effect of these factors by comparing different ethnic minorities within the same society will allow one to understand variation on ethnic identity across ethnic minorities. Rosenthal and Hrynevich (1985) conducted a study involving Greek- and Italian-Australian adolescents that illustrates research on these issues. According to the authors, the Greek community in Australia is highly organized, cohesive, and structured, with substantial institutional supports (e.g., churches and language schools) and cultural distinctiveness (e.g., Greek Orthodox religion), while the Italian community is characterized as more fractured and permeable, with considerable tendencies to assimilation into the dominant Anglo-Australian culture (pp. 725–726). Using factor analytic techniques, it was shown that the structure of ethnic identity among Greek-Australian adolescents ($N = 285$) included a dimension identified as "pride in cultural background" associated with strong involvement with their ethnic background; among Italian-Australian adolescents ($N = 176$) such a factor was absent. Instead, a factor associated with positive attitudes toward assimilation into the majority emerged.

Individuals' Demographic Characteristics

Ethnicity, socioeconomic status, education level, and gender have been issues of major importance within research on the relationship between demographic variables and ethnic identity. Because of structural barriers imposed to ethnic minorities, individuals' demographic features such as education level, occupation, or income usually reflect the relative low status of the groups in the larger society. However, measured at the individual level, demographic characteristics can contribute to an understanding of why across and within ethnic minorities some members tend toward individual mobility while others prefer collective strategies.

The relation between ethnicity, that is, the ascription to an ethnic group via objective markers such as race or physical appearance, and individuals' psychological relationship with the group is not as simple as it seems. Previous research has shown that criteria such as parents' ethnicity do not always correspond with the ethnic label used to describe the self in ethnic terms (Phinney & Alpuria, 1996). Clearly, objective criteria are highly relevant for ethnic self-definition as bases for the social and psychological meaning attributed to them.

In general terms, research indicates that ethnic-minority members attribute more importance to their ethnicity than ethnic-majority members (Martinez & Dukes, 1997; Phinney & Alpuria, 1990; Phinney & Tarver, 1988). In concordance, Verkuyten (1990) found that Turkish adolescents ($N = 237$) evaluate their ethnic identity as more positive than their Dutch classmates do ($N = 2,710$). Furthermore, ethnic identity varies across minority members. In a study involving Asian-, African-, and Mexican-American adolescents, Phinney (1989) found that significantly more Asian Americans reported they would prefer to belong to another group (mostly to the White group) than did Black and Mexican Americans. Using Phinney's (1992) multigroup ethnic identity measure, Martinez and Dukes (1997) found that Native Americans and White Americans scored lower in ethnic identity than Blacks and Hispanics. Applying the same measure, Lorenzo-Hernández and Ouellette (1998) reported that Puerto Rican Americans and African Americans scored higher in ethnic identity than Dominican Americans.

Findings regarding gender are also rather inconsistent. Some studies suggest that females score lower on ethnic identity than males (e.g., Phinney et al., 1993; Verkuyten, 1992), while others report the opposite pattern (Crocker et al., 1994; Martinez and Dukes, 1997). Most studies, however, report no gender differences (e.g., Brookins et al., 1996; Kinket & Verkuyten, 1997; Rosenthal & Feldman, 1992).

Within the same group, ethnic identity also varies depending on individuals' demographic features. Broman, Jackson, and Neighbors (1989) examined the effects of age, gender, education, family income, urbanicity (urban versus rural), and region (South, North, West) on ethnic identification (affective component) using data from a national sample of Black adults ($N = 2,107$). In general terms, rural and southern respondents exhibited higher levels of ethnic identification. Correlational data showed that ethnic identification was stronger as age increased and education decreased. Regression models indicated that age, education, urbanicity, and region were significant predictors of strong ethnic identification. No effects for gender and income were found. Furthermore, significant interactions between education and region indicated that in the South and North (but not in the West), highly educated Black Americans have stronger feelings of closeness to their ethnic group. This suggests that ethnic identity is influenced by interactions between individual-level and context-level variables.

Developmental Factors

Variation on ethnic identity also may be associated with individuals' developmental changes. This relationship has attracted researchers' attention since the seminal work of the Clarks and Horowitz in the 1930s (see Clark & Clark, 1939; Horowitz 1939) on the tendency of preschool and young school-age minority children to perceive themselves as similar to Whites and to express an evaluative preference for White stimuli (see Aboud, 1987; Banks, 1976; Brand, Ruiz, & Padilla, 1974).

Since the pro-White bias was reported, several developmental models have been proposed to describe the consolidation of ethnic identity and attitudes among children (e.g., Aboud & Skerry, 1984; Ramsey, 1987; Vaughan, 1987). In general, the models propose an age-related progression from the unawareness of ethnic membership to the "correct" and constant use of an ethnic category to describe the self, which generally occurs between age three to four and seven to eight, and is related to the acquisition of cognitive competences such as categorization, conservation, and causality (Ramsey, 1987). With regard to the attitudinal responses to ethnic affiliation, findings suggest different patterns across ethnic groups: Majority children exhibit a definite and constant in-group preference, approximately from the age of four on, and tend to be more ethnocentric than ethnic-minority children (see P. Katz, 1987). The latter express less in-group preference at early ages. This decreases with age, while positive attitudes toward the in-group emerge progressively, approximately from the age of twelve on (see Aboud & Doyle, 1995).

It has been suggested that social change might interact with a child's individual development. Cross (1991) and Vaughan (1987) have drawn attention to the fact that pro-White bias was reported more frequently in studies carried out between 1939 and 1960, while positive attitudes toward the in-group emerged more frequently in studies conducted in the late 1960s, during the rise of the Black power movement in the United States or the brown power movement in New Zealand.

With improvements of the abstract thinking abilities (Piaget & Inhelder, 1968), it is expected that adolescents and adults will label themselves "correctly." Therefore, models of ethnic identity development beyond childhood concentrate on individuals' decision-making processes about the role of ethnicity in their lives. Several models have been proposed to describe ethnic identity formation (e.g., Cross, 1991; Phinney, 1989), mostly based on Erikson's (1973) ego-identity development theory as operationalized by Marcia (1980). In general, the development of ethnic identity is conceived as progression from an unexamined ethnic identity, characterized by the lack of interest in or understanding of ethnic issues, through a period of active exploration or moratorium, which includes "immersion" in the history, culture, and traditions of the in-group, to an achieved ethnic identity, characterized by a deeper understanding and appreciation of ethnicity and ethnic background.

Research within developmental models is incipient, but evidence suggests that the importance of and concern with ethnic identity increases with age (Phinney & Chavira, 1992; Martinez & Dukes, 1997). Perhaps the major contribution of developmental approaches is the assumption that attitudes and behaviors toward the in-group and consequently toward out-groups might vary during individuals' psychosocial development. Both theory and research suggest that especially during the period of exploration or moratorium, ethnic identity is highly salient. For instance, one might expect for this period that individuals are more likely to exhibit group behavior. In fact, Cross (1991) describes this stage of ethnic identity development among Black Americans as a transition period characterized by "a very dichotomized view of the world in which all that is White becomes evil, oppressive, inferior, and inhuman, and all things Black are declared superior" (p. 202). It is also a period in which a "person's main focus in life becomes a feeling of 'togetherness and oneness with the [Black] people'" (p. 207).

SUMMARY

This chapter has focused on the first dimension of acculturation, referred to here as the level of identification with the ethnic groups of reference or ethnic identity. Using the social identity approach as the principal theoretical basis for the analysis, it is assumed that group-based self-categorizations are the result of the interaction of cognitive self-definition processes, individuals' motivation for positive group distinctiveness, and the specific features of intergroup relations in society.

Empirical data on antecedents of ethnic identity are consistent with several predictions of the social identity approach. Findings show that in those intergroup situations in which ethnic identity is threatened, individuals elicit two distinct paths of identity management. Some ethnic-group members distance themselves (at least psychologically) from their groups, showing low levels of identification with the ethnic in-group. Other ethnic-group members manage identity threats through more collective strategies, maintaining or reinforcing their ethnic identification and eliciting group behavior. These strategies vary according to several variables, such as the ethnic composition of the immediate context and the support provided by the organization, structure, and cohesiveness of the group. Further variables affecting ethnic identity are such sociodemographic features as ethnicity, socioeconomic status, gender, and age. Evidence also confirms the multidimensional nature of ethnic identity, suggesting that the effect of these factors varies across its components. Kinket and Verkuyten's (1997) data show that salience of the ethnic category might influence the cognitive and evaluative aspects but not the affective component of ethnic identity, while findings from Ethier and Deux's (1994) study suggest that threat might affect all components. In general, further research is necessary in order to detect the specific relationships between all these factors.

The literature here provides relevant insights for the present research. In line with the framework for research proposed in Chapter 1, research on ethnic identity corroborates the need to look at the level of attachment, pride, and esteem derived from belonging to an ethnic group as important sources in adaptation to ethnically plural societies. The next chapter examines the second dimension of acculturation, its correlates and determinants.

NOTES

1. The following review focuses exclusively on conceptualizations of ethnic identity in the empirical and theoretical literature published since 1990. For research conducted before that date, see Aboud (1987), Banks (1976), Brand et al. (1974), Cross (1991), or Phinney (1990).

2. Why and how these components are expected to relate will be discussed in more detail in the next section.

3. This is to the extent that it is a social categorization based in objective markers such as religion, geographical origin, language, race, physical appearance, history, and/or customs (see Giddens, 1993; Gurin, Hurtado, & Peng, 1994).

4. For a historical overview of the approach, see Hogg and Abrams (1988, 1999) and Turner (1996, 1999).

5. On this point, social identity theory and self-categorization theory differ, in that the latter focuses more on the cognitive aspects of self-categorization rather than on the role of self-enhancement motives (Hogg & Abrams, 1999). However, it should be noted that although the self-categorization theory does not develop a motivational analysis of self-categorizations, it acknowledges "that self-categories tend to be evaluated positively and that there are motivational pressures to maintain this state of affairs" (Turner et al., 1987, p. 57).

6. Clearly, there are no reasons to think that high-status group members will not elicit intergroup behavior as a means to protect an insecure social identity. On the contrary, an important assumption of the social identity theory is that "any threat to the distinctively superior position of a group implies a potential loss of positive comparisons and possible negative comparisons, which must be guarded against" (Tajfel & Turner, 1979, p. 45).

3

Intergroup Attitudes
and Behaviors

This chapter focuses on the second dimension of acculturation, contact and participation, which refer to the extent to which individuals desire to maintain positive relations with the larger society and other ethnic groups. When working with members of long-established ethnic groups in plural societies, it seems necessary to focus on their attitudes and behaviors toward relevant out-groups. This will be especially helpful to understand what leads them to engage in positive interethnic contact. Somewhat surprisingly, until quite recently most studies on acculturation have focused only on how members of acculturating groups accept and practice the customs, values, and traditions of out-groups. The specific issue of intergroup relations has been virtually neglected (see Ward & Kennedy, 1994, for a similar criticism). This chapter highlights the utility of the intergroup-relations literature for the conceptualization of both the dimension of contact and participation and the acculturation strategies derived from it.

Some basic processes of intergroup attitudes and behaviors were described in Chapter 2. Since there is no in-group without at least one out-group, it was impossible to ignore phenomena such as out-group derogation and homogeneity when referring to the psychological process of social or ethnic identity. However, while in the last chapter the focus was on individuals' psychological relations with their in-group, this chapter concentrates exclusively on their psychological relations to out-group members.

The first section presents several fundamental concepts in social psychology of intergroup relations in order to provide a basis for later discussion. The second part deals with intergroup hostility. Research shows that negative stereotypes, prejudice, and discrimination are determined by motivational forces, cognitive mechanisms, as well as situational and social structural variables. Therefore, relevant individual-level variables and context factors will be reviewed in this section. The third part deals with intergroup "harmony" as a metaphor of an intergroup situation characterized by positive and effective intergroup communications, mutually positive intergroup attitudes, and no discrimination. The major question here is under which conditions intergroup contact contributes to reach such a goal in ethnically plural societies (see Allport, 1954; Pettigrew, 1998). In the last two sections, relevant theories and empirical examples will be presented.

GROUPS IN CONTACT: BASIC CONCEPTS IN THE SOCIAL PSYCHOLOGY OF INTERGROUP RELATIONS

The social psychology of intergroup relations deals with causes and consequences of individuals' actions and perceptions toward others as members of different social groups. Sherif and Sherif (1979) specified the field of research as follows: "Only those behaviors and associated attitudes that stem from membership in or aspired membership in a human group are properly cases of intergroup relations" (p. 8). Consequently, this area of research focuses on individuals' intergroup behavior (Tajfel & Turner, 1979); that is, on the similarities and uniformities in behavioral patterns that emerge from the intermediate level of self-categorization (Turner, Hogg, Oaks, Reicher, & Wetherell, 1987).[1]

Intergroup relations defined in this way are based on the notion of social groups as cognitive representations of the self and others as belonging to the same social category (Turner, 1999). In line with the social identity approach, a group is a collection of individuals who identify themselves as members of the same category, identify with that social category, and are ready to act according to in-group norms (Turner et al., 1987).

The notion of a social group as a cognitive entity is perhaps the simplest and (because of this) the most comprehensive way to define it. However, groups have been differentially defined over years of research on group processes (see Brown, 2000). For example, Lewin's (1952) definition of a group "as a dynamic whole" (p. 146) was based on the interdependence of its members. Along similar lines, Cartwright and Zander (1968) defined it "as a collection of individuals who have relations to one another that make them interdependent to some significant degree" (p. 46). Finally, Sherif, Harvey, White, Hood, and Sherif (1961) included in their definition several structural characteristics, such as "more or less definite interdependent status and role relationships [and] a set of norms or values regulating the behavior of the individual members" (p. 8). The common assumption of these definitions is that groups consist of people interacting with each other on a face-to-face basis.

While based in social categorization processes, the concept of social group adopted here omits any requirement for face-to-face interactions. It assumes that under certain conditions the self-categorization as member of a group is sufficient to produce some kind of intergroup behavior (Turner et al., 1987). This definition does not deny the fact that social groups have specific structural characteristics (e.g., roles, leadership) and particular internal dynamics (e.g., group think, group polarization) that are important for understanding them. On the contrary, it is applicable to both small interactive groups and large-scale social categories such as ethnic minorities, and is especially appropriate to understanding uniformities of thoughts, feelings, and behaviors among members of the same social category (e.g., Black Costa Ricans), despite the high possibility that some of them will never interact face to face with each other.

Several analyses of group processes have been based on Floyd Allport's (1962) assumption that such phenomena "*lay only in the psychology of the individual as he operated in situations with others*" (p. 5, italics in original). Following this premise, the features of a group have been conceived as the sum (or some other arithmetic procedure) of the particular characteristics of its members. The distinction between interpersonal and intergroup behavior is addressed here as a matter of aggregation of individuals and interindividual interactions; that is, as interpersonal processes among a number of people interacting face to face.

An alternative perspective of group processes assumes that individual-level variables (although important) account only for a partial explanation of group phenomena. This idea can be traced back to writers such as Mead (1934), Lewin (1952), and the Sherifs (1979), and is presently pursued by the social identity approach (Hogg & Abrams, 1988; Tajfel, 1981; Turner et al., 1987; Turner, 1999). Within this perspective, groups and intergroup behavior are conceived as qualitatively distinct from individuals and interpersonal behavior. Consequently, it is assumed here that the analysis of intergroup processes requires the development of alternative or additional conceptualizations.

In particular, research within the second perspective has provided important insights for the analysis of several outcomes of intergroup relations, principally on conflictual outcomes such as stereotypes, prejudice, and discrimination. Almost simultaneously, research has been devoted to the development of effective strategies for reducing these manifestations of intergroup hostility and to promote positive intergroup relations. Before theory and research on these issues will be presented, the following sections focus on the definition and operationalization of stereotype, prejudice, and discrimination in order to provide a "common language" for the next sections.

Stereotypes and Stereotyping

Stereotypes are commonly defined as consensual beliefs about the attributes (e.g., personality traits, expected behaviors, or personal values) of a group of people. Recent conceptualizations distinguish between stereotypes and stereotyping. According to Oaks, Haslam, and Turner (1994), the former are perceptions of persons in terms of their group memberships, while the latter refers to the process of ascribing certain features to people by virtue of their group memberships. In a similar vein, Leyens, Yzerbyt, and Schadron (1994) distinguish between stereotypes as shared beliefs about members of a social category and stereotyping as "an intra-psychic process" (p. 12) of applying stereotypical judgments to individuals as interchangeable members of a social category.

However, several divergences have characterized the discussion about stereotypes since they were introduced in the social sciences by Lippmann (1922) as "the pictures in our heads" of social groups. Thus, in spite of the general agreement about the definition presented here, there has been much less consensus about the specific characteristics or unique properties of stereotypes.

For several authors stereotypes are best defined as "bad"; that is, as factually incorrect, rigid, and/or pathologic beliefs (e.g., Katz & Braly, 1933, 1935; Adorno, Frenkel-Brunswik, Levinson, & Sanford, 1950). By contrast, supporters of the kernel-of-truth hypothesis asserted that some stereotypes may not be totally invalid, at least in a consensual validity sense (see Allport, 1954; Brigham, 1971; Brown, 1995, for a review). Furthermore, contrary to the idea that stereotypes are fixed impressions, several authors define stereotypes as context-dependent, fluid categorical judgments (e.g., Oaks et al., 1994). Finally, in opposition to the pathologic view, other writers assume that stereotypes derive from normal and natural cognitive processes such as social categorization (Allport, 1954; Leyens et al., 1994; Oaks et al., 1994; Tajfel, 1981).

Some authors confine the term "stereotype" to the set of beliefs held by an individual toward a social group and the term "cultural stereotype" to community-shared beliefs (e.g., Ashmore & del Boca, 1981). This is an important distinction for conceptual clarity. It is true that stereotypes are differently shared across individuals. However, when the focus of interest is the processes through which people perceive and are perceived as group members, individuals' idiosyncratic stereotypes might be less relevant. Therefore, it is worth keeping the consensual nature of stereotypes in the foreground (see Hogg & Abrams, 1988; Katz & Braly, 1933; Oaks et al., 1994; Tajfel, 1981; but see also Leyens et al., 1994). Furthermore, since stereotypes are related to in-groups and out-groups, they are not evaluatively neutral (Brown, 1995). Evidence shows that stereotypes about out-group members and minorities are more likely to have negative connotations than those about in-group members and majorities (Ganter, 1997; Hilton & von Hippel, 1996). In addition, negative stereotypes have been shown to be more predictive of intergroup attitudes than positive stereotypes (Stangor, Sullivan, & Ford, 1991).

For many decades the operationalization of stereotypes was determined by Katz and Braly's (1933) checklist. In their seminal study, Katz and Braly asked college students to select from a previously prepared list of eighty-four traits (e.g., intelligent, artistic, aggressive, lazy) those that they considered as typical of ten national or ethnic groups. After that, subjects were asked to go back over the ten lists of words chosen for each group and mark those they considered the five most typical of the group in question. Katz and Braly operationalized stereotypes of a group as the traits most commonly attributed to that group. In general, results revealed considerable agreement between subjects in assigning traits. It was found, for example, that Black Americans were portrayed as "superstitious" by 84% of the sample and as "lazy" by 75%, Jews as "shrewd" by 79% and as "mercenary" by 49%, Germans as "scientifically minded" by 78%, and as "industrious" by 65% of the sample. This study was replicated by Gilbert in 1951 and by Karlins, Coffman, and Walters in 1969 at the same university, showing both stability and change in the endorsement of stereotypes over the time.

A further variant of trait assignment has been proposed by Brigham (1971, 1973). With his percentage estimate procedure, subjects are asked to indicate the percentage of individuals in a given group who they believe possess a particular trait. An extension of Brigham's method is the diagnostic ratio proposed by McCauley and Stitt (1978). It indicates the extent to which the perception of an attribute in a particular social group differs from the perception of that trait in the general population.

Issues related to potential social desirability effects have been addressed through nonreactive measures of stereotyping such as the bogus pipeline (Jones & Sigall, 1971). In this procedure, subjects are convinced that the researchers have a reliable and valid way to detect their "true" feelings and responses. Usually, it involves a bogus psychophysiological apparatus. It is assumed that if subjects believe in the efficacy of the equipment their motivation to distort responses will be reduced. Using this procedure to address stereotypical judgments about "Negroes" and "Americans" among White male students ($N = 60$), Sigall and Page (1971) found that "Negroes" were more negatively stereotyped under the bogus-pipeline condition than in the control (rating) condition. Conversely, "Americans" were more favorably rated under the bogus pipeline than in the rating condition. Other studies report similar effects (see Brown, 1995; Mummendey, Bolten, & Isermann-Gerke, 1982).

Stereotypes also are measured with reaction-time methods, often coupled with priming paradigms (see Dovidio & Gaertner, 1986; Hamilton, Stroessner, & Driscoll, 1994; Locke & Walker, 1999; Lepore & Brown, 1997). These techniques involve the activation of a group label through the presentation of a lexical term (e.g., Blacks) or a photograph, which is followed by the presentation of stereotypical word (e.g., fun loving). Differences in response latencies are commonly used as evidence of the associative strength between stereotypical terms and category labels. These paradigms have been used, for example, to measure the automatic activation of stereotypes when subjects judge ethnically ambiguous targets (Lepore & Brown, 1997).

Prejudice

Prejudice is widely defined as the holding of derogatory attitudes toward members of a group because of their membership in that group. Like stereotypes, prejudices have been characterized in diverse ways. In his review of the literature, Duckitt (1992) identified eighteen (more or less) different definitions of prejudice. Brown (1995) provides four more examples, and Dovidio and Gaertner (1986) add two more to the vast list. Unlike stereotypes, however, there is a stronger consensus among researchers on defining prejudice as derogatory attitudes or disposition. For instance, Allport (1954) defined it as "an antipathy based upon a faulty and inflexible generalization" (p. 9). Harding, Kutner, Proshansky, and Chein (1954) conceived it as "an ethnic attitude in which the reaction tendencies are predominantly negative" (p. 1022). More recently, Brown (1995) defined prejudice as "the holding of derogatory social attitudes or cognitive beliefs, the expression of negative affect, or the display of hostile or discriminatory behavior towards members of a group on account of their membership of that group" (p. 8).

Because prejudice is consensually defined as a negative intergroup disposition, it has been commonly studied as a special case of attitude. In line with the predominant three-component view of attitude, it is assumed (at least theoretically) that prejudice has cognitive, affective, and conative dimensions. According to this view, negative responses toward and negative judgments about group members (affective source) are supported by a particular belief structure of their characteristics (cognitive dimension or stereotypes), which is susceptible to result in hostile actions (conative component). A tripartite model in the conceptualization of prejudice has been adopted by several authors (e.g., Allport, 1954; Brown, 1995; Dovidio & Gaertner, 1986; Harding et al., 1954; Stangor et al., 1991; Tajfel, 1981).

Besides the discussion about the complexity of the "attitude-to-behavior process" (see Ajzen & Fishbein, 1977), the relative contribution of each component in understanding prejudice has also received considerable attention among researchers. For example, Hilton and von Hippel (1996) conceived prejudice as the application of social stereotypes, more specifically as an "outgrowth" of stereotyping (p. 256). By contrast, Stangor and colleagues (1991) argue that affective responses may be relatively stronger predictors of intergroup attitudes than stereotypes to the extent that the former are based on direct, self-relevant experiences, while stereotypes are often learned through secondary sources. Allport (1954) characterized stereotypes as "rationalizers"

(p. 204) developed to justify prejudice and discriminatory behaviors. Similarly, Dovidio and Gaertner (1986) conceived stereotypes as consequences rather than central causes of prejudice.

Once placed in the broader context of research on attitudes, prejudice has been assessed with standard attitude measurement techniques. Traditionally, the assessment of prejudice has included items such as "although social equality of the races may be the democratic way, a good many Negroes are not yet ready to practice the self-control that goes with it" (Woodmansee & Cook, 1967, p. 245) or "the Negroes would solve many of their social problems by not being so irresponsible, lazy, and ignorant" (Adorno et al., 1950, p. 105). Nonreactive measures of prejudice include bogus-pipeline procedures (e.g., Wagner & Zick, 1995), psychophysiological indexes (see Guglielmi, 1999), priming techniques (e.g., Fazio, Jackson, Dunton, & Williams, 1995), and implicit-association tests (Greenwald, McGhee, & Schwartz, 1998).

Recently, considerable attention has been paid to historical changes in the extent of prejudice and the form of its expression. Particularly in the United States, a fading-out effect in the expression of racial hostility and discrimination has been documented over the past three decades (see Dovidio & Gaertner, 1986; Oskamp, 2000). This might reflect, as many authors think, changes in sociocultural norms that make the expression of old-fashioned forms of prejudice less socially acceptable. In the context of the discussion about "symbolic racism" (e.g., Kinder & Sears, 1981) or "modern racism" (e.g., McConahay, 1986), Pettigrew and Meertens (1995) introduced the concepts of blatant and subtle prejudice to distinguish the "hot, close and direct" expression of blatant prejudice from the "cool, distant and indirect" form of subtle prejudice (p. 58). According to the authors, the blatant variant of prejudice includes the direct rejection of ethnic minorities on the basis of a racist belief structure. By contrast, the subtle form rests in the exaggeration of cultural differences, the defense of traditional values, and the denial of positive emotions toward ethnic minorities.

Based on this conceptualization, Pettigrew and Meertens (1995) developed a scale of each variety of prejudice. Blatant prejudice is assessed through items such as "West Indians have jobs that the British should have" or "I would not mind if a West Indian person who had a similar economic background as mine joined my close family by marriage." Subtle prejudice was measured through items such as "West Indians living here teach their children values and skills different from those required to be successful in Britain," and through direct questions of cultural distance and positive feelings toward members of ethnic minorities. The measures were tested in large probability samples from four West European countries ($N = 3,810$). This and other studies support the relative independence of the constructs, as well as their differential contribution in predicting interethnic attitudes (e.g., van Dick & Wagner, 1995; Pettigrew et al., 1998).

Discrimination

Discrimination, in sociological terms, involves complex social processes leading to the production and reproduction of inequalities in the access to socially valued resources such as wealth, income, property, and cultural products (see Giddens, 1993; Pettigrew, 1991). In a more restricted social psychological meaning, discrimination is usually understood as differential treatment based on membership in social categories. More specifically, it refers to those behaviors that limit or deny "individuals or groups of people equality of treatment" (Allport, 1954, p. 51).

Discriminatory behaviors (or individual discrimination) have been assessed via unobtrusive studies (see Crosby, Bromley, & Saxe, 1980). Recently, Klink and Wagner (1999) conducted a series of field experiments on the differential treatment of ethnic minority members in Germany, which exemplified research within these paradigms. In some experiments, Klink and Wagner observed helping behavior in interethnic contexts (confederate asked passers-by for a direction or money for a pay phone). Other studies addressed helping behavior with the lost-letter paradigm (Milgram, Mann, & Harter, 1965). The response of landlords toward home seekers was examined in further experiments. Differential treatment in bars or restaurants was also observed. In all experiments, ethnic-group membership systematically varied (through name, accent, or clothing of confederates). A meta-analysis of the fourteen experiments revealed that ethnic-minority confederates were treated worse than German confederates. Social-distance scales (e.g., Bogardus, 1933; Verkuyten, 1997b), social-attraction measures (e.g., Masson & Verkuyten, 1993), and dating-partner preferences (Liu, Campbell, & Condie, 1995) have been also employed as indicators of behavioral responses toward minority members.

To summarize the picture so far, research on intergroup relations deals with several outcomes of intergroup encounters. Because of their direct policy relevance, stereotypes, prejudice, and discrimination have attracted the most attention. Stereotypes have been widely defined as consensual beliefs about the attributes of social groups and their members; prejudice as derogatory attitudes toward members of a group by virtue of their membership in their group; and discrimination as those behaviors that deny people equality of treatment because of their group membership. Decades of empirical research have provided different methods to assess several characteristics of stereotypes, prejudice, and discrimination. While traditional procedures concentrated in their content, stability, and intensity, recent research paradigms have been employed to address relevant processes underlying them.

Research on stereotypes, prejudice, and discrimination has produced an extensive and complex literature (see, for an overview, Oskamp, 2000). In effect, each of these constructs represents a vast research field in itself. However, since negative stereotypes, prejudice, and discrimination represent conflictual outcomes of intergroup relations, they will be approached here as distinct manifestations of a general phenomenon of intergroup hostility. The following section presents an overview of research on these issues.

UNDERSTANDING INTERGROUP HOSTILITY

According to the social identity approach, intergroup attitudes and behaviors should be conceived as a function of the psychological processes underlying individuals' self-categorizations as group members and structural characteristics of the objective relations between social groups in a given social system. As Tajfel (1981) argued, "A psychological theory of intergroup relations must provide a two-way link between situations and behavior, and it can do this through an analysis of the motivational and the cognitive structures which intervene between the two" (p. 129). Following this theoretical argument, this section examines theory and research on both individual-level and context-dependent determinants of intergroup hostility.

Individual-Level Factors

At the individual level of analysis, intergroup-hostility literature has addressed both motivational and cognitive mechanisms as important causes of stereotypes, prejudice, and discrimination. Within motivational factors, special attention has been paid to personality, feelings of frustration and deprivation, as well as motivated social-comparison processes. Cognitive phenomena such as categorization, perceptual salience of stimuli, out-group homogeneity, and attributional biases received the attention of researchers as well. Both motivational forces and cognitive processes are also responsible for a further important determinant of intergroup attitudes; namely, individuals' levels of commitment to the in-group. Empirical evidence suggests that individuals' demographic features, such as education level, socioeconomic status, gender, and ethnicity, also contribute to the understanding of prejudiced attitudes. Gender has usually been included in the analysis as a control variable. Differences in interethnic attitudes across different ethnic groups have also been less studied. Nevertheless, some empirical evidence of variation in intergroup attitudes across gender and ethnicity will be included in the next sections.

Motivational Sources

Within motivational approaches, some researchers have attempted to detect the "type of individual" (i.e., the type of personality) most likely to elicit negative intergroup attitudes and behaviors. Often cited as the prototypical example of such approaches, the authoritarian personality theory posits that intergroup hostility rests in individuals' intrapsychic conflicts (Adorno et al., 1950). According to the theory, the basic motivational conflict underlying the authoritarian personality emerges from a strict and punitive parental socialization, in which socially unacceptable impulses (e.g., sex, aggression) are unusually harshly restricted. It follows that idealized parental figures are introjected and become generalized to all authority figures, while resentment and hostility toward the parental authorities are repressed and displaced onto others, who are seen as subordinates who violate roles and norms.

The product of these psychodynamics is a syndrome of specific covarying personality traits: "The authoritarian individual is conventional; has aggressive feelings toward 'legitimate' targets (e.g., homosexuals); and is submissive to authoritative or strong leadership" (Stone, Lederer, & Christie, 1993, p. 4). The next logical step in the explanation of intergroup hostility is that as a consequence of this specific personality syndrome some individuals (namely the authoritarians) are more susceptible to supporting stereotypic belief systems, express more negative affect and derogatory attitudes toward minorities, and elicit more discriminatory behavior than others.

Combining large-scale psychometric testing (e.g., F-scale) and individual clinical interviews, the research program initiated by Adorno and his colleagues (1950) developed and tested a number of measures of intergroup attitudes and personality traits (see Stone, Lederer, & Christie, 1993, pp. 3–21, for a detailed review). In general, results seem to support the idea that the motivation to repress intrapsychic conflict leads authoritarians to employ prejudice as a kind of "safety valve." More recently, Meloen (1993) explored the validity of authoritarianism measures (F-scale or derivatives) as predictors of antidemocratic and pro-fascist tendencies in studies carried out between 1945 and 1985. In general, the results showed that supporters of ideologies associated with Nazism, fascism, racism, or nationalism scored higher in authoritarianism than the general population. Finally, van Dick and colleagues (1997) found that measures of authoritarianism were significantly correlated with rejection of multicultural society across four different West German samples.

Aside from its conceptual and methodological shortcomings, the authoritarian personality theory has been intensively criticized because of its proclivity to individualistic reductionism (see Brown, 1995; Pettigrew, 1996; Zick, 1997, for a detailed account of the principal deficits). Several alternative models have been proposed in order to place authoritarianism in the situational and social structural context of intergroup relations. Altemeyer's (1988) cognitive-learning approach to authoritarianism as a network of beliefs and attitudes, Duckitt's (1989) conception of authoritarianism as a particular orientation to the in-group, and Pettigrew's (1999) authoritarianism-in-context model represent important attempts to avoid dispositional and compositional fallacies in the interpretation of intergroup hostility at the individual level of analysis.

Theories derived from the frustration–aggression hypothesis (Dollard, Doob, Miller, Mowrer, & Sears, 1939) still follow a psychodynamic logic stressing motivational conflicts as an explanation of intergroup hostility. According to this view, derogatory attitudes toward out-group members are responses to frustration; that is, they result from the motivation to restore the psychological equilibrium lost by the impossibility of achieving personal goals and necessities. However, in contrast to Adorno and colleagues (1950), these models do not hold a pathologic view of the psychological processes underlying intergroup hostility.

The basic assumption of the frustration–aggression hypothesis is that "the occurrence of aggressive behavior always presupposes the existence of frustration and, contrariwise, that the existence of frustration always leads to some form of aggression" (Dollard et al., 1939, p. 1). Here, the displeasure and psychic tension caused by the blocking of goal achievement is assumed to be relieved only via aggression, which is usually directed at the source of frustration. However, when the sources of frustration are either not easily identifiable or are powerful enough to retaliate, the aggression is redirected onto alternative, usually vulnerable and "legitimate" targets. Hovland and Sears's (1940) famous study of the relationship between economic recession and anti-Black violence seems to support the hypothesis.

In response to several criticisms, especially regarding the explanation of the selection of targets, the scapegoat theory specifies under which conditions the displacing process occurs (see Berkowitz, 1962; Hovland & Sears, 1940). For instance, Berkowitz (1962) suggested that aggression against specific targets is only expressed when the act will not elicit counteraggression or punishment; the target is visible, distinctive, or "strange"; there exists previous dislike toward the scapegoat; and the perceived characteristics of the target groups (i.e., stereotypes) justify and permit the scapegoating. Berkowitz also suggested that dissatisfaction and unrest derive from intragroup comparisons, especially "when we look at objects we believe we have some chance of getting, because we regard ourselves as relatively similar to the person having those things, that we are frustrated at the inability to realize our hopes" (p. 88). However, issues concerning the choice of specific scapegoats and the conditions for the displacement are still vague. Clearly, an approach based exclusively on intraindividual motivational factors suffers a basic conceptual deficiency: It fails to explain by itself the historical uniformity of prejudice toward certain social groups.

Models based in the construct of *relative deprivation* also stress personal dissatisfaction as the basis for intergroup hostility (Crosby, 1976; Gurr, 1970). Crosby (1976) defines relative deprivation as the feeling "that one has been unjustly deprived of some desired thing" (p. 88). Thus, relative deprivation refers to the psychological state derived from discrepancies between expectations and achievements. This state is characterized by feelings of dissatisfaction and, in extreme forms, by anger or antagonism. Deprivation is assumed to be relative to the extent that (1) objective deprivation criteria do not always correspond with subjectively experienced deprivation, and (2) deprivation results from negative discrepancies when making comparisons. Walker and Pettigrew (1984) summarize the basic conceptualization of relative deprivation as follows: "Persons may feel deprived of some desirable thing *relative* to their own past, another person, persons, group, ideal, or some other social category" (p. 302, italics original).

The idea that social comparisons are important sources of deprivation makes the construct of relative deprivation especially suitable for a social psychological analysis of intergroup relations. Particularly the distinction between egoistic deprivation and fraternal deprivation introduced by Runciman (1966) represents a shift in the conceptualization from an exclusively microlevel of analysis to a more compressive explanation of intergroup hostility incorporating contextual factors. Egoistic or individual deprivation occurs when individuals engage in intragroup comparisons, while fraternal or collective deprivation derives from intergroup comparisons.

Following this distinction, Vanneman and Pettigrew (1972) proposed four types of relative deprivation and gratification. Double-gratified people are those who feel their economic situation is better or equal than both in-group and out-group members. Fraternally deprived individuals are those who think they do well personally, but poorly as group members. Egoistically deprived people feel their group does well relative to out-group members but they do poorly compared with in-group members. Double-deprived individuals are faced with negative discrepancies relative to both in-group and out-group members.

A logical derivation of this distinction is that fraternal deprivation should be more predictive of intergroup attitudes and behaviors than egoistic deprivation. In their classic study on the relationship between relative deprivation, racial attitudes, and voting behavior, Vanneman and Pettigrew (1972) provided empirical support for this assumption. They found among Whites that perceived deprivation relative to Blacks was positively related to anti-Black attitudes. In addition, it was found that fraternally deprived Whites were less willing to vote for Black politicians and evaluated them less favorably than those experiencing egoistic deprivation. Similar attitudinal patterns have been found in West Europe (see Pettigrew et al., 1998). Using data from the 1988 Eurobarometer 30 survey these authors show that measures of fraternal deprivation are positively correlated with measures of prejudice (particularly with the blatant variant), while egoistic deprivation scales are not. Finally, in a recent study on the relationship of discontent and assertive actions in working women ($N = 70$), Hafer and Olson (1993) found that collective deprivation, but not individual discontent, predicted collective reactions (e.g., support of a walkout or strike in order to protest against the status of working women).

A further model that posits special attention to the interactive effects of motivation and social comparison is the social identity theory. As pointed out before, the social identity approach argues that negative discrepancies in the evaluation of the in-group relative to a relevant out-group mobilize individuals to maximize the positive distinctiveness of the in-group, particularly on dimensions that are relevant for social identity. Under certain structural conditions (i.e., impermeability, instability, and illegitimacy of intergroup relations), this process can lead to collective actions and intergroup hostility (Tajfel & Turner, 1979).

This process, indeed, depends to some extent on the level of self-categorization that has been made salient in the intergroup situation (Turner et al., 1987). If personal identity is salient, it is expected that people engage in interpersonal comparisons. Consequently, negative outcomes derived from interpersonal comparisons will probably lead to egoistic deprivation. In this case, such individualistic symptoms as stress or depression rather than collective actions are expected. By contrast, when individuals perceive themselves as group members it is more likely that they engage in intergroup comparison, which (in case of negative outcomes) can lead to fraternal deprivation, and in turn to collective behaviors and intergroup hostility.

In effect, Vanneman and Pettigrew (1972) found that fraternal deprivation was especially great among members highly identified with their in-group. Empirical data reported in Chapter 2 show similar results: When faced with illegitimate low status (a clear example of collective deprivation), high identifiers, but not low identifiers, react through collective strategies, reinforcing their ethnic identification and eliciting group behavior (see Branscombe, Ellemers, Spears, & Doosje, 1999; Ethier & Deux, 1994).

There are important similarities between some relative-deprivation models and the social identity approach. Both perspectives stress the importance of motivational factors and social-comparison processes in the emergence of intergroup hostility, and both attempt to address how structural realities are subjectively perceived to affect individuals' feelings, thoughts, and actions. Walker and Pettigrew (1984) argue that theories derived from research on collective relative deprivation represent important formalizations of the social identity theory. However, the authors draw attention to the predominant tendency among some researchers to emphasize only the egoistical variant of deprivation and its mechanisms to account for collective responses (e.g., Crosby, 1976). The result is a reductionistic view of relative deprivation in line with Floyd Allport's (1962) conception of group phenomena.

The major differences between the social identity theory and the relative-deprivation theory lay precisely in this point. They hold different assumptions about the psychological processes underlying personal and collective discontent. The social identity theory provides an analysis of individuals' self-perception to understand when collective deprivation is more likely to be experienced. It also predicts when group behavior will occur, depending on the perceived structural relations between groups. Finally, the social identity theory explicitly acknowledges the need to consider not only motivational but also cognitive processes affecting the perception of both the self and the intergroup context.

Cognitive Underpinnings

As pointed out in Chapter 2, the social identity approach assumes that individuals' tendency to form relevant groups or categories affects the perception of both in-group and out-group members via perceptual overestimation of intracategory similarities and intercategory differences. Such accentuation effects are expected to be particularly strong when people are themselves implicated in one of the categories (Tajfel, 1981). More specifically, it is assumed that the activation of social categories lays in the interaction between (1) perceiver's motivations, past experiences, and current intentions; (2) the characteristics of the stimulus relative to the context; and (3) the perceived characteristics of intergroup relations (Turner et al., 1987; Oaks et al., 1994).

A similar idea was proposed by Allport (1954). He argued that the categorization processes of prejudice are an outgrowth of normal processes of creating groups and generalizations. He also assumed that categories are not merely descriptive, but evaluative in their nature. Once they make the "separation of human groups," individuals use the salience of particular social and physical cues (i.e., race, sex, age) as "faulty" principles of organization leading to the grouping of "similar" people into discrete categories.

Along similar lines, the social-cognition literature conceives social categories or schemas as cognitive structures that contain and organize individuals' knowledge about social reality (Fiske & Taylor, 1991). The use of these shortcuts is assumed to affect encoding, memory, inference, and evaluation processes. Again, this literature posits that individuals use distinctive cues (race, sex, age) to organize the complexity of environmental information based on similarity versus dissimilarity criteria (Bruner, 1957; Taylor, 1981).

These propositions suggest that both categorization and perceived salience of the stimulus (although normal and adaptive) are a potential basis for group behavior. There is considerable empirical support for these assumptions. Research in laboratory settings has shown that the activation of social categories occurs extremely rapidly when coupled with stereotypes (see Fiske, 2000). Furthermore, in both the physical and social domains people tend to minimize within-category differences and maximize between-category differences (see Tajfel, 1981). Once categorization occurs, behaviors of group members are perceived in stereotypical terms. For instance, Taylor, Fiske, Etcoff, and Ruderman (1978) reported experimental data in which male stimulus persons were seen as more analytical and less sensitive than female stimulus persons, although the behavior showed by the stimuli was held constant.

In addition, data show that the salience of physical or social cues (by virtue of numerical distinctiveness or "solo status") reinforces the categorization (Taylor et al., 1978), and that stimulus salience combined with prior knowledge produce polarized evaluations of the categories (A. Nesdale, Dharmalingam, & Kerr, 1987). As described in Chapter 2, when individuals are involved in the categorization as members of one category they usually evaluate the in-group more favorably than out-groups on dimensions relevant to in-group definition (Wagner, 1994; Ellemers, van Rijswijk, Roefs, & Simons, 1997). Empirical data also suggest that categorization effects interact with social norms. Socially "marked" groups are more likely categorized than "unmarked groups"; that is, Blacks tend to be categorized as Blacks regardless of their gender (see Fiske, 2000).

The tendency to accentuate out-group homogeneity is also a function of categorization, stimulus salience, previous knowledge, and cultural norms (e.g., prevailing stereotypes). That is, not only out-groups are perceived as more homogeneous than the in-group. The numerical relation between in-group and out-group also affects judgments of variability. Research suggests that majority members conceive minority members as more homogenous than they view themselves (Lorenzi-Cioldi, 1998), and that minorities share this perception when the dimension of comparison is important for the maintenance of social identity (Simon, 1992).

Categorization and stimulus salience (in this case, via infrequency of occurrence) are responsible for the emergence of the *illusory correlation effect* (Chapman & Chapman, 1967). Hamilton and colleagues (see Hamilton, 1981) showed that the overestimation of the relationship between two classes of events responds to the overestimation of the cooccurrence of distinctive and infrequent stimulus events. The combination of two types of infrequency, one involving a social category (e.g., ethnic-minority members), the other involving undesirably behaviors (e.g., physical attacks), will be especially relevant for the formation of stereotypes.

Finally, causal attribution for socially desirable versus undesirable behaviors are also deeply shaped by social categorization, stimulus salience, previous knowledge, and cultural norms, which facilitate the emergence of what Pettigrew (1979) calls the *ultimate attribution error*; that is, the tendency to attribute undesirable behaviors to internal, dispositional causes when elicited by out-group members. Research also shows that these factors interact with motivational forces (e.g., the need for positive social identity). Recent experimental data by Hunter, Reid, Stokell, and Platow (2000) illustrate these issues. Group members in the experimental condition, who were given the opportunity to display group-serving attribution biases, showed higher levels of collective self-esteem than group members in the control condition.

In sum, while acknowledging the role of cognitive factors, several writers show that intergroup hostility is not exclusive of "ill" individuals, but applicable to all group members. Category-based intergroup perceptions fulfill several functions. These structures serve to understand the social world; that is, to organize and simplify the social environment, reduce uncertainty, preserve important social values, and regulate social interactions (Allport, 1954; Oaks et al., 1994; Tajfel, 1981).

In-Group Commitment

Peoples' behaviors are not only guided by the need for understanding, but also by the need for belonging (see Fiske, 2000). Affiliations in social categories deeply shape self-perception and attitudes toward others. The social identity approach explicitly acknowledges the role of commitment to the in-group in these issues. It posits that people, when acting as group members, engage in various forms of intergroup discrimination in order to achieve and maintain a positive group-based self-regard (see Hogg & Abrams, 1988; Tajfel & Turner, 1979). A number of empirical studies support the idea that group behavior is stronger among individuals who feel highly identified with the in-group than those who feel less committed (see Doosje, Ellemers, & Spears, 1999; but see also Hinkle & Brown, 1990). However, research on acculturation predicts that among some individuals (i.e., integrationists), a secure sense of commitment with the own culture will be related to positive interethnic attitudes. There is also some empirical support for this idea (e.g., Lambert, Mermigis, & Taylor, 1986; Szapocznik et al., 1980).

In fact, the relation between in-group identification and intergroup attitudes is by no means straightforward. In-group preference does not always imply less positive out-group attitudes. In their review of several studies on intergroup attitudes and behaviors, Hinkle and Brown (1990) show that in-group and out-group attitudes might be positively and negatively related and even unrelated. In a recent study on intergroup attitudes among ethnic minority adolescents (133 African Americans, 219 Latinos, and 195 Asian Americans) by Phinney, Ferguson, and Tate (1997), path analyses revealed that strong commitment to the in-group predicted positive in-group attitudes, and these in turn predicted positive (rather than negative) out-group attitudes.

By contrast, Tzeng and Jackson (1994) found among White, African, and Asian Americans (total $N = 484$) that in-group favoritism affected interethnic hostility in line with Sumner's (1906) ethnocentrism prediction. Respondents high in in-group favoritism expressed the most hostile behavioral intentions, anti-out-group affective reactions, and negative out-group evaluations toward out-groups compared with subjects neutral and low in this measure. However, when the impact of in-group favoritism was examined separately for each group, data patterns were less consistent. Among Blacks, for instance, those low in in-group preference expressed more hostile affect toward out-group members than those high in ethnocentrism.

Verkuyten (1997b) found among 410 Dutch adolescents (between fourteen and sixteen years old) that respondents with high collective self-regard expressed less favorable attitudes toward out-groups than those with low collective self-esteem, confirming the classical assumption. He also explored the relative contribution of stereotypes, symbolic beliefs, affective responses, and social distance in predicting attitudes toward out-groups, controlling for individuals' levels of collective self-regard. Data show that out-group attitudes were better predicted by these predictors among respondents with high in-group pride than among participants low in collective self-regard.

These results highlight the complexity of the issue. Chapter 2 showed that identification with the in-group depends on several individual-level variables and contextual factors. Evidence also suggests that the effect of these factors varies across the specific components of ethnic identity. Thus, it is reasonable to think that the same factors will interact with individuals' in-group identification in affecting out-group attitudes, and that some components of social identity will be more responsible for these effects than others. Phinney, Ferguson, and Tate (1997) found that commitment (affective component) had only an indirect effect on out-group attitudes via in-group attitudes (evaluative component). Tzeng and Jackson (1994) found the effect using an evaluative measure of the in-group implying direct comparisons between in-group and out-group. Finally, Verkuyten (1997b) demonstrated the predicted relation using Luhtanen and Crockers's (1992) private collective self-esteem subscale, which measures in-group pride. Further research is necessary in order to detect the specific contribution of each component on out-group attitudes.

Another difficulty in the analysis of the relationship between in-group commitment and intergroup attitudes concerns the interpretation of the causal direction. On the one hand, Doosje and colleagues (1999) report data from laboratory settings in which the level of commitment was manipulated, suggesting that identification was sufficient to produce group behavior irrespective of structural-context variables such as permeability of group boundaries. On the other hand, Duckitt and Mphuthing (1998) reported longitudinal data from Black African students in South Africa ($N = 101$), suggesting a causal impact from attitudes to identification and not the reverse.

Thus, research on the relation between individuals' commitment to the group and intergroup attitudes corroborates Tajfels's (1981) idea that intergroup relations should be understood as a function of individuals' (as group members) variables and context-dependent factors. A further key variable that could help to clarify such contradictory results is the nature and quality of intergroup contact, which can potentially affect the self-categorization, affecting the affective responses toward in-group and out-group members (see Pettigrew, 1998). The specific contribution of intergroup contact will be discussed later. First, the role of further individual-level variables in shaping intergroup attitudes should be addressed briefly.

Individuals' Demographic Characteristics

One of the most frequently documented phenomena in research on intergroup attitudes is that formal education and (in a less consistent way) economic status are negatively related to derogatory attitudes toward out-group members (see Zick, 1997, for a review). Several explanations for the so-called poor-White-racism thesis have been developed. From a cognitive point of view, educational differences in ethnic attitudes will respond to differences in cognitive capacities, such as verbal intelligence, cognitive complexity, and associative flexibility. An impression-management explanation posits that higher-educated people might be especially sensitive to social desirability. Finally, a cognitive-motivational perspective argues that lower-educated people might react to social-identity threats by engaging in intergroup comparisons with those groups that allow them positive outcomes; that is, socially "marked" groups such as ethnic and racial minorities, asylum seekers, and immigrants (see Wagner, 1994, for a review).

Recently, Wagner and Zick (1995) examined the relationship between education and prejudice in both survey data and laboratory settings. Survey data (1988 Eurobarometer 30) showed that the negative covariation between formal education and intergroup attitudes (feelings of antipathy, subtle and blatant prejudice) was highly consistent across seven representative samples from Western Europe, controlling for socioeconomic status and target group. In addition, an experimental study involving German young adults ($N = 130$) corroborated the effect of formal education on devaluation of ethnic minorities using bogus-pipeline controls for social-desirability effects. Less-educated individuals expressed more negative evaluations toward out-groups than higher-educated subjects. These differences were greater in the bogus-pipeline condition than in the paper–pencil condition, indicating that self-presentation biases do not account for the observed differences between the groups. Finally, Wagner and Zick examined the potential effect of several social psychological variables as mediating variables that could explain the educational differences in the expression of prejudice. These were relative deprivation (both fraternal and egoistic); perceived incongruency between in-groups' and out-groups' values, traditions, and practices; political conservatism; national pride; and interethnic contact. Feelings of group relative deprivation, conservatism, incongruency, and contact were found to be especially important mediating variables of the education effect, confirming motivational and cognitive explanations of the poor-White-racism thesis. However, these controls did not remove the predictive quality of formal education; that is, a significant direct causal path remained from education to less prejudice even after these mediating effects were considered.

Gender has commonly been included as a control variable, but in most cases it is virtually neglected in the analysis. Some authors have explicitly examined gender differences in intergroup attitudes, assuming that men's tendency to competitiveness and women's communal and emotional concerns affect their attitudes toward out-groups (e.g., Verkuyten, 1997b). Empirical evidence seems to support the idea that males tend to express more negative attitudes toward out-groups than females (e.g., Phinney, Ferguson, & Tate, 1997; Masson & Verkuyten, 1993; Wagner, 1983). Male subjects have been found to be more sensitive to perceive threats to social identity and more xenophobic than females (Watts, 1996). Females express more acceptance toward racial minorities and homosexuals than males (Qualls, Cox, & Schehr, 1992). However, many studies show no gender differences in intergroup attitudes, and in some of them females have been found to elicit more prejudice than males (e.g. Pettigrew, 1959).

Finally, research on intergroup attitudes has shown that some effects, such as in-group bias, are consistent across diverse ethnic groups and cultural set-

tings (see Gudykunst & Bond, 1997). However, variation on out-group attitudes across ethnic groups have also been reported, pointing out the need to
look at the role of ethnicity in the analysis of these issues. Research with
children suggests that out-group attitudes develop among majority and minority children differently. Commonly, majority children show negative attitudes
toward out-groups from four to five years of age on (Aboud, 1987). By contrast, the initial out-group attitudes among minority children are not equally
negative (recall the pro-White bias). Among adolescents, Phinney, Ferguson,
and Tate (1997) found that African Americans showed more positive out-group
attitudes than Latinos (school district 1), and that Latinos expressed more positive out-group attitudes than Asian Americans (school district 2). Among adults,
Liu and colleagues (1995) found that Latinos were less ethnocentric in dating
preference than White, African, and Asian Americans.

In summary, research has shown that individual-level variables play an important role in several expressions of intergroup hostility. The literature reviewed here shows that individual-level variables and context-dependent factors
are strongly related. Even the simplest act of categorization is deeply influenced by both the immediate setting in which the categorization takes places
and the broader context of cultural norms and values that influence the content
of the category. It seems clear that the analysis would be incomplete if contextual factors were not taken into account.

Contextual Factors

Contextual factors affecting intergroup hostility are related to the structural
features of the intergroup situation and how it is experienced by group members. These issues have been systematically addressed through three major
theories: the realistic group conflict theory (Sherif, 1979), the social identity
theory (Tajfel & Turner, 1979), and the intergroup contact theory (Allport,
1954; Pettigrew, 1998). The following paragraphs focus on the central principles and empirical evidence of the two first theories. The intergroup contact
theory will be considered later.

Conflicting Group Interests

The realistic group conflict theory posits that intergroup hostility emerges
from the direct competition between groups for scarce and valued resources,
such as power, prestige, or wealth. According to the theory, unfavorable stereotypes, in-group biases, and derogatory attitudes toward out-group members are more likely to occur when groups are competitively interdependent;
that is, when the gain of desired goals by one group results in loss for the
other. In addition, conflicting interests are assumed to enhance intragroup solidarity and cohesiveness and increase members' attachment with the group. By
contrast, when groups are cooperatively interdependent through the presence

of a superordinate goal, intergroup hostility will decrease. These general postulates were initially validated by Sherif and collaborators (1961) in their famous "summer camp studies," and replicated in both experimental and field settings with children and adults (see Brown, 2000, for a review).

Some realistic group conflict models emphasize both objective and perceived conflict between groups (e.g., Bobo, 1983). While incorporating considerations from relative deprivation and modern racism theories, other approaches concentrate on subjectively perceived threats from an out-group (e.g., W. S. Stephan & Stephan, 2000). These writers distinguish between realistic and symbolic threats. The former concern threats to the physical, material, economic, and political power of the in-group (e.g., "Mexican immigrants are contributing to the increase in crime in the United States"). By contrast, symbolic threats concern threats to the cultural system (e.g., "Mexican immigration is undermining American culture"). Thus, in concordance with the conceptualization of subtle prejudice (Pettigrew & Meertens, 1995), symbolic threats refer to perceived differences in values, beliefs, and practices. According to this view, the greater an out-group is perceived to produce a threat to the in-group, the more negative the attitudes toward that group will be.

Empirical evidence is relatively consistent with these general principles. Perceived conflict was found to have a significant impact on cognitive evaluation, affective reactions, and behavioral disposition among Whites and African and Asian Americans in Tzeng and Jackson's (1994) study. Subjects with greater perception of conflict showed significantly higher hostility than those who perceived little or no conflict with an out-group. Again, separate analyses for each group revealed cross-ethnic differences. Among subjects high in conflict perception, Whites expressed more out-group hostility than Asian and African Americans. This finding suggests that social status may interact with the perception of conflict.

Research inspired in the integrated threat theory (W. S. Stephan & Stephan, 2000) has found that both realistic and symbolic threats are significant predictors of attitudes toward immigrant groups in the United States (W. G. Stephan, Ybarra, & Bachman, 1999). However, outside of the United States, results are less consistent. In Spain, for example, realistic threats were only marginally significant predictors of attitudes toward Moroccan immigrants, and symbolic threats failed to reach statistical significance at all (see W. G. Stephan, Ybarra, Martinez, Schwarzwald, & Tur-Kaspa, 1998).

Structural Characteristics of Intergroup Relationships

The social identity theory also acknowledges the effect of structural characteristics of intergroup relations in stratified societies on the emergence of intergroup hostility. However, it qualifies several assumptions of the initial realistic conflict theory.

First, Tajfel and Turner (1979) argued that conflicting interests do not necessarily lead to intergroup hostility. In such a case, cognitive alternatives to the status quo will be required. Moreover, even if the relationship between the groups is experienced as unstable and illegitimate, intergroup hostility will depend on the perceived permeability of group boundaries, which offers a great range of options, from individual mobility through social creativity to direct competition. Second, the social identity theory posits that competition for limited resources is not a prior condition for intergroup discrimination. As pointed out before, the mere categorization into relatively meaningless categories has been shown to be sufficient to trigger certain in-group bias, suggesting that there are additional sources of competitive tendencies. Third, with the notion of social competition (Turner, 1975) it is assumed that people could engage in competitive aims irrespective of objective gains and losses. In this case, intergroup hostility will emerge from the perception of threats to the prestige and distinctiveness of the in-group relative to meaningful out-groups. Finally, it is assumed that the emergence of hostility will be mediated by the dynamics of social identity (cognitive and motivational sources) that are activated when in-group prestige and distinctiveness are threatened.

Empirical evidence of these assumptions has been discussed already in previous chapters (see Chapter 2). Intergroup behavior seems clearly to depend on the interaction between structural beliefs and identification with the in-group (see Ellemers et al., 1988, 1997; Branscombe & Wann, 1994). As pointed out before, the evidence is supportive but far from conclusive. Issues related to the role of each component of the "threatened" social identity in the emergence of group behavior and the question of how people perceive the different threats are addressed in current research programs (e.g., Branscombe et al., 1999), but still deserve more empirical testing. The cross-cultural validation of the theory still represents an important challenge.

To summarize research on intergroup hostility so far, decades of experimental and field research have resulted in a vast and complex literature reflecting the multiple causation of intergroup hostility. Fiske (2000) organizes the history of research on these issues into three periods: Having commenced with an exclusively motivational emphasis in the 1930s, research and theory became more exclusively cognitive in the 1970s and 1980s, followed by a cognitive–motivational balance in the 1990s. In this way, the literature has identified a number of important factors influencing the way in which individuals act and react toward out-group members. At the individual level, motivational and cognitive mechanisms as well as educational level and socioeconomic status seem to have great impact. At the group level, the specific characteristics of the contact situation and the perceived characteristics of the intergroup boundaries appear as central determinants of intergroup hostility. Research illustrates clearly the interactive effect of individual-level and context variables on intergroup attitudes and behaviors.

INTERGROUP HARMONY:
PRECONDITIONS AND MECHANISMS

As pointed out already, intergroup attitudes are largely defined by characteristics of the intergroup situation and how they are experienced by the participants in the interaction. Intergroup contact can occur in terms of competition or interdependent cooperation in the pursuit of common goals, groups in contact can be equal or unequal in status, and participants in the interaction can perceive themselves as unique individuals or as representative members of their social groups, and so contact can be interpreted as a threat or as an opportunity of enrichment. In the literature of intergroup relations, these issues have been addressed through intergroup contact theory (Allport, 1954).

Optimal Intergroup Contact

Intergroup contact theory postulates that under certain conditions intergroup contact will contribute to reduce intergroup hostility. Obviously, bringing members of different social groups into contact does not assure positive outcomes per se. Allport (1954) demonstrated the complexity of the issue by distinguishing several situational variables affecting intergroup contact outcomes. These include quantitative and qualitative aspects such as frequency, duration, and variety of contact, status and role relationships within the interactions, the atmosphere surrounding the contact situation, and the different areas in which contact takes place. However, from the vast list of conditions, Allport identified four assumed to be necessary for optimal intergroup contact: (1) equal status, (2) common goals, (3) intergroup cooperation, and (4) institutional support. Later refinements of the theory (see Brown, 1995; Cook, 1978; Brewer & Miller, 1984; Pettigrew, 1998) highlighted a further critical condition, labeled "acquaintance potential" (Cook, 1978) or "friendship potential" (Pettigrew, 1997).

An intergroup situation structured in this way is assumed to provide stereotype-disconfirming information to the extent that group members are equal in ability and worth (see Brown, 1984). It also will contribute to positive interdependence because group members need each other to achieve a superordinate goal (see Gaertner, Dovidio, & Bachman, 1996; Sherif, 1979). Finally, it will facilitate the development of meaningful relationships, the discovery of interpersonal similarities, and, in turn, interpersonal attraction and mutual positive affect (see Cook, 1978).

The contact hypothesis has generated extensive research in both naturalistic contexts and laboratory settings (for extensive reviews, see Brewer & Kramer, 1985; Brown, 1995; Pettigrew, 1998). In general, empirical evidence is consistent with the central idea of the theory. Supportive evidence has been found among children (e.g., Rich, Kedem, & Shlesinger, 1995), adolescents (e.g.,

Masson & Verkuyten, 1993), and adults (e.g., Hamberger & Hewstone, 1997) across different cultural settings on all continents (see Pettigrew, 1998).

Recent meta-analytical findings by Pettigrew and Tropp (2000) summarize the vast research literature on these issues (see also Pettigrew, 2000). Data from 376 studies, 525 independent samples, and more than 156,000 subjects reveal an overall contact-prejudice mean effect of $r = -0.19$. Several important predictors of the strength of the relationship between contact and prejudice were found. The specific setting in which the contact takes place is one of them. Studies conducted in work or organizational settings yield the largest effects, followed by laboratory and school settings, while contact studied in recreational contexts had the lowest effect sizes. Group status was also related to the link between contact and prejudice. Effect size for minority members' samples was smaller than for majority samples, indicating that the intergroup situation might be understood differently depending on the social status of the participants in the interaction. A further predictor was the type of measure used to tap prejudice. Studies using measures of emotions showed the strongest effects, while stereotype and sociometric measures yield the weakest. Tests using intergroup friends as a contact measure yield a contact-prejudice mean effect remarkably higher than the mean effect of those studies in which friendship was not addressed. In addition, although contact seems to have positive effects with and without the presence of all critical conditions, effect sizes were higher in those studies in which most of the critical conditions were met than in studies without them. Finally, these data suggest that intergroup contact effects usually generalize from the group members participating in the contact situation to the entire group, and even to groups not involved in the contact situation (see Pettigrew & Tropp, 2000; Pettigrew, 2000).

It is with these results in mind that one of the principal debates in the literature of intergroup contact can be addressed briefly: the question of how positive attitudes toward participants in the optimal contact situation can be generalized to (1) the entire group, (2) distinct situations, and (3) other groups not involved in the situation.

Generalization of Contact Effects: How Does Contact Work?

Considerable efforts have been made to examine the psychological changes involved in an optimal contact situation that might be responsible for the cross-level, cross-situation, and cross-group generalization of positive effects (see Brown, 2000; Pettigrew, 1997, 1998). Three different models have been developed to address these issues: the personalization model (Brewer & Miller, 1984), the distinct social identity model (Hewstone & Brown, 1986), and the common in-group identity model (Gaertner et al., 1996). Each of these models starts from the same assumption: Positive effects of optimal intergroup contact are mediated by changes in individuals' cognitive representations of in-group, out-group, and their relationship. Each model, however, suggests a different pathway to reduction of intergroup hostility.

The Personalization Model

This model is based in the assumption that positive contact effects are mediated by decategorization. It is assumed that contact reduces in-group biases because it facilitates the elimination of group boundaries via two processes: differentiation and personalization. Differentiation refers to changes in the perception of the participants in the interaction. It implies attending to their unique characteristics as individuals. Personalization implies paying "attention to personalized information about others that is self-relevant and not correlated with category membership" (Brewer & Miller, 1984, p. 288). In other words, personalization represents a change in the level of self-categorization from the intermediate (social-identity) to the subordinate (personal-identity) level (Turner et al., 1987). Thus, an optimal contact situation reduces intergroup hostility because it promotes interactions between unique individuals rather than group members. In addition, it is assumed that through the frequent use of personalized information participants in the interaction will learn to act and react more as individuals and less as group members in different situations, leading to generalization of positive contact effects.

Empirical support for this model has been provided mostly by laboratory studies in which group memberships are experimentally created. Evidence indicates that positive outcomes emerge especially when individuals participate in cooperative team tasks with out-group members under personalized conditions (Brewer, 1996). However, in "real-world" settings using "natural" groups, results are much less consistent (see Rich et al., 1995).

The Distinct Social Identity Model

This model is based on the assumption that positive effects are mediated by subcategorization. According to this model, the optimal contact situation reduces prejudice because it facilitates mutual differentiation within an interdependent cooperative context. Contrary to the personalization model, the distinct social identity model warns of attempts to eliminate the existing in-group–out-group divisions. This might be perceived as a threat to preexisting value-laden social categories, which in turn would mobilize individuals to restore positive distinctiveness by perceiving in-group homogeneity, increasing self-stereotyping, and eliciting out-group derogation. According to this model, the generalization of the contact benefices lays precisely in keeping the salience of the subgroup identity in the optimal situation. As Brown (1995) argues, "If this can be successfully arranged then any positive change engendered during contact is likely to transfer readily to other members of the outgroup because one's contact partners are seen as somehow typical of that group" (p. 262).

Supportive evidence for this model has been provided by Dechamps and Brown (1983), who asked art and science students to cooperate in a superordinate goal (to produce a magazine article). Here, more positive intergroup attitudes were found when group members assumed distinctive but complementary roles (e.g., one group working in layout, the other on text) than when the two groups adopted similar roles. More recently, Brown, Vivian, and Hewstone (1999) reported survey data from European countries concordant with the idea that frequent and cooperative contact is strongly related to positive intergroup attitudes, particularly when (1) the contact persons were seen as typical representatives of their national categories and (2) when the distinctiveness of their nationalities was salient during the contact.

The Common In-Group Identity Model

The common in-group identity model assumes that positive effects are mediated by recategorization. According to this model, contact is beneficial in part because it "transforms members' cognitive representations of the membership from two groups to one" (Gaertner et al., 1996, p. 273). This will be the case when Blacks (us) and Whites (them) become part of a more inclusive category (we). According to this model, the induction of a superordinate social identity will make possible generalization to out-group members absent in the contact situation, because the "new identity" will maintain "the associative link to these additional out-group members" (p. 275). The rationale for these considerations is the observation that intergroup hostility usually begins as in-group enhancement rather than out-group derogation. Thus, inducing a new more inclusive social identity that encompasses both in-group and out-group will redirect the cognitive and motivational processes that usually are activated in intergroup situations.

Consistent with the model, data from both laboratory and field settings show that a greater perception of a superordinate identity is predictive of lower levels of intergroup bias toward former out-group members (see Gaertner et al., 1996; Dovidio, Kawakami, & Gaertner, 2000, for reviews).

Integrative Issues

The different models reviewed here provide well-founded but divergent points of view about the processes and consequences of an optimal contact situation. Given real differences between groups, sometimes it is impossible, undesirable, and even counterproductive to neglect intergroup boundaries. However, a situation that promotes the interaction between unique individuals via personalization or common in-group identity seems to be necessary to disconfirm stereotypes and facilitate interethnic acquaintance or friendship. Yet if contact takes place only on an interpersonal basis, the general intergroup attitudes might remain intact.

Brewer (1996, 2000) suggests a potential solution of this apparent paradox by combining elements of all models. She suggests an integrated perspective in which a salient superordinate level of categorization allows for subordinated differentiation and individualization. This would be possible by making people aware of multiple, cross-cutting group memberships. In a cross-cutting cooperative context, members of different groups are assigned roles or functions that are necessary to achieve a common goal, and are independent of (i.e., cross-cut) the original social categories. For instance, some members of each group will assume leadership roles, while others follower roles. This will allow the perception of cross-cutting similarities between in-group and out-group members and personalization, but at the same time it provides them opportunities for optimal distinctiveness.

Gaertner, Dovidio, and colleagues (Gaertner et al., 1996; Dovidio et al., 2000) also acknowledge the importance of maintaining subgroup distinctiveness. They posit that the adoption of the superordinate identity does not require the loss of the subgroup identity. From this point of view, members' subgroup and superordinate group identities can exist simultaneously in a "dual identity." In effect, their empirical findings show that group members who identify with both the subgroup and the superordinate group elicit lower bias than those with only subgroup identity (see Gaertner et al., 1996, study 2).

Pettigrew (1998) introduces the time dimension to disentangle the contradiction. He suggests thinking of decategorization, mutual differentiation, and recategorization as different stages leading to prejudice reduction with generalization. According to his longitudinal intergroup contact theory, the first phase of contact should minimize the salience of the initial group membership. It will allow the discovering of similarities, which enhance attraction and friendship potential. Once initial anxiety and potential negative expectations are diminished, he suggests introducing the mutual distinctiveness facilitating generalization. Finally, recategorization is assumed to yield the maximum reduction of prejudice, if time and the optimal conditions promote participants to conceive themselves as members of different "subgroups on the same team."

Clearly, there are factors affecting contact outcomes that are not intrinsic to the situation, but are related to participants' characteristics, actual expectations, and past experiences. For instance, W. S. Stephan and Stephan (2000) emphasize the role of individuals' intergroup anxieties. They posit that people might experience the intergroup situation as a threat because they might expect negative outcomes for the self, such as being embarrassed, ridiculed, exploited, or rejected. The authors suggest that intergroup anxiety is more likely to occur when group members belong to groups having a history of antagonism, perceive that their groups are highly different, have little prior personal contact, know little about the out-group, are ethnocentric, and interact in competitive intergroup contexts in the minority status. As Pettigrew (2000) pointed out recently, intergroup anxiety can affect the contact processes in three ways: by increasing contact avoidance, limiting positive effects, and mediating contact effects.

A further meaningful variable is the subjectively perceived importance of contact. As noted, people can perceive intergroup contact as a threat or as an opportunity for enrichment. Individual differences in the perceived importance of intergroup contact seem to be an important variable affecting contact effects, as recently demonstrated by van Dick and colleagues (2001). Using structural equation models, they demonstrate that the relation between contact (both distal and proximal) and intergroup attitudes is largely mediated by respondents' perceptions of contact as valuable and meaningful. The mediating effect of perceived importance was found across nine different samples ($N = 24{,}325$) involving both minority and majority members in diverse cultural settings (Germany and Costa Rica), using different dependent measures such as antipathy toward out-group members, blatant and subtle prejudice, immigration attitudes, and acculturation attitudes.

To summarize research on intergroup contact so far, efforts to improve intergroup relations originally concentrated almost exclusively on the characteristics of optimal intergroup contact. Several facilitating conditions have been proposed over years of research. However, it seems that equal status, common goals, intergroup cooperation, institutional support, and "friendship potential" are critical. Later on researchers focused on the processes mediating changes predicted by the intergroup contact theory, producing important insights on the cognitive and affective changes underlying contact effects. Recent developments have begun to integrate more explicitly the subjective experiences that individuals bring to the intergroup contact situation. In this section, two examples of individuals' perceptions of intergroup contact have briefly addressed intergroup anxiety and perceived importance. Further research is needed to understand the specific roles of these factors and their interaction with each situational variable.

SUMMARY

This chapter has focused on an overview of relevant theories of intergroup relations in order to detect important processes underlying the second dimension of acculturation. Decades of research on these issues has demonstrated that there are multiple paths leading individuals to engage in positive interethnic contact (see Oskamp, 2000). In this chapter the focus has been on those individual-level variables and situational factors that have been found to be especially relevant to understanding the role of intergroup attitudes and behaviors on adjustment to ethnically plural societies among ethnic-group members. Individuals' in-group commitment and their education level, socioeconomic status, gender, and ethnicity seem to have great impact. The objective and perceived characteristics of the contact situation appear as central determinants of intergroup attitudes and behaviors. Clearly, any intergroup situation is deeply influenced by social context (e.g., societal norms, integration policies, laws, mass media), which structures both the form and the effects of contact (see Pettigrew, 1998).

Central to the present research is the observation that intergroup contact, under optimal conditions, leads to reduction of intergroup hostility. It indicates that neither the avoidance of contact (e.g., separatism or segregationism) nor absorption into the host society (e.g., assimilation) will solve the problems of intergroup relations in ethnically plural societies. Reducing prejudice by eliminating group boundaries could be perceived as a threat to distinctiveness leading to intergroup hostility (at least among those group members who identify strongly with the subgroup category, given certain structural conditions). On the other hand, attempts to maintain the groups segregated, even in the form of a "separate but equal" structure, reinforce ignorance, preserve stereotypes unchallenged, and facilitate the emergence of intergroup anxiety. Interacting in such a system will require a strong normative structure against open forms of intergroup hostility, as Pettigrew and Meertens (1996) demonstrated in their analysis of intergroup relations in The Netherlands. However, such political systems are rare in the world, and even the strongest normative structure can easily be destabilized by economic or political crisis.

Rather, theory and research support the idea that the best contact outcomes emerge from mutual differentiation within an interdependent cooperative context, as assumed by recent models of intergroup contact (Brewer, 1996; Dovidio et al., 2000; Gaertner et al., 1996; Hewstone & Brown, 1986; Pettigrew, 1998). This conceptualization is compatible with the notion of multiculturalism at the macrolevel, and is comparable with the concept of the integration strategy at the individual level. The next chapter examines the thesis that integration strategy provides the best outcomes not only for individuals' collective self-regard but also for their personal self-esteem.

NOTE

1. As pointed out by Pettigrew (personal communication, March 2001) from a more comprehensive view, a social psychology of intergroup relations should also include group-to-group considerations apart from individuals-as-group-members analyses. The definition presented here does not concur with Pettigrew's suggestion (as he also noted). It rather stresses the importance of including the processes of psychological group formation in the social psychological analysis of intergroup relations, as will be seen later.

4

Psychological Adaptation

This chapter focuses on the psychological outcomes of acculturation or psychological adaptation. As pointed out in Chapter 1, the adjustment to ethnically plural contexts implies decision-making processes leading to (at least) four modes of acculturation. The central proposition of this research is that acculturation and adaptation among ethnic groups is primarily determined by their psychological relations to both their ethnic group of reference (ethnic identity) and other ethnic groups (interethnic attitudes and behaviors) within a superordinate structure; namely, the larger society. Following this assertion, in Chapters 2 and 3 relevant processes underlying each dimension of acculturation were examined. This chapter attempts to integrate the general findings reported in previous chapters in order to describe and explain the specific outcomes of the two dimensions and four strategies of acculturation for individuals' personal adjustment to ethnically plural societies.

This chapter begins with a general definition of psychological adaptation and several related concepts. The second part examines the way in which acculturation might relate to psychological well-being. The third part describes empirical evidence of the predicted outcomes. The chapter ends with an overview of the hypothesis guiding this research.

PSYCHOLOGICAL ADAPTATION
TO ETHNICALLY PLURAL SETTINGS

In a general sense, adaptation refers to the processes of adjustment to the prevailing conditions in the environment. Within acculturation research, adaptation has been commonly referred to as the level of "fit" between the acculturating individual and the mainstream cultural context (Berry & Sam, 1997). Adaptation, in this sense, represents the long-term psychological outcomes of individuals' acculturation processes. In recent literature, a distinction between psychological and sociocultural adjustment has been introduced (e.g., Ward & Kennedy, 1993). The former is particularly associated with psychological well-being, while the latter is related to the ability to interact effectively in the mainstream cultural environment.

Specifically, psychological adaptation includes a positive sense of personal identity, life satisfaction, and "good" mental health. It has been commonly assessed with measures of self-esteem (e.g., Grossman, Wirt, & Davids, 1985) and psychological adjustment (e.g., Roccas, Horenczyk, & Schwartz, 2000), including specific checklists to measure anxiety, depression, and psychosomatic symptoms (e.g., Ryder, Alden, & Paulhus, 2000) and dysfunctional behaviors such as alcohol and drug abuse (e.g., Szapocznik, Kurtines, & Fernández, 1980). Sociocultural adaptation is characterized by the development of adequate social and cultural skills to deal with everyday social situations and demands in the mainstream cultural context. It has been measured in terms of individuals' difficulty performing daily tasks such as making friends, participating in social activities, understanding the local language, or managing work- or school-related issues (e.g., Ward & Rana-Deuba, 1999).

From the point of view of research on intergroup relations, adaptation can be understood as the development of cultural and social competencies, which allow individuals to interact effectively with both the ethnic group of reference and other ethnic groups. Adaptation implies the development of sensibility to the beliefs, values, and norms of the culture. It also presupposes the acquisition of adequate communications skills, beginning with the ability to communicate clearly in the language of the given cultural group. A culturally and socially competent individual can maintain active social relations and perform effectively within institutional structures (see LaFromboise, Coleman, & Gerton, 1993). For many group members, adaptation comprises the development of strategies to cope with issues such as prejudice and discrimination (see Crocker & Major, 1989). Finally, the development of effective cultural and social competencies should be reflected in a positive personal and ethnic identity, personal satisfaction, and good mental health.

Adaptation is by no means absolute. Depending on a great variety of factors, it can take place in the form of increased "fit" between the individual and the mainstream society. As mentioned in Chapter 1, the characteristics of the intergroup relations prevailing in the society represent important factors affecting how individuals acculturate, and in turn how satisfied they feel as individuals and as members of a subgroup within the larger society. Positive psychological outcomes are expected when both dominant-community members' and minority members' orientations match regarding integration and assimilation. Likewise, less "fit" and even conflicts are expected when there is discordance between majority and minority members' acculturation modes, as, for instance, when ethnic minority groups aim to integrate while mainstream community members prefer them to assimilate (see Berry & Sam, 1997; Bourhis, Moise, Perreault, & Senéca, 1997).

Acculturation per se does not compromise individuals' mental health. However, in extreme cases individuals' capacity to cope with the demands of the mainstream cultural context can be exceeded, leading to high levels of psychological distress. Experience of prejudice and discrimination is just one example of the many stressors for acculturating individuals (see Clark, Anderson, Clark, & Williams, 1999; Jasinskaja-Lahti & Liebkind, 2001). The concept of *acculturative stress* has been developed to address the opposite outcomes of successful adaptation. Williams and Berry (1991) defined it as a special type of stress derived from the processes of acculturation, "often resulting, in a particular set of stress behaviors, that include anxiety, depression, feelings of marginality, and alienation, heightened psychosomatic symptoms, and identity confusion" (p. 634).

Further variables affecting positive adaptation are related to the phase of acculturation (e.g., initial contact, conflict, crisis) and the personal resources of the acculturating individuals. Thus, the time people have been exposed to the mainstream culture, their coping styles (e.g., task-oriented versus emotion-focused coping), perceived social support, personal characteristics (e.g., demographic features), and acculturation orientations are important personal resources influencing the psychological outcomes of acculturation (see Berry, 1997; Liebkind, 1996; Nesdale, Rooney, & Smith, 1997; Szapocznik et al., 1980; Ward & Kennedy, 1993; Williams & Berry, 1991).

For the purposes of this research, *global self-esteem* will be used as the primary indicator of positive psychological adaptation. Self-esteem has been widely defined as feelings of personal worth. Rosenberg and Kaplan (1982) used the notion of self-esteem to refer to the evaluative-dimension self-concept. Coopersmith (1967) defined it as "the evaluation which the individual makes and customarily maintains with regard to himself: it expresses an attitude of approval or disapproval, and indicates the extent to which the individual believes himself, to be capable, significant, successful, and worthy" (p. 4). Porter and Washington (1982) refer to self-esteem as a general evaluative view of the self, "which, if high, comprises feelings of intrinsic worth, competence, and self-approval rather than self-rejection, and self-contempt" (p. 225).

A global feeling of self-regard is only one of many indices of psychological adjustment. However, it is widely recognized as a central aspect of psychological functioning and well-being (see Wylie, 1979, for a review). Self-esteem has been shown to be positively related to optimism, personal satisfaction, and self-efficacy (see Crocker & Major, 1989), and negatively to depressive symptoms (see Harter, 1996). Crocker and Quinn (1998) describe self-esteem as "a central aspect of the subjective experience and quality of life, . . . powerfully related to variables that influence the affective tone of one's daily experience" (p. 169).

As such, the concept of self-esteem is a relevant construct for understanding psychological adaptation among ethnic groups because of its theoretical link to ethnic identity. The conceptual basis for the relationship between ethnic identity and self-esteem derives largely from the social identity theory (Tajfel & Turner, 1979), with the assumption that both personal and social identities represent two subsystems of self-concept. However, the idea that membership in social categories is an important source of self-evaluations has a long history within social psychology (see Mead, 1934; Allport, 1954; Sherif & Sherif, 1979).

Thus, a positive sense of belonging to one's group is assumed to be related to positive self-esteem, while negative attitudes and feelings toward the ingroup will be related to low self-esteem (see Phinney, 1991). Empirical research within the social identity approach is consistent with this idea (see Chapter 2). In addition, since membership in social categories is an important source of self-regard, the prevailing intergroup attitudes and behaviors in a given social system are assumed to affect the self-perception of a member of an ethnic group and in turn the self-esteem (Tajfel, 1981). However, it is inappropriate to see a deterministic relation between ethnic identity, intergroup attitudes, and self-esteem. As will be seen later, there are several psychological processes mediating the impact of intergroup phenomena on self-esteem (Crocker & Major, 1989). For the moment, it is important to emphasize that feelings of self-regard are theoretically and empirically associated with psychological adjustment, acculturation, and intergroup phenomena.

In sum, research on acculturation has defined adaptation as the level of "fit" between the acculturating individual and the cultural environment. Positive adaptation is reflected in a clear sense of personal and cultural identity, good mental health, and the achievement of efficient cultural and social competencies. The term acculturative stress has been employed to address the negative outcomes of acculturation, which comprise anxiety, depression, and feelings of anomie, psychosomatic symptoms, and identity confusion. Because of its theoretical links to the dimensions of acculturation, self-esteem is assumed here to be an important hint of the level of adaptation in ethnically plural societies.

Although most research on acculturation and adaptation has been carried out to address adjustment problems among immigrants, refugees, or sojourners in the "new" cultural context, it is argued here that these concepts are also appropriate to describe acculturation experiences among members of long-established ethnic groups in ethnically plural societies. Furthermore, adaptation in terms of acquisition of cultural and social competencies represents a cultural requirement for both ethnic minority and majority members in modern societies, since both are faced with the cultural demand of interacting in social settings that are becoming (more than ever) ethnically and racially diverse (see LaFromboise et al., 1993, for a similar argument). The next section examines more closely how acculturation might relate to psychological well-being.

ACCULTURATION OUTCOMES

Because of its practical relevance, the relationship between acculturation and psychological well-being has been the subject of extensive research over the past decades (see Berry, 1997, for an overview). Several predictions about the psychological outcomes of intercultural contact have been formulated in line with the two predominant formulations of acculturation; namely, the linear–bipolar view and the two-dimensional perspective.

Unidimensional models predict that psychological adaptation should increase as individuals relinquish their "old" and adopt the "new" culture. In line with the idea that acculturation is a gradual and inevitable process of absorption into the host society, it is expected that low-acculturated individuals experience anxiety, isolation, stress, and low self-esteem as a result of difficulties in coping with the new environment and the gradual loss of support provided by the ethnic group of reference. However, adjustment problems will decrease once "successful" assimilation gradually takes place. In other words, assimilation is assumed to relate positively and linearly with psychological adaptation (see Szapocznik, Scopetta, Kurtines, & Aranalde, 1978; Grossman et al., 1985).

However, a number of important studies reveal inconsistent and even contradictory results (see Rogler, Cortes, & Malgady, 1991). As pointed out by Ryder and colleagues (2000), this is in part because the predictions derived from linear models are themselves unclear. The question remains whether adaptation occurs because of the loss of the original culture, or rather because of the acquisition of the new culture. In addition, since researchers within these approaches assume mutual exclusion between ethnic subgroup and mainstream identification, they are clearly not sensitive to the possibility of testing the idea that both contribute positively to psychological adjustment.

Contrary to linear models, two-dimensional approaches assume that strong identification with the ethnic group of reference and positive orientations toward other ethnic groups and the mainstream society represent orthogonal dimensions that might contribute differentially to individuals' positive adjustment, leading to different types of adaptation. It should be noted that two-dimensional approaches also acknowledge that, with time, some long-term positive adaptation might occur. However, they propose an alternative conceptualization to the somewhat deterministic linear–bipolar models, arguing that adaptation is rather probabilistic depending on several individual- and group-level moderating factors.

At the individual level, acculturation strategies are well-known factors shaping individuals' positive adaptation (Berry, 1997). A review of the literature suggests that integration affords the best psychological outcomes and marginalization the worst, while assimilation and separation are linked with an intermediate level of adjustment (see Berry, 1997; Doná & Berry, 1994; Phinney, 1991; Ward & Rana-Deuba, 1999).

Integration seems to be the most adaptive strategy because it provides individuals with two social support systems and represents the absence of intergroup conflict (Berry, 1997). It is known from research on intergroup contact that a dual identity assures individuals optimal distinctiveness as subgroup members and provides them with pride and esteem derived from both the subgroup and the superordinate social identity (Brewer, 1996; Hewstone & Brown, 1986; Gaertner et al., 1996). Finally, integration can be interpreted as the successful achievement of effective social and cultural competencies when interacting with both the ethnic group of references and other ethnic groups, which in turn provides individuals with a sense of self-efficacy (LaFromboise et al., 1993).

By contrast, marginalization is related to the worst outcomes because of the absence of these support systems and the presence of potential intergroup conflicts (Berry, 1997). As seen in Chapters 2 and 3, membership in social categories provides individuals with a frame for orientation in the social world and self-definition. As such, social categories are important tools to understand and organize the social environment, reduce uncertainty, preserve social values, and regulate social interactions (Tajfel, 1981). Finally, psychological distance from both the ethnic group of reference and the mainstream culture is also indicative of low cultural and social competence.

People who favor separation have the benefits from the self-protective properties of membership in a value-laden social category (Crocker & Major, 1989). Interacting in predominantly in-group settings (with similar people) allows individuals to have self-affirmation. However, the lack of experience in bicultural or mainstream settings could have negative consequences for the development of effective cultural and social competencies, including the ability to develop strategies to manage prejudice and discrimination (see Phinney, 1991). As seen in Chapter 3, the avoidance of intergroup contact might reinforce ignorance about out-groups and negative stereotypes, and can be associated with high intergroup anxiety, which represents an important stressor for members of both ethnic-minority and ethnic-majority members (see W. S. Stephan & Stephan, 2000).

Finally, people who prefer assimilation compromise their group membership. This might represent a strategy to manage a negative social identity, indicating low satisfaction with the in-group (see Ethier & Deux, 1994). These attempts at individual mobility will expose individuals to derogatory attitudes toward the own group that prevail in mainstream settings (Rogler et al., 1991). Phinney (1991) points out that such attempts might also provoke negative sanctions from members of the in-group, who may see them as a kind of betrayal.

However, assimilation can also be interpreted as a successful adaptation to bicultural settings, providing individuals with feelings of self-efficacy (see LaFromboise et al., 1993).

In sum, a brief review of the literature on the relationship between acculturation and psychological adjustment highlights the complexity of the issues. Contrary to the parsimony of traditional models, which predict positive outcomes of assimilation, two-dimensional perspectives emphasize a multiple causation of individuals' adjustment to ethnically plural environments. This research examines the specific contribution of acculturation dimensions and strategies, which are assumed to relate in a predictable fashion to individuals' well-being. Everything else being equal, integration is assumed to afford the best psychological adaptation, while marginalization is assumed to be the least adaptive strategy. Separation and assimilation are conceived as intermediate strategies regarding their contribution to personal satisfaction in ethically plural societies. The next section examines empirical evidence testing these predictions.

EMPIRICAL EVIDENCE

The separate consideration of the psychological relation to the ethnic group of reference and the mainstream culture might be especially helpful in understanding acculturation and adaptation. However, most research on acculturation has focused on strategies at the expense of the study of the two underlying dimensions of acculturation. From the conceptualization of acculturation strategies, one can deduce that both dimensions have an additive effect on psychological adaptation. However, the impact of each dimension might vary across acculturating groups, depending on their particular characteristics, so that both dimensions might display different patterns of association with psychological adaptation. In order to address these and other related issues, this section begins with an overview of research on the specific relationship between each dimension of acculturation and measures of well-being. After that, their interactive effect (i.e., acculturation strategies) on self-esteem and other related constructs will be reviewed.

Ethnic Identity and Self-Esteem

In general, research results are consistent with the assumption that a positive sense of ethnic identity is related to feelings of self-regard. Lorenzo-Hernandez and Ouellette (1998) report positive correlations between ethnic identity and self-esteem among Dominicans ($N = 102$), Puerto Ricans ($N = 45$), and African Americans ($N = 31$). Similarly, Martinez and Dukes (1997) found in a large sample of adolescents from different ethnic groups, including White, Native, African, Hispanic, and Asian Americans ($N = 12,386$), that ethnic identity was positively related not only to self-esteem but also to self-confidence and purpose in life. In a recent study with Vietnamese immigrants in Australia by Nesdale and colleagues (1997), affective and evaluative components of ethnic identity were found to be significant predictors of self-esteem. Ward and Rana-Deuba (1999) showed that the preference for maintaining the heritage culture predicted greater psychological adjustment among international workers in Nepal. Ward and Kennedy (1994) report similar findings among sojourners in New Zealand ($N = 98$). Those with strong ties to their own group exhibited less psychological adjustment problems than those low in coethnic identification. Finally, Doná and Berry (1994) found that the best predictor of low psychological stress among Central American refugees in Canada ($N = 101$) was the tendency to maintain the Latin culture.

On the contrary, Ryder and colleagues (2000, study 2) found that mainstream orientations, but not heritage-culture orientations, were significant predictors of psychological adjustment among Chinese Canadians ($N = 150$). Similarly, ethnic identity was found to be unrelated to measures of well-being among Italian Australians ($N = 82$), as reported by Rosenthal and Cichello (1986). Verkuyten (1990) found that ethnic identity (evaluative component) had only a marginal impact on predicting global self-esteem among Turkish adolescents in The Netherlands. Other sources of self-evaluation, such as body image and popularity, had a greater impact.

One reason for such inconsistencies seems to be the particular experience and the specific characteristics of the acculturating groups in question. Note, for example, that Ryder and colleagues (2000) worked with members of long-established ethnic minorities (first- and second-generation Chinese Canadians), for whom a successful adaptation to the mainstream society will be central for their psychological well-being, while Ward and Rana-Deuba's (1999) sample was composed predominantly by Western European and North American international aid workers on temporary assignment to Nepal.

In effect, several factors might moderate and even explain the link between ethnic identity and self-esteem. Prior research suggests that (1) the particular characteristics of immediate context, (2) specific features of the ethnic group of reference, (3) demographic characteristics of the individuals (especially gender and socioeconomic status), and (4) individuals' developmental changes are particularly important for personal self-esteem.

Regarding the characteristics of the immediate context, proponents of the insulation hypothesis (e.g., Rosenberg & Simmons, 1972) argue that minority members in predominantly majority settings will be more likely to have lower levels of self-esteem that those interacting within the ethnic group of reference. The rationale for this assumption is that in a majority context minority members are exposed to prevailing negative attitudes toward the own group. In addition, it is assumed that in mainstream settings norms and values differ from those of the own group. Finally, the comparison groups in mainstream settings, namely the privileged majority, will reinforce relative deprivation. Evidence supporting this assumption is rather inconsistent and even contradictory. While Rosenberg and Simmons (1972) found that Black children in segregated schools exhibited higher self-esteem than those in integrated settings, Krause (1983) as well as Zirkel and Moses (1971) found no relationship between ethnic composition of the immediate environment and self-esteem.

On the contrary, ethnic identity might be positively related to self-esteem precisely by virtue of numerical distinctiveness. Phinney and colleagues (Phinney, 1992; Phinney, Cantu, & Kurtz, 1997) found some empirical support for this argument among White adolescents. Only in those settings in which they were a small minority (e.g., in predominantly non-White schools) was ethnic identity positively correlated with self-esteem. Thus, being in a minority situation can reinforce in-group solidarity, and in turn enhance the importance of the in-group for self-evaluation.

Research also shows that the link between ethnic identity and self-esteem varies across ethnic groups. More specifically, findings indicate that ethnic identity is more predictive of self-esteem for ethnic minorities than for ethnic majorities (Verkuyten, 1990; Arroyo & Zigler, 1995; Phinney, Cantu, & Kurtz, 1997). Clearly, since ethnic identity has been found to be less relevant for self-perception among ethnic-majority members, it is reasonable to think that it may also only make a small contribution to their feelings of self-regard.

Gender has a variable influence on self-esteem and other measures of psychological well-being. Females show generally lower levels on self-esteem than males (Martinez & Dukes, 1997; Phinney & Alpuria, 1996; Verkuyten, 1986). In addition, research on acculturation indicates that females exhibit higher levels of acculturative stress than males (Berry, 1997; Jasinskaja-Lahti & Liebkind, 2001; Liebkind, 1996). However, these findings vary across ethnic groups and depend on the values and norms prevailing in their cultures. For example, Phinney, Cantu, and Kurtz (1997) found that gender was predictive of self-esteem among Latino and White adolescents, but not among African American adolescents. Empirical data in Australian settings reported by Phinney and Rosenthal (1992) indicate that minority girls are more likely to be exposed to psychological distress when they come from cultures in which relative gender status and roles are strongly differentiated.

Concerning socioeconomic status, research has shown that individuals from lower socioeconomic groups have lower self-esteem than those from higher socioeconomic backgrounds (e.g., Phinney & Alpuria, 1996). Once more, these findings vary across studies, ethnic groups, and cultural or social settings, and are less consistent than findings regarding gender. For example, in a classic study on social class and global self-esteem, Rosenberg and Pearlin (1978) found virtually no association between socioeconomic status and self-esteem among children, and only a moderate relationship among adolescents and adults.

Within developmental approaches, it is assumed that subjects with achieved ethnic identity will show higher self-esteem than those in earlier phases of ethnic-identity development. In effect, Phinney (1989) found among Black-, Asian-, and Mexican-American adolescents ($N = 91$) that those at higher stages of ethnic identity showed higher scores on different measures of well-being, including self-evaluation and sense of mastery. However, in an exploratory longitudinal study on ethnic identity among Asian, Black, and Hispanic Americans ($N_{time\ 1}$ = 64, $N_{time\ 2}$ = 18), Phinney and Chavira (1992) found that ethnic identity and self-esteem were significantly related to each other, irrespective of changes to higher stages of ethnic identity over a three-year period. As pointed out in Chapter 2, research within developmental approaches is rather incipient and needs further empirical validation.

Finally, variation on the relationship between ethnic identity and self-esteem might be due to the multidimensionality of ethnic identity. From Chapter 2, it is known that ethnic identity is better defined as a broad construct involving cognitive, affective, evaluative, and behavioral components. These components are expected to contribute differentially to individuals' sense of belonging to an ethnic group. Accordingly, one might argue that each component has a particular impact on self-esteem and, going further, that the evaluative component should have the greatest impact on self-esteem.

Luhtanen and Crocker (1992, study 2) found that the four subscales of their collective self-esteem scale relate differentially with personal self-esteem as measured with Rosenberg's (1965) self-esteem scale. Here, the most evaluative subscales (membership, private, and public) were significantly correlated with personal self-esteem (e.g., I often regret that I belong to some of the social groups I do), while the identity subscale, which measures the significance attributed to membership in the own group, was unrelated to self-esteem. Similarly, Verkuyten and Lay (1998) found that the public and membership subscales, but not identity, were predictive of personal self-esteem.

In a further study, Verkuyten (1995) found those Dutch, Turkish, and Moroccan adolescents living in The Netherlands with higher scores on positive in-group evaluation had a more positive self-concept than those scoring low on in-group evaluation. Interestingly, among Surinamese adolescents, those who identified strongly with their ethnic group and (also) had a relatively negative evaluation of their in-group elicited the lowest score for global self-esteem. These findings suggest that ethnic identity contributes to personal self-regard only among those individuals for whom membership in ethnic groups is relevant.

Intergroup Attitudes and Self-Esteem

Research on intercultural contact is also consistent with the idea that positive attitudes toward other groups are related to positive self-esteem and adjustment. However, these seem to have less impact on self-esteem compared with ethnic identity. Phinney and Devich-Navarro (1997) reported that attitudes of African-American and Mexican-American adolescents toward other groups were strongly and positively related to self-concept. In a further study,

Phinney, Cantu, and Kurtz (1997) found that attitudes toward other groups were significant predictors of self-esteem among Latino adolescents, but not among Whites and African Americans. Similarly, Ryder and colleagues (2000) showed that positive orientations toward the mainstream society predicted lower levels of depression among Chinese-Canadian students. By contrast, positive orientations toward the host society were found to be unrelated to psychological adjustment among sojourners in Nepal (Ward & Rana-Deuba, 1999).

Intergroup attitudes and behaviors affect self-esteem in another way; namely, via *reflected appraisals*. Especially when working with ethnic-minority members, the impact of majority members' attitudes and behaviors on minority members' self-esteem should be examined as potential moderating factors of the relationship between acculturation and adaptation. Empirical data support the idea that under certain conditions the perception of prejudice, discrimination, and/or low status have a negative influence on feelings of personal self-regard (see Berry, 1997; R. Clark et al., 1999; Cross, 1991; Helms, 1990; Phinney, 1991).

For instance, in her study on acculturation and stress among young Vietnamese refugees and their parents in Finland (N = 280), Liebkind (1996) found that negative attitudes of the host population (e.g., prejudice and discrimination) were a significant predictor of stress symptoms among adult males. Similarly, Jasinskaja-Lahti and Liebkind (2001) reported that perceived discrimination is one of the major psychological stressors affecting psychological adjustment among Russian-speaking immigrant adolescents (N = 170). Interestingly, they found that perceived discrimination had a rather indirect effect on psychological adjustment via self-esteem, which was associated with higher levels of psychological well-being. Finally, Verkuyten and Lay (1998) showed that the expected relationship between perceived group status on personal self-esteem was no longer significant once collective self-esteem (more specifically, public collective self-esteem) was controlled. Thus, these results suggest that the relationship between interethnic attitudes and self-esteem is by no means straightforward.

In effect, after an exhaustive review of the literature on self-esteem among socially "marked" groups, including ethnic- and racial-minority members, homosexuals, obese persons, and mentally retarded individuals, Crocker and Major (1989) concluded that "prejudice against members of stigmatized or oppressed groups generally does not result in lower self-esteem for members of those groups" (p. 611, italics original).

Crocker and Major (1989) distinguish three major strategies that members of stigmatized groups might employ to protect their personal self-esteem from social prejudice and discrimination: (1) by attributing negative feedback to prejudice toward their own group, (2) by making in-group rather than out-group comparisons, and (3) by a selective valuation of the dimensions of comparison. Specifically, the self-concept is less likely to be affected when there are opportunities to display external attributions for negative events; that is, when negative experiences and outcomes are attributed to prejudice held by others rather than when they are taken as reflections of personal shortcomings. Similarly, individuals' self-concepts will be protected when they make comparisons with other people who are similar, because in this way, potential negative discrepancies from social comparisons and, in turn, feelings of deprivation are more likely to be avoided. Finally, since positive social comparisons depend on the relevance of the comparative dimension, the self-concept will be protected when people attribute a positive value to those dimensions in which the in-group performs well and confers less meaning to those dimensions in which it performs poorly.

Crocker and Major (1989) provide several empirical examples supporting these assumptions. In general, evidence suggests that members of stigmatized groups are by no means passive victims of prejudice and discrimination. Members of oppressed groups tend to employ several strategies to manage the negative consequences of prejudice and discrimination. However, to say that members of stigmatized groups widely use these strategies is not to say that prejudice and discrimination do not affect self-perception. As Crocker and Major (1989) pointed out, it is unwise to assume that these strategies "are used by every member of every stigmatized group every time a negative outcome occurs" (p. 618).

To illustrate the complexity of the issues, the authors mention several factors that moderate the use of the strategies described here, including how the stigma is perceived, the specific features of the stigma, the immediate context in which the stigma occurs, and characteristics of the stigmatized person (see also Crocker & Quinn, 1998). Thus, the buffering effect of these strategies will depend on (1) the salience of the membership in the stigmatized group, (2) the acceptance of the negative feedback, (3) the centrality of the stigma in the self-concept, (4) the ambiguity of the causes of negative feedback or outcomes, and (5) individual differences in the extent to which self-esteem is based on the opinions and approval of others.

Recent studies reported by Crocker and Quinn (1998) indicate, for example, that self-protective attribution (e.g., the belief that negative outcomes are caused by others' prejudices) is more likely to be elicited under conditions of *attributional ambiguity*; that is, when there is uncertainty about the cause of the negative event. Thus, when it is clear that prejudice is not the cause of the negative feedback, individuals have less opportunity to employ this strategy and personal self-esteem might be hurt. In addition, Crocker and Quinn found that the extent to which social stigma leads to low self-esteem is related to the tendency to employ the approval and opinions of others as a basis for self-esteem. Thus, the negative impact of social stigma might differ across individuals and groups, depending on how their self-esteem is contingent on "reflected appraisals."

Acculturation Strategies and Self-Esteem

Research with ethnic groups and long-established immigrants shows that the adoption of integration is related to positive psychological outcomes, while marginalization appears to be the less adaptive strategy. Evidence regarding separation and assimilation is much less consistent. For instance, in their study on the relationship between acculturation strategies and self-esteem among high school students from different ethnic backgrounds, Phinney and coworkers (1992) found that integration was positively correlated with self-esteem among Asians and Hispanics, but not among Whites and Blacks. Assimilation was negatively correlated with self-esteem only among Asians. When controlling for place of birth (American-born versus foreign-born subjects), the correlation between assimilation and self-esteem was statistically significant only among foreign-born adolescents. Finally, separation was unrelated to self-esteem among all ethnic groups.

After reviewing thirty publications on acculturation and mental heath among Hispanics in the United States, Rogler and colleagues (1991) concluded that psychological adjustment stems from an optimal combination of both cultural retention and successful adaptation to the mainstream society or integration. More specifically, the data suggest that both the loss of cultural identity and the rejection of mainstream culture are associated with low mental health status. Similarly, Rivera-Sinclair (1997) found among Cuban immigrants ($N = 254$) that biculturalism (i.e., integration) was positively correlated with psychological adjustment. Finally, among Portuguese youth born in France ($N = 519$), Neto (1995) showed that life satisfaction was positively related to integration and negatively associated with marginalization.

Research involving other acculturating groups presents a similar picture. For instance, Doná and Berry (1994) found Central American refugees in Canada who adopted the integration strategy exhibited fewer psychological problems than respondents who endorsed assimilation and separation. In her study of Vietnamese refugees in Finland, Liebkind (1996) reported that the rejection of the mainstream culture was associated with psychological distress among adult females. As predicted by Ward and Rana-Deuba (1999, integrated sojourners in Nepal experienced significantly less depression than those adopting other strategies. However, the prediction that marginalized sojourners would exhibit more depression than other groups was not confirmed. In a further study involving Malaysian students in Singapore ($N = 156$), Ward and Kennedy (1993, study 2) found that evaluative preferences for separation from the mainstream culture was predictive of psychological distress.

As can be seen, although empirical data are relatively consistent with theoretical predictions, it should be taken with caution that the link between acculturation strategies and self-esteem varies highly across and within acculturating groups. In addition, studies reveal great variability in the operationalization of the strategies and psychological adjustment. Finally, in many cases not all strategies have been assessed, so that an interpretation of potential trends is not feasible.

PREDICTING ACCULTURATION OUTCOMES: RESEARCH HYPOTHESES

This section provides a detailed description of the rationale and hypotheses regarding acculturation and psychological adaptation guiding the empirical part of this book. The literature reviewed here shows that the study of the relative impact of acculturation dimensions and strategies on self-esteem implies a careful control of other relevant factors that might affect the entire acculturation process. Therefore, the first step in the analysis will be a test of the impact of the control variables on the focal variables under study. Afterward, the focus will be on the expected relationships between the primary variables of interest.

Self-Esteem

In line with empirical data presented in this chapter, several hypotheses regarding the impact of socioeconomic status, gender, perceived ethnic discrimination, perceived in-group status, and ethnic composition of the immediate environment on self-esteem can be advanced.

Socioeconomic Status

Empirical data on the relationship between socioeconomic status and self-esteem present an inconsistent picture. Some data support the idea that individuals from lower socioeconomic groups have lower self-esteem than those from higher socioeconomic backgrounds (e.g., Phinney & Alpuria, 1996), while other studies found virtually no association between socioeconomic status and self-esteem (Rosenberg & Pearlin, 1978). Because of the conflicting results, no specific predictions about the effects of socioeconomic status on self-esteem are advanced.

Gender

Females show generally lower levels on self-esteem than males (Martinez & Dukes, 1997; Phinney & Alpuria, 1996; Verkuyten, 1986, 1995). However, gender has been found to be predictive of self-esteem among some but not all ethnic groups, depending on their specific social and cultural features. Therefore, gender is included in the analysis but no specific predictions can be developed for its effects.

Perceived Ethnic Discrimination

Research on stigma and self-esteem shows that membership in a stigmatized group does not lead automatically to low levels of self-esteem (Crocker & Major, 1989). Several factors determine when feelings of self-regard are more likely to be affected by stigma. It should be noted, however, that in general terms the belief that one is the target of prejudice and discrimination because of one's membership in specific social categories has an important impact on feelings of self-regard. Empirical data are largely consistent with the idea that perceived discrimination is one of the major psychological factors affecting self-esteem negatively (see Berry, 1997; R. Clark et al., 1999; Cross, 1990; Helms, 1990; Jasinskaja-Lahti & Liebkind, 2001; Liebkind, 1996; Phinney, 1991). Therefore, it is expected that the perception of discrimination will be negatively correlated with self-esteem.

Perceived In-Group Status

With Tajfel and Turner (1979), social status of the in-group is used here as the social position of that group in terms of its prestige in a given society. Like perceived ethnic discrimination, perceived in-group status might represent an important source of threat affecting self-esteem. Thus, using the same argumentation of the previous hypothesis, it is expected that the perception of low in-group status will be associated with lower levels of self-esteem.

Ethnic Composition of the Immediate Environment

Empirical data regarding the effect of ethnic density on self-esteem are somewhat inconsistent. While some research suggests that self-esteem is more protected when people interact in predominantly in-group settings (Rosenberg & Simmons, 1972), other studies found no relationship between ethnic composition of the immediate environment and self-esteem (Krause, 1983; Zirkel & Moses, 1971). Because empirical data are highly inconsistent, ethnic composition of the place of residence will be included in the analysis, but no specific predictions about the effects of ethnic composition of place of residence on self-esteem will be advanced.

Ethnic Identity

Consistent with research reviewed in Chapter 2, this research pays special attention to the potential effects of ethnicity, socioeconomic status, gender, age, perceived ethnic discrimination, perceived in-group status, and ethnic composition of the immediate environment on ethnic identity. The following hypotheses emerge from this literature.

Ethnicity

Empirical data regarding variation on ethnic identity across ethnic groups suggest that ethnic identity is an issue of special relevance for ethnic minorities. Ethnic identity has been found to be higher among ethnic-minority members than among ethnic-majority members in different cultural settings (e.g., Martinez & Dukes, 1997; Phinney & Alpuria, 1990; Phinney & Tarver, 1988; Verkuyten, 1990). Therefore, it is predicted here that Black participants will show higher scores on ethnic identity than White adolescents.

Socioeconomic Status

Research on the impact of socioeconomic status and ethnic identity is inconclusive. Using both education level and family income as indicators for socioeconomic status, some studies suggest that ethnic identity is more likely to be maintained among lower educated than highly educated group members (e.g., Broman et al., 1988). On the contrary, other studies have found that education and socioeconomic status are positively correlated with the maintenance of cultural distinctiveness indicated by the endorsement of separation and integration strategies (see Berry et al., 1989). Other studies found no relationship between these variables (e.g., Phinney, 1989; Phinney & Alpuria, 1990). Because of these conflicting results, socioeconomic status is included in the analysis but no specific predictions can be formulated.

Gender

The relationship between gender and ethnic identity is also unclear. Some studies suggest that females score lower on ethnic identity than males (e.g., Phinney et al., 1993; Verkuyten, 1992), while others report the opposite (Crocker et al., 1994; Martinez and Dukes, 1997). Most studies report no gender differences on ethnic identity (e.g., Brookins, Anyabwille, & Nacoste, 1996; Kinket & Verkuyten, 1997; Rosenthal & Feldman, 1992). Therefore, gender is included in the analyses but no specific predictions are made about its effects on ethnic identity.

Age

From a developmental perspective, it is assumed that the importance of and concern with ethnic identity increase with age. Although research on these issues is incipient, there is evidence supporting this hypothesis (Phinney & Chavira, 1992; Martinez & Dukes, 1997). Therefore, it is expected that age correlates positively with ethnic identity.

Perceived Ethnic Discrimination

Research on ethnic identity has demonstrated the importance of the characteristics of intergroup relations in a given social system for psychological relations to social categories. As posited by the social identity theory (Tajfel & Turner, 1979), perceived ethnic discrimination might affect the sense of pride toward the own ethnic group negatively, which is likely to be expressed in low levels of identification with the ethnic in-group. Some empirical evidence supports this hypothesis (Ichiyama, McQuarrie, & Ching, 1996; Rosenthal, Whittle, & Bell, 1989; Verkuyten & Lay, 1998). However, as shown in Chapter 2, group members might manage identity threats with more collective strategies, maintaining or reinforcing their ethnic identification (e.g., Ethier & Deux, 1994; Phinney et al., 1993). Perceived discrimination, in these cases, should have no impact on ethnic identity, or even can reinforce the commitment with the ethnic group. Because of the conflicting results, no specific predictions will be made regarding the effect of perceived ethnic discrimination on ethnic identity.

Perceived In-Group Status

As pointed out before, perceived in-group status represents a further potential threat to the social identity. According to the social identity theory, the perception of low in-group status could lead under certain conditions to less satisfaction with the in-group, expressed in a psychological dissociation with the in-group. Empirical data are relatively consistent with this prediction (e.g., Ellemers, van Knippenberg, de Vries, & Wilke, 1988; Ellemers, van Rijswijk, Roefs, & Simons, 1997; Spears, Doojse, & Ellemers, 1997; Wagner, 1994; Wagner, Lampen, & Syllwasschy, 1986). However, as in the case of perceived ethnic discrimination, threats to ethnic identity might rather lead to in-group reaffirmation. Therefore, no specific predictions regarding the effects of in-group status on ethnic identity are made.

Ethnic Composition of the Immediate Context

Research on the impact of ethnic density on ethnic identity provides another inconsistent picture. On the one hand, it has been shown that the use of an ethnic category to self-categorization increases with the number of coethnics in the immediate context (e.g., Broman, Jackson, & Neighbors, 1989; Hutnik & Sapru, 1996). On the other hand, evidence also suggests that ethnic identity might become more important for self-definition as the number of coethnics decreases; that is, by virtue of numerical distinctiveness or when opportunities for interethnic contact increase because of the presence of other ethnic groups in the immediate context (e.g., Phinney, 1992). Furthermore, these effects were found to vary highly across groups and according to the components of ethnic identity. For instance, they have been observed on the cognitive component of ethnic identity but not on affective components (e.g., Kinket & Verkuyten, 1997). Because of the discrepant findings regarding these issues, ethnic density is included in the analyses but no prediction is made of its effects on ethnic identity.

Interethnic Attitudes

Empirical data reviewed in Chapter 3 show that socioeconomic status, gender, perceived ethnic discrimination, perceived in-group status, and interethnic contact are important determinants of interethnic attitudes. The central hypotheses of their impact on interethnic attitudes are as follows.

Socioeconomic Status

In concordance with the predictions derived from research on poor-White racism, it is expected that participants of higher economic status express less negative interethnic attitudes than participants of lower socioeconomic status (see Wagner & Zick, 1995).

Gender

In line with previous research (e.g., Phinney et al., 1997; Masson & Verkuyten, 1993; Qualls, Cox, & Schehr, 1992; Wagner, 1983; Watts, 1996), it is expected that females display more positive interethnic attitudes than males. This prediction is based on the idea that socialization patterns reinforce men's competitiveness and women's communal and emotional concerns, which in turn affect their attitudes toward out-groups (Verkuyten, 1997b).

Perceived Ethnic Discrimination

Like fraternal relative deprivation (e.g., Vanneman & Pettigrew, 1972), perceived intergroup conflict (see Tzeng & Jackson, 1994), or realistic and symbolic threats (W. S. Stephan & Stephan, 2000), the perception of discrimination is an important source of threat that can be reflected in negative responses to out-groups (e.g., Branscombe & Wann, 1994). Therefore, it is expected that perceived ethnic discrimination relates negatively with interethnic attitudes.

Perceived In-Group Status

Following the same line of reasoning, it is expected that the perception of low in-group status will be associated with less positive interethnic attitudes.

Contact

Research derived from the intergroup contact theory predicts that contact will have positive effects on intergroup attitudes and behaviors (Pettigrew, 1997, 1998; Pettigrew & Tropp, 2000). Hence, it is predicted that higher levels of interethnic contact will be associated with more positive interethnic attitudes.

The Impact of Acculturation Dimensions and Strategies on Self-Esteem

Ethnic Identity

Research within the social identity approach has largely demonstrated that membership in a value-laden social category provides individuals with a positive sense of self-regard (see Tajfel & Turner, 1979). Research with ethnic groups in ethnically plural settings is consistent with this principle (see Lorenzo-Hernández & Ouellette, 1998; Martinez & Dukes, 1997; Nesdale et al., 1997; Ward & Rana-Deuba, 1999; Doná & Berry, 1994). Therefore, it is expected that strong ethnic identity will be associated with higher levels of self-esteem.

Interethnic Attitudes

In addition to a positive identification with the in-group, attitudes toward other relevant ethnic groups are assumed to be related to individuals' views of themselves. In ethnically plural contexts, positive attitudes toward other groups are indicative of less conflict, less intergroup anxiety, effective social and cultural competencies, and more optimal intergroup contact (see Berry, 1997; W. S. Stephan & Stephan, 2000; La Fromboise et al., 1993). Therefore, positive interethnic attitudes will be associated with positive self-esteem.

Integration

Because of the benefits of membership in the subgroup and the superordinate group (see Crocker & Major, 1989; Gaertner et al., 1996), and the positive adaptation to the mainstream culture (Phinney, 1991), participants who prefer the integration strategy are expected to show the highest levels of self-esteem compared to participants who adopt separation, assimilation, and marginalization.

Separation and Assimilation

These strategies are expected to afford intermediate levels of self-esteem (Berry, 1997). However, because of the limited research on the differential effects of these strategies on self-esteem, no predictions about their specific impact will be formulated.

Marginalization

Since marginalization has been found to be the least adaptive acculturation strategy across almost all acculturating groups in different cultural contexts (see Berry, 1997), it is predicted that participants adopting this strategy will show the lowest levels of self-esteem compared to participants favoring the other strategies.

SUMMARY

This chapter has focused on the specific psychological outcomes of acculturation. Overall, the empirical evidence presented here is consistent with the idea that a strong sense of ethnic identity is related to positive outcomes for individuals' self-esteem. These findings generalize across a variety of acculturating groups, including refugees (e.g., Doná & Berry, 1994), sojourners (e.g., Ward & Kennedy, 1994), and long-established ethnic groups (e.g., Phinney, Cantu, & Kurtz, 1997). Not surprising, the ethnic (sub)community must be viewed as an organized entity providing individuals with norms, values, and interaction patterns, which are important for self-perception and social action. This community is different from the mainstream culture, but not deficient or pathological. Patterns such as kinship-based networks (i.e., the extended family) and mutual exchange are important sources of support and personal satisfaction. In addition, research suggests that positive attitudes toward other groups are related to positive evaluation of the self-concept. Findings are also consistent with the idea that among all acculturation strategies integration affords the best psychological outcomes, while marginalization seems to be the least adaptive.

When attempting to understand the specific contribution of the acculturation dimensions and strategies on self-esteem, one should take into account that there are several other individual-level and context-dependent factors that might also affect the psychological outcomes of acculturation predicted by the theory. On the basis of prior research, the characteristics of intergroup relations within the mainstream society (e.g., majority members' attitudes and behaviors toward the in-group), the features of the immediate context, the particularities of the ethnic group in question, individuals' demographic characteristics, developmental changes, and personal attributes were examined here.

One important insight from this literature is that dimensions and strategies of acculturation are only one source of individuals' feelings of self-regard. Especially when working with ethnic-minority members, researchers often neglect the distinction between collective and personal self-esteem and forget that many factors contribute to feelings of self-worth. This leads to a remarkable amount of confusion in analysis. Similarly, the data suggest that intergroup attitudes and behaviors affect feelings of self-regard, but only in some circumstances and for some individuals. For instance, perceived discrimination might not affect self-esteem when individuals have the opportunity to attribute negative outcomes to external causes such as others' prejudice. By contrast, experiences of discrimination might be particularly prejudicial for individuals whose self-esteem depends highly on others' opinions, or when membership in the stigmatized group is highly relevant for self-perception.

A further important finding is that the effect of acculturation dimensions and strategies are context dependent; that is, their consequences for self-definition become important when opportunities of interethnic contact increase. Finally, when working with ethnic minorities in stratified societies, such individuals' features as ethnicity can be confounded with other demographic characteristics (e.g., socioeconomic status). One might expect variation in self-esteem within ethnic groups according not only to socioeconomic status but also to gender and age. These variables should be controlled in order to understand the specific impact of acculturation on adaptation.

The specific hypotheses guiding this research are as follows:

H1. Perception of ethnic discrimination will be negatively correlated with self-esteem.

H2. Perception of lower in-group status will be associated with lower levels of self-esteem.

H3. Black participants will show higher levels of ethnic identity than White participants.

H4. Age will be positively related to ethnic identity.

H5. Participants of higher economic status will express more positive interethnic attitudes than participants of lower socioeconomic status.

H6. Females will display more favorable interethnic attitudes than males.

H7. Perceived ethnic discrimination will be negatively associated with interethnic attitudes.

H8. Low perceived in-group status will relate to less favorable interethnic attitudes.

H9. Interethnic contact will be positively associated with interethnic attitudes.

H10. Strong identification with the ethnic group of reference will be associated with higher self-esteem.

H11. Positive interethnic attitudes will be positively related to self-esteem.

H12. Respondents who adopt an integration strategy will show higher levels of self-esteem than individuals who adopt the assimilation, separation, and marginalization strategies.

H13. Individuals who adopt the marginalization mode will have lower levels of self-esteem than individuals classified in the other three groups.

5

Acculturation and Psychological Adaptation: Methodological Issues

In addition to the central empirical goals, this research has two methodological interests. First, it examines the utility and validity of the measures across ethnic groups in Costa Rican settings. For this purpose, the instruments were extensively reviewed to arrive at the final version used in the present research. The processes of adaptation included a pilot study with Black and White Costa Rican adolescents and youths. Second, this research explores an alternative way to assess acculturation strategies by classifying participants into four categories representing integration, separation, assimilation, and marginalization on the basis of their responses to measures of ethnic identity and interethnic attitudes.

This chapter addresses these issues while describing the method and procedures of the present research. The first part provides a description of the participants. The next section describes the original measures and the process of scale adaptation, including the preliminary results of their psychometric properties (pilot study). The chapter ends with a description on the concrete procedures of sampling, data collection, and analysis.

PARTICIPANTS

The sample, comprising all those who completed usable questionnaires, consisted of 1,174 Costa Rican high school students. Participants were recruited from public schools in San José and Limón. The schools, all located in urban districts, served communities of middle and working class (Projecto Estado de la Nación, 1998). Table 5.1 shows descriptive statistics of the sample by ethnicity and city of residence.

The sample included 408 Afro-Caribbeans and 766 Whites. White participants were equally distributed in both cities, whereas 72% of Black participants lived in Limón. According to recent statistics, females represent 50% of the student body in Costa Rican public urban schools (Ministerio de Planificación, personal communication, February 2000). In this sample, however, females were overrepresented within both ethnic groups (59.4% for White participants, 59.6% for Black participants).

Participants' ages ranged from thirteen to twenty-two years, corresponding to the age range of students attending public schools in Costa Rican urban zones (Projecto Estado de la Nación, 1998). The mean age for Black participants was 16.27 ($SD = 1.58$), while the average age for White participants was 15.93 ($SD = 1.48$). On the other hand, participants from Limón (mean age 16.30 years, $SD = 1.57$) were somewhat older than participants from San José (mean age 15.68, $SD = 1.39$). Age differences were statistically significant, $F(3,1160) = 13.09$, $p < 0.01$ for the main effect of ethnic group and $F(3,1160) = 40.55$, $p < 0.01$ for the main effect of city of residence. There were no significant age differences between males and females in any ethnic group, $F(3,1160) = 1.19$, $n.s.$ for the main effect of gender. There were no interactions between any of the factors.

Results of chi-square analyses indicated significant differences in socioeconomic status between Blacks and Whites. Here, the percentage of students of low SES was significantly higher among Whites than Blacks (χ^2 [1, $N = 1106$] = 11.08, $p > 0.001$).[1] Within each ethnic group, significant differences in SES were also found between students from Limón and San José. Among White participants, the percentage of students of low SES was significantly higher in Limón than in San José (χ^2 [1, $N = 731$] = 19.92, $p > 0.001$). Among Black participants, the percentage of students of middle SES was higher in San José than in Limón (χ^2 [1, $N = 375$] = 12.06, $p > 0.001$).

Overall, data indicate that Blacks are higher in SES than Whites. However, these results should be interpreted attending to the particular features of the educational system in Costa Rica as well as the differential access to resources across regions in the country. It should be noted that public schools in Costa Rica represent the educational option for the low class (many middle-class Whites attend private schools), and that the city of Limón is located in one of the poorest regions of the country (Projecto Estado de la Nación, 1998). With this background information, data show an interesting phenomenon. For both Blacks and Whites, the opportunities for social mobility are higher in San Jose than in Limón. In San José, however, these opportunities seem to be restricted to Whites: While middle-class Whites attend private schools, low-class Whites and middle-class Blacks only have access to the public system. Further research is needed in order to test the validity of this interpretation.

Table 5.1
Descriptive Statistics of the Sample by Ethnicity and City of Residence

		Blacks			Whites		
		San José	Limón	Total	San José	Limón	Total
Total		112	296	408	384	382	766
Female		56	188	244	214	242	456
Male		56	108	164	170	140	310
Age	Mean	15.83	16.42	16.27	15.64	16.21	15.93
	SD	1.48	1.60	1.58	1.37	1.54	1.54
SES	Low	37	150	187	199	244	443
	Middle/high	69	119	188	178	110	288

Note: SES is based on parent's occupation (5% missing).

In summary, demographic data show that participants come from heterogeneous social and cultural backgrounds. In large part, however, the sample showed a comparable distribution with the student body of urban schools in San José and Limón.

MEASURING ACCULTURATION AND PSYCHOLOGICAL ADAPTATION

The questionnaire constructed for the present research included measures of each of the constructs specified in Figure 1.5; that is, self-esteem, ethnic identity, interethnic attitudes, perceived ethnic discrimination, perceived in-group status, and interethnic contact.[2] Measures were distributed in three sections. The first section contained the measures of self-esteem. Items measuring ethnic identity, interethnic attitudes, and in-group status were randomly distributed in the second section. Measures of contact and perceived ethnic discrimination were included in the third section. Toward the end of the questionnaire the following demographic items were included: participants' ethnicity, parents' ethnicity, participants' gender, age, place of residence, parents' education level, and parents' occupation. Table 5.2 shows the operationalization of the variables.

In line with the need to provide comparative data, measures used in this research were largely derived from existing scales that (1) have been widely applied in different cultural settings and (2) demonstrate adequate psychometric characteristics across groups and cultural settings. As seen in Table 5.2, only one instrument was specially developed for the research. The measures were translated from the original language into Spanish by a native speaker (the author). The aim was not to achieve a literal translation of each item, but

Table 5.2
Operationalization of the Theoretical Constructs

Class of variable	Specific variable	Operationalization
Dependent	Self-esteem	Rosenberg Self-Esteem Scale (Rosenberg, 1965)
		Erikson Psychosocial Stage Inventory (Rosenthal, Gurney, & Moore, 1981)
Independent	Ethnic identity	Multigroup Ethnic Identity Measure (Phinney, 1992)
	Interethnic attitudes	Other Group Orientation Measure (Phinney, 1992)
Control	*Group-Level*	
	Perceived discrimination	Perceived Ethnic Discrimination Measure (new)
	In-group status	Public Collective Self-Esteem Scale (Luhtanen & Crocker, 1992)
	Ethnic composition of the environment	City of residence: San José = 1, Limón = 2
	Individual-Level	
	Interethnic Contact	"Kontaktskala" (van Dick & Wagner, 1995)
	Demographics	
	Ethnicity	Self-ethnic label (multiple-choice item)
	Gender	Female = 1, Male = 2
	Socioeconomic Status	Parents' occupation
	Age	Age in years

rather an adaptation of the measures to Costa Rican adolescents. Therefore, the language level was simplified as much as possible. The Spanish version was evaluated by five independent judges (all Spanish native speakers), who revised each scale and in some cases improved the translation. The scales were reviewed once more and were then administrated to the Costa Rican adolescents and youths in the pilot study.

Participants in the pilot study were 124 (76 White and 48 Black) Costa Rican adolescents and youths, who ranged in age from 14 to 25 years, with a mean of 18.6 years. Of the participants, 47% were female; 72% were university students. In order to examine the psychometric properties of the scales, each measure was submitted to principal components analyses with varimax rotation and to reliability analyses using Cronbach's alphas, and item-total correlations as indices of internal consistence.[3] Measures were then revised and improved on the basis of item analyses to arrive at the final version used here. An overview of the psychometric characteristics of the measures is presented in Table 5.3. The interested reader can find a more detailed description of psychometric data in Appendix D.

The Assessment of Self-Esteem

Feelings of self-regard were measured by selected items from two scales: Rosenberg's (1965) self-esteem scale (RSES) and the Erikson psychosocial stage inventory (EPSI) developed by Rosenthal, Gurney, and Moore (1981) based on Erikson's (1973) ego-identity development theory.

The Rosenberg self-esteem scale is a ten-item Likert measure that taps global feelings of self-worth (e.g., "I feel that I am a person of worth, at least on an equal basis with others"). Items are usually scored using a four-point scale from 1 (strongly agree) to 4 (strongly disagree). Individuals' scores on self-esteem are indicated by the sum of the ten items, resulting in a scale range of 10 to 40 with high scores indicating high self-esteem. Here, the response scale ranges from 1 (totally disagree) to 6 (totally agree).[4]

From the Erikson psychosocial inventory, eight items of the identity versus identity diffusion subscale were used. This subscale assesses self-acceptance

Table 5.3
Descriptives and Reliabilities for All Measures among Black and White Participants in the Pilot Study

Measure	No. of items	Blacks		Whites		Total
		M	SD	M	SD	α
Self-esteem	16	4.95	.64	4.66	.88	.87
Ethnic Identity	12	4.68	.84	3.82	1.00	.88
Interethnic attitudes	6	5.06	.76	5.06	.83	.67
Perceived ethnic discrimination	4	-	-	-	-	-
Perceived ingroup status	4	3.92	1.23	4.76	1.08	.75
Interethnic contact	9	3.16	.57	2.71	.57	.84

Note: Means and standard deviations are presented for each ethnic group for descriptive purposes. Item-total correlations and factor loadings are calculated for the whole sample. Perceived ethnic discrimination was not assessed in the pilot study. All items were answered on a six-point scale from 1 (totally disagree) to 6 (totally agree), except for the interethnic contact measure, which was answered on a four-point scale from 1 (never/not at all intensive/not at all important) to 4 (very often/very intensive/very important). High scores indicate high levels in each construct. *N*s vary from 114 to 123 because of missing values (max. missing values < 9%).

and ego-identity stability (e.g., "I like myself and am proud of what I stand for"). Each item requires agreement or disagreement on a scale from 1 (hardly ever true) to 5 (almost always true). Scores on self-acceptance are obtained by reversing negative items, summing across them, and obtaining the mean. High scores indicate positive self-acceptance and identity stability. A six-point scale from 1 (totally disagree) to 6 (totally agree) was used here.[5]

Preliminary analyses of the pilot-study data revealed that both measures are highly correlated ($r = 0.65$, $p < 0.001$), suggesting that they might form a single indicator of feelings of self-regard. A principal-components analysis with varimax rotation was undertaken to explore this possibility. The first five Eigenvalues were 6.12, 2.19, 1.29, 1.17, and 0.97, accounting for 34%, 12.2%, 7.1%, 6.5%, and 5.4% of the variance in the measure. Thus, the strong Eigenvalue of the first factor and the low variance accounted for by the remaining factors corroborate the unidimensional structure underlying the eighteen items.

After removing two items that loaded less than 0.30 ("All in all, I am inclined to feel that I am a failure" and "I wish I could have more respect for myself"), the loadings of the remaining sixteen items was in the single factor range from 0.45 to 0.75. Therefore, the items were combined to form the measure of self-esteem.

Individuals' scores on self-esteem were derived by reversing negative items, summing across them, and obtaining the mean. High scores indicate high self-esteem. Reliability analysis of the composed measure yielded a Cronbach's alpha of 0.87. All items showed an item-total correlation above 0.33.

The Assessment of Acculturation Dimensions and Strategies

The possibility of testing the independent effects of acculturation dimensions and strategies on self-esteem is largely determined by the operationalization of these constructs. Traditionally, acculturation strategies have been measured with four independent measures of attitudes toward each of the four acculturation modes. Each scale includes a number of statements reflecting the acculturation mode in questions referringto several areas of the everyday life, such as friends, education, intergroup relations, and so on (e.g., "Most of my friends are Koreans because I feel comfortable around them, but I don't feel as comfortable around Canadians"). As pointed out before, the measures have been widely adapted and used across cultural groups and contexts. However, several authors, including Berry (see Doná & Berry, 1994), have drawn attention to some conceptual and methodological shortcomings regarding the measurement of acculturation strategies via four different subscales.

Ward and Rana-Deuba (1999) draw attention to several difficulties with this technique. First, they argue that the more fundamental components of acculturation have received less attention than they deserve. In effect, since both dimensions have been shown to relate differently to psychological adjustment depending on the acculturating group under research (e.g., Ryder,

Alden, & Paulhus, 2000), it seems necessary to examine their particular contribution to adaptation separately.

The second problem is related to the operationalization of the dimension of "contact and participation." Ward and Kennedy (1994) argue that research has focused on how acculturating group members accept and practice the customs, values, and traditions of out-groups, but not on how they relate to out-groups in specific terms of intergroup attitudes and behaviors. In fact, the interscale correlations reported by Berry, Kim, Power, Young, and Bujaki (1989) indicate that the dimensions are not operationalized in the same way in the four subscales. For instance, Berry and colleagues have reported positive correlations between assimilation and marginalization (between 0.24 and 0.36), indicating, somewhat illogically, that individuals who adopt a positive orientation to the mainstream society (assimilation) at the same time reject relations with both the mainstream society and the ethnic group of reference (marginalization).

These inconsistencies might be also related to the third problem; namely, the item content. As Berry and Doná (1994) noted, acculturation strategies have commonly been assessed by combining attitudes toward both the in-group and out-groups in a single statement. Consider, for example, the statement, "Most of my friends are Koreans because I feel very comfortable around them, but I don't feel as comfortable around Canadians." As can be seen, such items do not reflect the assumption of dimensions' orthogonality posited by the theory.

The fourth problem is a practical one. As Ward and Rana-Deuba (1999) point out, measures place unnecessary demands on the respondents: They are too long, repetitive, and even complicated. This is due to the fact that (1) items contain two different pieces of information, (2) more than one item is employed to measure each dimension, and (3) each strategy is measured with reference to several domains (education, food preference, media usage, etc.). In addition, this approach implies the development of culture-specific measures, depending on the areas or domains under study, which in turn depends on each acculturating group in question. This requires considerable effort in test construction and complicates data comparison.

Although recent measures of acculturation strategies clearly overcome these limitations (e.g., van Dick, Wagner, Adams, & Petzel, 1997), the use of four separate scales for the measurement of integration, separation, assimilation, and marginalization restricts the exploration of the independent effect of dimensions and strategies on self-esteem. An alternative approach is taken in this research by measuring the two dimensions separately. Two independent scales of in-group identification and interethnic attitudes in combination with a dichotomization technique were employed to classify participants into four categories representing integration, separation, assimilation, and marginalization.

An increasing number of published studies have employed this technique in recent years (e.g., Doná & Berry, 1994; Piontkowski et al., 2000; Ryder, Alden, & Paulhus, 2000; Sayegh & Lasry, 1993; Ward & Rana-Deuba, 1999). This technique addresses the problem of divergent information in the item content, is evidently more economical than original versions, and is perhaps the best way to explore some of the central assumptions of bidimensional models; namely, the orthogonality of acculturation dimensions.

The present research explores the advantages and limitations of this procedure. The utility of this methodological technique can be established if the measures employed to tap both dimensions are reliable and independent, or at least not strongly correlated.

Ethnic-Identity Measure

Ethnic identity was assessed using a version of the multigroup ethnic identity measure (MEIM) developed by Phinney (1992). The original measure consists of fourteen items, which are rated on a four-point scale ranging from strongly agree to strongly disagree. Items assess three aspects of ethnic identity that have been shown to be common across groups. Seven items assess ethnic-identity achievement (e.g., "Think a lot about how my life will be affected by my ethnic group membership"). Five items tap feelings of attachment and pride toward the ethnic group of reference (e.g., "I feel a strong attachment towards my own ethnic group"). Two further items assess ethnic behaviors (e.g., "I participate in cultural practices of my own group, such as special food, music or customs").

Although conceptually distinct, previous research has shown that these components form part of a single indicator of ethnic identity (Lorenzo-Hernández & Ouellette, 1998; Martinez & Dukes, 1997; Phinney, 1992; Phinney, Cantu, & Kurtz, 1997). An individual's ethnic-identity score is derived by computing the mean of the items. High scores indicate strong ethnic identity.

On the basis of recent work, the measure has been subjected to some modifications. Two items have been dropped in the new version and the item content has been improved (J. S. Phinney, personal communication, August 1998). The twelve-item version was employed here, and a six-point answering scale from 1 (totally disagree) to 6 (totally agree) was used. In addition, for a better account of the component of ethnic behaviors, one item was added to the scale: "I am active in organizations or social groups that promote the traditions of my own ethnic group."

Principal-component analyses with varimax rotation yielded three factors for the sample in the pilot study. However, as indicated by the Eigenvalues (5.31, 1.33, and 1.10, respectively), data seem to replicate the unidimensionality of the scale reported in previous research. Therefore, a one-factor solution was examined. About 40% of the variance in the scale was accounted for by this factor (10.2% variance explained by factor 2, and 8.5% by factor 3). After removing one item that loaded less than 0.10 on the factor ("I think a lot about how my life will be affected by my ethnic group membership"), the remaining factor loadings ranged from 0.41 to 0.83.

Reliability analysis of the twelve items revealed Cronbach's alpha of 0.88. All items had an item-total correlation above 0.32. The elimination of further items would not lead to an increase in the alpha coefficient. Therefore, the twelve items were retained. The additional item of ethnic behaviors demonstrated consistent association with the original measure, yielding a factor loading 0.64 and an item-total correlation of 0.57.

Interethnic Attitudes Measure

Attitudes toward ethnic out-groups were assessed using the other-group orientation measure (OGOM) developed also by Phinney (1992). The scale consists of six items assessing attitudes and orientations toward other groups (e.g., "I like meeting and getting to know people from ethnic groups other than my own"). Items are rated here on a four-point scale from 1 (strongly agree) to 4 (strongly disagree).

Individuals' scores on interethnic attitudes are obtained by reversing negative items, summing across the six items, and obtaining the mean. Higher scores indicate more positive attitudes toward out-groups. In the present research, a six-point responding scale from 1 (totally disagree) to 6 (totally agree) was used.

In concordance with the original conceptualization (Phinney, 1992), factor analysis indicates that the measure is largely unidimensional (factor 1, Eigenvalue 2.41, 40.2% variance explained; factor 2, Eigenvalue 1.10, 18.4% variance explained; factor 3, Eigenvalue 0.84, 14% variance explained). In the one-factor solution, factor loadings ranged from 0.41 to 0.77. Reliability analysis revealed a Cronbach's alpha of 0.67. Item-total correlations ranged from 0.24 to 58. The deletion of the item with the lowest item-total correlation did not provide substantial improvements in the alpha value. Therefore, the six items were retained for the main study.

The Operationalization of Control Variables

The framework guiding this research classifies variables affecting the acculturation processes in group- and individual-level variables. As pointed out in Chapter 1, several variables can serve as indicators of group-level factors affecting adaptation. Majority members and attitudes toward specific ethnic groups, citizenship laws, education policies, or financial and social support to cultural activities have been suggested and used as features of a large society affecting acculturation. At the level of the specific acculturating groups, their social prestige, structure, organization, size, and distribution have been proposed (see Berry, 1997; Bourhis, Moise, Perreault, & Senéca, 1997; Piontkowski, Florack, Hoelker, & Obdrzálek, 2000).

In this research, however, self-report measures of perceived ethnic discrimination and perceived in-group status are employed. Strictly speaking, only the ethnic composition of the immediate context is operationalized at the group level. Nevertheless, perceived ethnic discrimination and subjective status are still classified as group-level variables because they give information on how the objective characteristics of intergroup relations are subjectively perceived.

Group-Level Variables

Perceived Ethnic Discrimination

On the basis of previous research (Luhtanen & Crocker, 1992; Phinney, Madden, & Santos, 1998), a 4-item scale was developed to assess to what extent participants believe that they have been personally discriminated against because of their membership in their ethnic group. The scale includes statements referring to three domains of everyday life: occupation, education opportunities, and economic success (e.g., "To what extent do you feel that your ethnic background hinders your opportunities to find a good job?"). Each item requires agreement or disagreement on a scale from 1 (totally disagree) to 6 (totally agree). Individuals' scores on perceived ethnic discrimination are computed by summing across the items and obtaining a mean. Higher scores indicate more perception of ethnic discrimination. Perceived discrimination was not assessed in the pilot study.

Perceived In-Group Status

In line with Tajfel and Turner (1979), the social status of the in-group is defined as the social position of the group in terms of its prestige and value in a given society. Consequently, perceived in-group status is operationalized here as individuals' judgments of how other people evaluate their in-group. Luhtanen and Crocker's (1992) 4-item public subscale from their collective self-esteem scale was employed to assess these reflected appraisals because their conceptualization of public self-esteem is equivalent with this definition (see the first section of Chapter 2). Construct validity for this scale as a measure of in-group status has been reported by Luhtanen and Crocker by showing that racial minorities in the United States (Blacks and Asians) report lower public collective self-esteem than Whites. In addition, Verkuyten and Lay (1998) report a correlation of 0.40 between this scale and other measures of perceived in-group status.

The public scale includes positively and negatively worded items (e.g., "In general, others think that the social groups I am a member of are unworthy"). Items are rated on a 7-point scale from 1 (strongly disagree) to 7 (strongly agree). High scores indicated high (perceived) in-group status. Here, a 6-point Likert scale from 1 (totally disagree) to 6 (totally agree) was administrated, and the words "social group" were replaced by "ethnic group." This type of adaptation has been successfully used in previous studies (Crocker, Luhtanen, Blaine, & Broadnax, 1994; Ethier & Deux, 1994; Verkuyten & Lay, 1998).

Data analysis of the pilot study shows that the four items represent a consistent unidimensional measure of perceived in-group value and status. Principal-component analysis yielded one factor with an Eigenvalue 2.35, accounting for 58.7% of the variance in the measure (factor 2, Eigenvalue 0.77, 19.3% variance explained). Factor loadings ranged from 0.68 to 0.84. Reliability analyses yielded a Cronbach's alpha of 0.75. All items had an item-scale correlation greater than 0.47.

Ethnic Density

To examine potential effects of the ethnic composition of the immediate environment, participants were recruited from two cities: San José and Limón. The former is the capital of the country, with about 600,000 inhabitants. The latter, with about 84,000 inhabitants, is the central canton of the province of Limón, which is situated on the Atlantic coast. Estimates indicate that 90% of the Black community lives in the province of Limón. Blacks constitute the second largest ethnic group (after the White community), comprising about 32% of the total population of this province. By contrast, in the city of San José the Black community represents less than 2% of the population (Sawyers & Perry, 1996). The distribution of the Black population in these cities is used here as a criterion of ethnic density. Therefore, in terms of the presence of the Black community, San José was classified as the low-ethnic-density city, while Limón as the high-ethnic-density city. Thus, as part of the demographics questionnaire, participants provided information on their place of residence (San José = 1, Limón = 2).

Individual-Level Variables

Interethnic Contact

Participants' experience of interethnic contact was assessed through a version of a contact scale developed by van Dick and Wagner (1995) for German settings. The original measure consists of eight items assessing direct personal contact with foreigners (*Ausländer*). Participants were asked to indicate whether they had personal contact with foreigners in the following fields: (1) among family and relatives, (2) at work, (3) in the neighborhood, (4) among the circle of acquaintances, and (5) among the circle of friends. The answering scale ranged from 1 (never) to 4 (very often). Three additional items assess frequency, intensity, and importance of contact, respectively. Each item is rated on a Likert scale from 1 (never/not at all intensive/not at all important) to 4 (very often/very intensive/very important).

An individual's score on interethnic contact is obtained by summing across the items and computing the mean. High scores indicate frequent and intensive contact characterized by the respondents as meaningful or relevant (i.e., frequent and positive interethnic contact). In the present research, the same answer format was used, but some content modifications were undertaken in order to adapt the measure to Costa Rican settings. First, the term "foreigners" was replaced by "members of other ethnic groups." Second, the field of acquaintances was dropped to focus on friends. Third, "sport activities" and "other activities" were added to the list to tap further areas of potential contact that might be particularly important among adolescents.

In the pilot study, principal-components analysis with varimax rotation suggest that the nine items form a largely unidimensional measure (factor 1, Eigenvalue 4.12, 45.8% of variance explained; factor 2, Eigenvalue 1.39, 15.4% variance explained; factor 3, Eigenvalue 0.91, 10% variance explained). Therefore, a one-factor solution was investigated. Factor loadings ranged from 0.41 to 0.82. Reliability analysis yielded a Cronbach's alpha of 0.84. Item-total correlations ranged from 0.28 to 0.74. Although item eight (importance of contact) shows a low item-total correlation, its drop would not lead to an improvement of the alpha coefficient. Therefore, the nine items were retained for the main study.

Demographics

Ethnicity

Participants were asked to select the appropriate ethnic label to define themselves and their parents from a list of Costa Rica's principal ethnic groups:

1. Black Costa Ricans (or Afro-Caribbeans)
2. White Costa Ricans (or Mestizos)
3. Indígenas (indigenous people)
4. Asian Costa Ricans
5. Other ethnic groups

Only participants who identified themselves as Black Costa Ricans or White Costa Ricans were included in the sample. Six cases were discarded because of their membership in other ethnic groups.

Socioeconomic Status

Since participants were all students from public high schools in San José and Limón and therefore their education level was highly homogenous, parental occupation was used as an approximation of the socioeconomic levels of the participants. Parents' occupations were assessed through an open-ended question. Participants were asked to fill in a blank with the profession or occupation of their mothers and fathers. Father's occupation was used as the primary criterion; when this was not available, mother's occupation was used. On the basis of this information, responses were coded into forty-seven different occupations or professions by the author (see Appendix B), which were, in turn, classified by two independent judges into two categories:

1. *Low socioeconomic status*: Father's occupation is unskilled work not requiring formal education.
2. *Middle/high socioeconomic status*: Father's occupation requires formal (technical or university) education.

Judges agreement was 85%. Interjudge agreement corrected for chance (Cohen's *kappa*) was 0.69. Disagreement was solved by a third judge. Of the cases, 5% ($N = 68$) did not report parents' occupation, and therefore were classified as missing.

Finally, participants reported their gender (female = 1, male = 2), age in years, and grade level (7 to 12).

PROCEDURE

The data were collected in May 1998 by the author and an undergraduate psychology student, who assisted in this phase. Two weeks prior to data collection, letters were sent to several schools in Limón and San José inviting them to participate. Three schools in Limón and five in San José took part in the research.

In the schools, randomly selected classrooms were visited. Students were informed about the project and invited to participate voluntarily. Only five students refused to participate. Confidentiality was always guaranteed. Questionnaires were then distributed in the classroom. There was always a person available to answer any question. Completion of the questionnaire took approximately thirty minutes.

Questionnaires were then screened. Sixty-four forms were discarded because of incomplete demographic information. Overall, the response rate was of 94% (there were sixty-four incomplete forms, six forms were discarded because of membership in other ethnic groups, and five participants refused to participate).

OVERVIEW OF THE ANALYSES

The data analyses were performed for each ethnic group separately. However, for the test of specific hypotheses or for descriptive purposes, cross-group comparisons were also undertaken. Analyses of the data were calculated with SPSS 9.01 and EQS 5.7 (Bentler, 1992).

The analyses included the following steps: First, exploratory factor analysis and reliability tests via Cronbach's alpha and item-total correlations were carried out in order to examine if the structure and psychometric properties of the scales replicated the pilot study results. The second step was the classification of respondents into the modes of acculturation. Participants' scores on the measures of ethnic identity and interethnic attitudes were used to classify them into four categories representing integration, separation, assimilation, and marginalization. Specifically, respondents scoring high in ethnic identity and interethnic attitudes were classified in the integration strategy. Participants scoring high in ethnic identity and low in interethnic attitudes were categorized in the separation modus. Low scores in ethnic identity and high in interethnic attitudes represented the assimilation mode. Finally, low ethnic identity and low interethnic attitudes represented marginalization.

There are two approaches for the splitting procedure. Some authors (e.g., Doná & Berry, 1994) employ the scalar midpoint as the cut point; other authors select the median score as the cutoff criterion (e.g., Ward & Rana-Deuba, 1999). The first approach represents a more direct approximation of participants' acculturation modes because it allows examination of the distribution of the strategies in the sample. However, previous research has shown that the scalar-mean method often results in the loss of one cell (i.e., marginalization), given the overwhelming preference for the other strategies (Doná & Berry, 1994). The second approach is a less "pure" approximation, because it is based on a relative "within sample" classification, and because of loss of those cases situated on the critical cutoffs. However, it allows comparisons with proportionate groups and the test of specific predictions about the relative contribution of each mode to psychological adaptation. Therefore, the second classification scheme was used for the subsequent analyses. However, the scalar-midpoint technique was also performed for descriptive purposes.

In a third step, preliminary analyses were conducted to (1) test for ethnic-group differences, (2) detect potential multicolinearity problems for subsequent analyses, and (3) examine the correlates and determinants of the focal variables. In order to test for ethnic-group differences, a multivariate analysis of variance (MANOVA) of all measures were carried out, using ethnic group as a factor. The subsequent analyses were carried out separately for each ethnic group. First, Pearson product moment correlations among all variables of interest were calculated. Second, ethnic identity, interethnic attitudes, and self-esteem were each regressed on the control variables. Third, a discriminant function analysis was performed to identify the predictors of the four acculturation strategies.

In a fourth step, primary analyses were conducted. To test the central hypotheses, self-esteem was submitted to a 2×2 analysis of variance (ANOVA) with ethnic identity (high versus low) and interethnic attitudes (high versus low) as factors, followed by planned comparisons for prior predictions using t

tests to examine differences on self-esteem across strategies. Three contrasts were performed. The mean score on self-esteem of the integration cell was compared to the mean of the remaining cells. Similarly, the mean score on self-esteem of the marginalization cell was contrasted to the mean of the remaining cells. Finally, the separation and assimilation cells were compared. To control for the effects of perceived discrimination, in-group status, interethnic contact, city of residence, socioeconomic status, gender, and age, a 2×2 analysis of covariance (ANCOVA) was conducted with these control variables as covariates. In this way the independent effect of the acculturation dimensions (main effects) as well as the effects of the acculturation strategies (interaction term) could be examined, while controlling for other relevant variables associated with the focal variables of interest. On the basis of these results, the data were analyzed using structural equation models from the EQS program (Bentler, 1992). Optimal models were calculated separately for each ethnic group. The models were first calculated on a random split of half of the total sample, and then cross-validated on the other half.

SUMMARY

This chapter described the methodological design developed to test the hypothesis under study, including a detailed description of participants, measures, and procedures.

Participants in the main study were 408 Black and 766 White high school students who attend public schools located in urban districts in San José and Limón. Analysis of the demographic data reveals that the sample is heterogeneous in several social and cultural dimensions, reflecting in this way the heterogeneity of the population from which it was selected; namely, the student body of urban schools in Costa Rica.

The measures used to tap the variables of interest were translated and adapted from scales extensively used in empirical research on intergroup relations and acculturation. Data from a pilot study involving more than 100 Black and White students indicated that the scales can be satisfactorily used to assess acculturation and psychological adaptation in Costa Rican settings.

The questionnaire (including demographic items and the adapted measures) was distributed in randomly selected classrooms of three schools in Limón and five in San José. A response rate of 94% was achieved.

The analytical strategy used here includes several steps: (1) a further test of the psychometric properties of the measures in the main sample, (2) the classification of participants into acculturation modes on the basis of their responses to the ethnic-identity measures and their interethnic attitudes, (3) a preliminary examination of the relationship among all variables, (4) the analysis of the specific impact of acculturation dimensions and strategies on self-esteem, and (5) a comprehensive examination of the multivariate causal relationship between the variables using structural equation modeling techniques.

NOTES

1. The second section of this chapter describes the operationalization of SES in more detail.

2. The questionnaire included several measures of the use of mass media in everyday life. These were included for other research purposes, and therefore will not be discussed here. To be sure that these measures would not affect the responses of participants, the scales were presented at the end of the questionnaire, after the demographic items.

3. Because of the small number of Black participants, data from the pilot study were analyzed for the whole sample. Ns reported here vary because of missing values (max. 8%).

4. For the Spanish version, the literal translation of "strongly disagree" or "strongly agree" ("fuertemente en desacuerdo" or "fuertemente de acuerdo") was considered inappropriate. Therefore, it was substituted by "totalmente en desacuerdo" or "totalmente de acuerdo" ("totally disagree" or "totally agree"), which are more common in Costa Rica).

5. The rationale for changing the scale range was to provide a more homogeneous answer format and to avoid participants' tendency to choose the midpoint of the scale.

6

Acculturation and Psychological Adaptation: Research Results

This chapter presents the results of the research in five main sections. The first section focuses on the structure and psychometric properties of the scales in the main study. The second section presents the classification of the participants into the acculturation strategies. The third section presents preliminary analyses of the data conducted to examine the relationships between control variables and focal independent and dependent variables. In this section, Hypotheses 1 to 9 will be tested. The fourth section addresses the main research questions. Here, data are examined to determine the effect of acculturation dimensions and strategies on self-esteem among Black and White adolescents (Hypotheses 10 to 13) when considering the potential effects of the control variables. Finally, the fifth section focuses on the development and test of a general model for predicting psychological outcomes of acculturation. The specific strategy of analysis will be discussed in each section.

A FURTHER TEST OF THE STRUCTURE AND PROPERTIES OF THE SCALES

To examine the factor structure of the measures in the main study, each scale was subjected to a principal-components analysis with varimax rotation. Reliability analyses were conducted using Cronbach's alpha coefficients and

corrected item-total correlations. The data were also screened for strong violations to normality assumptions. Analyses were conducted for Blacks ($N = 408$)
and Whites ($N = 767$) separately.[1] This allows examining the structure and
consistence of the scales across ethnic groups. Table 6.1 presents the psychometric characteristics of the measures. The interested reader is referred to
Appendix E for a more detailed description of the psychometric data.

Self-Esteem

Recall that self-esteem was assessed by a composite measure based on selected items from Rosenberg's (1965) self-esteem scale and Rosenthal, Gurney, and Moore's (1981) Erikson psychosocial stage inventory. In the
Afro-Caribbean group, principal-component analyses yielded three factors with
Eigenvalues above 1 (4.85, 1.77, and 1.22) that account for 30.3%, 11.1%,
and 7.7% of the total variance, respectively (successive Eigenvalues were 0.95,
0.89, and 0.83). The first factor included all positively worded items with factor
loadings between 0.50 and 0.73. The second factor involved all negatively
worded items with factor loadings ranging from 0.40 to 0.69. The third factor
included three items with similar content with factor loadings ranging from
0.56 to 0.72. These were, "I've got a clear idea of what I want to be," "I know
what kind of person I am," and "I can't decide what I want to do with my life."

The presence of the second factor deserves more scrutiny. In effect, several
studies using Rosenberg's (1965) self-esteem scale and similar measures have

Table 6.1
**Descriptives and Reliabilities for All Measures among Black and White
Participants in the Main Study**

Measure	No. of items	Blacks			Whites		
		M	*SD*	α	*M*	*SD*	α
Self-esteem	16	4.71	.80	.83	4.81	.79	.85
Ethnic Identity	12	4.51	.93	.85	3.98	.85	.78
Interethnic attitudes	6	4.77	.91	.65	4.68	1.04	.74
Perceived ethnic discrimination	4	3.89	1.14	.54	4.56	1.08	.59
Perceived ingroup status	4	2.43	1.39	.80	1.86	1.18	.81
Interethnic contact	9	3.17	.59	.83	2.90	.65	.86

Note: As in the pilot study, all items were answered on a 6-point scale from 1 (totally disagree)
to 6 (totally agree), except for the interethnic contact measure, which was answered on a 4-
point scale from 1 (never/not at all intensive/not at all important) to 4 (very often/very
intensive/very important). High scores indicate high levels in each construct. *N*s vary from
368 to 408 and from 717 to 766 for Blacks and Whites, respectively, because of missing
values (max. missing values < 8%).

reported the presence of two apparently distinct factors involving positive and negative items, respectively (see Robinson, Shaver, & Wrightsman, 1991, for a review). The question remains whether the two components reflect distinct constructs representing self-worth and self-derogation, respectively, or rather a single theoretical dimension that is contaminated by a method artifact. Supporters of the first hypothesis use the ratings of the negative and positive sets of items as separate subtotals, with the argument that each set underlies a different mechanism (e.g., Nesdale, Rooney, & Smith, 1997). Other authors draw attention to the problem of confounding important content issues with less relevant method effects (e.g., Marsh, 1996).

A critical test of these competing hypotheses has been proposed by Marsh (1996). He posits that young and less verbally able respondents have greater difficulty in responding to negatively worded items, leading to the appearance of two separate factors. According to this reasoning, correlations between the negative-item and positive-item factors should increase with age and verbal ability. In other words, the method effect should be smaller with increasing age, indicating that the distinction of two different constructs underlying self-esteem is rather unnecessary. To test this idea, Afro-Caribbean respondents were classified as "younger" (mean age 15 years, SD 0.89, min. 13 years, max. 16 years, $N = 218$) and "older" (mean age 17 years, SD 0.93, min. 17 years, max. 22 years, $N = 187$) using a median split procedure (median 16 years). The correlation between the negative-item and positive-item factors were then calculated separately for each group and compared after being transformed into Fishers's Z scores. Results show that both factors were significantly correlated in both groups ($r = 0.41$ and 0.56, $p < 0.001$ for younger and older, respectively) and that the correlation was significantly higher among older students ($z = 2.00$, $p < 0.05$).

Thus, the strong Eigenvalue of the first factor, the low variance accounted for by the second factor, and the correlational data presented here indicate that the second factor represents a largely irrelevant method component.[2] A single-factor solution was therefore chosen. Factor loadings ranged from 0.39 to 0.71. For White participants, the first five Eigenvalues were 5.42, 1.85, 1.27, 0.91, and 0.83, accounting for 33.8%, 11.6%, 8%, 5.7%, and 5.2% of the total variance, respectively. A similar factor structure pattern was found in this group. Therefore, one general factor was extracted. Factor loadings ranged from 0.42 to 0.75. On the basis of these results, the sixteen items were added to form the measure of self-esteem.

This scale has a theoretical range from 1 to 6 due to the response format used in the present study, where high scores represent high self-esteem. For Afro-Caribbeans, the measure ranged from 2.06 to 6, with a mean of 4.71 and a standard deviation of 0.80. Reliability analyses yielded a Cronbach's alpha of 0.83. Corrected-item total correlations ranged from 0.30 to 0.57. The distribution of the scale was negatively skewed (skewness = –0.85). The Kolmogorov–Smirnov test indicated deviations from normality ($z = 1.95$, $p < 0.01$). This is characteristic for this scale (or variations of it) when working with nonclinical samples (Robinson et al., 1991). Skewness coefficients above 0.60 have been previously reported (see Crocker, Thompson, McGraw, & Ingerman, 1987).

For White participants, the range of the self-esteem measure was from 1.81 to 6, with a mean of 4.81 and a standard deviation of 0.79. The internal consistency of a Cronbach's alpha of 0.85 was also satisfactory. All items had an item-total correlation above 0.33. The distribution was also negatively skewed (skewness = 0.68), the Kolmogorov–Smirnov test indicated deviations from normality ($z = 2.00, p < 0.01$).

Ethnic Identity

For the Afro-Caribbean sample, the first five Eigenvalues were 4.77, 1.56, 0.98, 0.77, and 0.72, accounting for 39.8%, 13%, 8.1%, 6.4%, and 6.0% of the total variance, respectively. The first two factors were highly interrelated ($r = 0.54, p < 001$). A one-factor solution was therefore suitable. Factor loadings on the single factor ranged from 0.47 to 0.74. For Whites, the five first factors had Eigenvalues of 3.64, 1.58, 1.08, 0.92, and 0.86 that accounted for 30.4%, 13.2%, 9%, 7.6%, and 7.1% of the variance in the measure, respectively. The three-factor solution was not easily interpretable. A one-factor solution was therefore chosen. Loadings on the single factor ranged from 0.36 to 0.68. As can be seen, factor analyses suggest that this version of the multigroup ethnic-identity measure represents a single measure of ethnic identity. Therefore the twelve items were added.

For Black respondents, the ethnic identity scores ranged from 1 to 6, with a mean of 4.51 and a standard deviation of 0.93. High scores indicate strong ethnic identification. Reliability analyses yielded a satisfactory internal consistency coefficient Cronbach's alpha of 0.85. All items had a corrected-item total correlation above 0.41. As indicated by the Kolmorov–Smirnov test (skewness = –0.72; $z = 1.40, p = 0.04$) the score deviates only slightly from a normal distribution.

For Whites, the score range was from 1.42 to 5.83, with a mean of 3.98 and a standard deviation of 0.85. Reliability analyses yielded a Cronbach's alpha of 0.78. Corrected item-total correlations ranged from 0.28 to 0.54. The deletion of the item with the lowest item-total correlation did not improve the alpha value. Therefore, the item was retained. The sum scores were also practically normally distributed (skewness = –0.30, $z = 1.40, p = 0.04$).

Interethnic Attitudes

Factor analyses showed the following picture: For Blacks, the first five Eigenvalues were 2.26, 1.17, 0.83, 0.67, and 0.65. Since the second factor seems to be a methodologically induced factor (the second factor contained the negatively worded items), a general factor was extracted that accounted for 37.7% of the variance in the scale. Factor loadings ranged from 0.39 to 0.72. For White participants, only one factor with an Eigenvalue of 2.73 was extracted, accounting for 45.5% of the total variance (successive Eigenvalues were 0.93, 0.79, 0.59, and 0.50). Factor loadings ranged from 0.51 to 0.82.

Since factor analyses indicate that the measure of interethnic attitudes has a nearly unidimensional structure, the six items were retained. For Blacks, scores of this measure ranged from 1 to 6, with higher scores indicating more positive interethnic attitudes. Scale mean and standard deviation were 4.77 and 0.91, respectively. Reliability analyses revealed a modest internal consistency, as indicated by a Cronbach's alpha of 0.65. Corrected item-total correlations ranged from 0.26 to 0.48. The distribution was negatively skewed (skewness $= -0.70$, $z = 1.78$, $p < 0.01$).

For Whites, the measure scored from 1 to 6, with a mean of 4.68 and a standard deviation of 1.04. Reliability analyses yielded a Cronbach's alpha of 0.74. All items had a corrected item-total correlation above 0.35. The scale was also negatively skewed (skewness $= -0.84$, $z = 2.81$, $p < 0.01$).

Perceived Ethnic Discrimination

Recall that the measure of perceived ethnic discrimination was not assessed in the pilot study. In the main study, principal-component analysis using varimax rotation showed that the four items form an unidimensional measure of perceived ethnic discrimination across groups. For Afro-Caribbeans, analyses yielded one factor with an Eigenvalue of 2.54, accounting for 63.6% of the variance in the measure (the successive Eigenvalues were 0.71, 0.48, and 0.27). Factor loadings on the single factor ranged from 0.64 to 0.82. For Whites, one factor was indicated with an Eigenvalue of 2.58 that explained 64.6% of the total variance (successive Eigenvalues were 0.67, 0.40, and 0.35). Factor loadings ranged from 0.68 to 0.85.

For Afro-Caribbeans, scores of the measure of perceived ethnic discrimination ranged from 1 to 6, with high scores indicating more perception of ethnic discrimination. Scale mean was 2.43 and the standard deviation was 1.39, showing that perceived ethnic discrimination was generally low. Clearly, the distribution was positively skewed (skewness $= 0.68$, $z = 3.05$, $p < 0.01$). Similar distributions have been reported in previous research involving adolescents from different ethnic groups (Phinney et al., 1998). The internal consistency of the scale was satisfactory, as indicated by a Cronbach's alpha of 0.80. Corrected item-total correlations ranged from 0.45 to 0.74.

For Whites, the measure ranged from 1 to 6, with a mean of 1.86 and a standard deviation of 1.18. The scale was also positively skewed (skewness $= 1.49$, $z = 6.44$, $p < 0.01$). Reliability analyses yielded a Cronbach's alpha of 0.81. All items had corrected item-total correlations above 0.36.

Perceived In-Group Status

The unidimensional structure of the public collective self-esteem scale was replicated in the main study across ethnic groups. For Blacks, the Eigenvalues were 1.70, 1.08, 0.64, and 0.58. The presence of a second factor with an Eigenvalue above 1 was associated with a substantially irrelevant method effect due to responses to the negatively worded items. Therefore, only one general factor was extracted that accounted for 42.6% of the total variance. Factor loadings ranged from 0.62 to 0.71. For Whites, the Eigenvalues were 1.82, 0.99, and 0.63, with the first factor accounting for 45.4% of the variance in the measure. Factor loadings ranged from 0.63 to 0.71.

For Blacks, scores of this measure ranged from 1 to 6. Scale mean and standard deviation were 3.89 and 1.14, respectively. High scores indicate high (perceived) in-group status. In contrast to the preliminary analyses (pilot study), the internal consistency was very low (Cronbach's alpha = 0.54). However, the lowest corrected item-total correlation was 0.30, so that elimination of single items would not lead to an increase in the alpha coefficient. The distribution was somewhat negatively skewed (skewness = –0.08, z = 1.46, p = 0.03). For Whites, the measure scored from 1 to 6, with a mean of 4.56 and a standard deviation of 1.08. Similarly, the internal consistency was low, as indicated by a Cronbach's alpha of 0.59. All items had a corrected item-total correlation above 0.35. The scale was also negatively skewed (skewness = –0.64, z = 2.50, p < 0.01).

One possible explanation for the substantial drop in the alphas with respect to the pilot study is that participants in the main study were somewhat less educated than participants in the pilot study (recall that in the pilot study 72% of the participants were university students). In effect, the public collective self-esteem scale was developed with university students and has been mostly employed among samples of young adults (see Luhtanen & Crocker, 1992). To test for grade-level effects on the internal consistency of this measure, Cronbach's alphas were computed separately for students from the first level (seventh, eighth, and ninth grades) and second level (tenth, eleventh, and twelfth grades) of secondary school. Cronbach's alphas for Blacks were 0.36 in the first-level group and 0.63 in the second-level group. For Whites, alphas were 0.48 and 0.66, respectively.

Thus, for students from higher grades, alphas were satisfactory (considering the low number of items involved) and comparable to previous results (see Verkuyten & Lay, 1992). By contrast, students from the first level seemed to have difficulties approaching this scale.[3] This should be taken into account in further analyses involving this scale.

Interethnic Contact

As in the pilot study, principal-components analysis with varimax rotation suggests that the nine items form a unidimensional measure of interethnic contact. In the Afro-Caribbean group, the first five Eigenvalues were 3.96, 1.12, 0.79, 0.69, and 0.66. A one-factor solution with 44% of the variance accounted for was therefore suitable. Factor loadings ranged from 0.48 to 0.79. For Whites, one factor with an Eigenvalue of 4.45 that explains 49.4% of the variance was indicated (successive Eigenvalues were 0.89, 0.80, 0.67, and 0.60). Factor loadings ranged from 0.51 to 0.84.

For Blacks, scores of the contact scale ranged from 1.22 to 4 out of a possible range from 1 to 4, with high scores indicating frequent and positive contact. Scale mean and standard deviation were 3.17 and 0.59. Reliability analysis revealed a satisfactory internal consistency, as indicated by a Cronbach's alpha of 0.83. Corrected item-total correlations ranged from 0.38 to 0.67. The distribution was slightly skewed toward the positive interethnic attitudes end of the scale (skewness = -0.48, $z = 1.84$, $p < 0.01$). For Whites, the measure scored from 1.11 to 4, with a mean of 2.90 and a standard deviation of 0.65. Reliability analyses yielded a Cronbach's alpha of 0.86. All items had a corrected item-total correlation above 0.41. The scale was also slightly negatively skewed (skewness = -0.32, $z = 2.05$, $p < 0.01$).

In sum, psychometric data in the main study was highly concordant with results from the pilot study. Results show that the scales are virtually unidimensional and have (with few exceptions) adequate internal consistencies. The scales present two particular features that deserve comment. First, for some of the scales, methodologically induced factors emerge due to the presence of negatively worded items. One way to approach such effects is the elimination of the negative items in the scores (see Marsh, 1996). However, in line with the reasoning of the authors of the scales, negatively worded items should be retained to control other response biases, such as acquiescence tendencies. Second, the scales present some deviations from normality. This should not be surprising when working with self-report instruments through which evaluations of the self and other meaningful social objects are assessed. In such cases, researchers can evaluate the possibility of data transformation. Since the sample size in this study is relatively large, the violations are small, and the techniques employed are robust tests, such transformations are not necessary for these scales.

MAPPING ACCULTURATION STRATEGIES

Recall that the conceptual basis for the classification of the participants into one of the four strategies of acculturation is Berry's (1984) idea that individuals' attitudes toward the dimensions of acculturation can be dichotomized, producing four cells representing the four acculturation modes (see Figure 1.3).

The central precondition for the categorization of four acculturation modes is that the scales measuring the dimensions of acculturation (i.e., ethnic identity and interethnic attitudes) are orthogonal. In effect, the zero-order correlations between these variables indicate that the scales were essentially independent ($r = 0.00$ and $r = 0.11$ for Blacks and Whites, respectively), allowing the subsequent classification. Participants were first classified using the scalar midpoint approach for descriptive purposes. Since the scales ranged from 1 to 6, the theoretical midpoint was 3.5. Participants whose scores were equal to or higher than 3.5 were classified as high in each scale. Thus, respondents scoring high in both measures were classified as "integrationists." Participants scoring high in ethnic identity and low in interethnic attitudes were categorized into the "separation" modus. Those participants scoring low in ethnic identity and high in interethnic attitudes were classified as "assimilationists." Finally, participants low in both measures were classified as "marginalized." Figure 6.1 shows the distribution of the acculturation strategies within each ethnic group.

For Blacks, the scalar midpoint split approach resulted in 322 (78.9%) participants classified as integrated, 41 (10%) as assimilated, 28 (6.9%) as separated, and only 3 (0.7%) as marginalized. Similarly, 493 (64.4%) White participants were classified as integrated, 150 (19.6%) as assimilated, 60 (7.8%) as separated, and 32 (4.2%) as marginalized. These trends are highly consistent with previous research indicating that integration is the most preferred strategy, while marginalization is the less adopted mode (see Berry, Kim, Power, Young, & Bajaki, 1989; Doná & Berry, 1994; Phinney, Chavira, & Williamson, 1992; Piontkowski, Florack, Hoelker, & Obdrzálek, 2000; Roccas, Horenczyk, & Schwartz, 2000). However, while most research shows that separation is pre-

Figure 6.1
Distribution of the Acculturation Strategies across Ethnic Groups

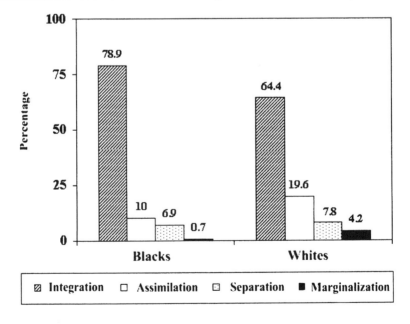

ferred over assimilation, in this study assimilation was preferred over separation. This classification approach provides important information about the distribution of acculturation strategies within and across groups, but the low number of cases in the marginalization mode does not allow further meaningful comparisons.

By contrast, the median split approach allows comparing features of four balanced groups, which is the primary interest of this study. For Black participants the median scores were 4.58 and 4.83 in ethnic identity and interethnic attitudes, respectively. For White participants the medians were 4.04 and 4.83 for ethnic identity and interethnic attitudes, respectively. Participants who scored equal to or higher than the median were classified as high in the respective scale. This allows the retention of the entire sample. For Blacks, the median split approach resulted in 115 participants classified as integrated, 97 as assimilated, 90 as separated, and 100 as marginalized. For Whites, 230 were classified as integrated, 181 as assimilated, 177 as separated, and 170 as marginalized. This classification approach was used for the subsequent analysis.

PRELIMINARY ANALYSES

In preparation for the main analyses, the relationships among the variables under study were examined. As pointed out before, the goal of these analyses was threefold: to test for differences across ethnic groups, to check for multicollinearity problems, and to examine the effect of the control variables on each of the focal variables.[4] For these purposes, several statistical techniques were employed. First, to test for ethnic-group differences, a multivariate analysis of variance of all measures was carried out, using ethnic group as factor. Second, Pearson correlations among all constructs were calculated to examine the relationships among the measures. Third, a series of linear regressions were computed. Ethnic identity, interethnic attitudes, and self-esteem were each regressed on the control variables. Finally, a discriminant function analysis was performed to identify the predictors of the acculturation strategies.

Preliminary analyses are guided by several predictions about the relationship between the variables under study. Therefore, the following paragraphs focus exclusively on the results that are relevant for the examination of these predictions. Recall the specific hypotheses: Self-esteem will be negatively correlated with perceived ethnic discrimination (H1) and positively with perceived in-group status (H2). With regard to ethnic identity, Afro-Caribbeans will show higher levels of ethnic commitment and pride than White participants (H3). Also, ethnic identity will correlate positively with age (H4). Regarding interethnic attitudes, participants high in SES and females will show more favorable interethnic attitudes than participants from lower socioeconomic status and males (H5 and H6). Interethnic attitudes will relate negatively to perceived ethnic discrimination (H7) and positively with in-group status (H8) and interethnic contact (H9).

Ethnic-Group Differences

Results of the MANOVA showed a significant multivariate effect for ethnicity, Wilks's lambda $F(6,1107) = 42.31, p < 0.001$. Table 6.2 summarizes means and standard deviations for all measures for each ethnic group, and the results of the univariate analyses.

Univariate analyses revealed significant ethnic differences on self-esteem, $F(1,1112) = 5.04, p < 0.05$, ethnic identity, $F(1,1112) = 78.92, p < 0.001$; perceived ethnic discrimination, $F(1,1112) = 52.92, p < 0.001$; perceived in-group status, $F(1,1112) = 91.19, p < 0.001$; and interethnic contact, $F(1,1112) = 42.32, p < 0.001$. As predicted by Hypothesis 3, Blacks show higher levels of ethnic identity than Whites. Not surprisingly, Blacks report significantly more ethnic discrimination, less in-group status, and more interethnic contact than Whites. No ethnic differences were found in the attitudes toward members of other ethnic groups. Finally, the small effect of ethnicity on self-esteem ($\eta^2 = 0.004$) suggests that ethnic minority and majority members elicit comparable levels of self-esteem. These results and the fact that Blacks and Whites differ in several demographic variables (see the first section of Chapter 5) reinforce the need for testing the research hypotheses separately for each ethnic group.

The Relationship between Control and Focal Variables

The zero-order correlations among the variables under study are presented in Table 6.3. Due to the large number of correlations involved, only those significant at a p-level of 0.01 are described here. A general look at the correlation matrix reveals modest but statistically significant intercorrelations among the measures, indicating that they assess related but distinct constructs.

Table 6.2
Univariate Analysis of Variance on the Effects of Ethnicity on All Measures

Measures	Blacks		Whites			
	M	SD	M	SD	$F(1,1112)$	η^2
Self-esteem	4.71	.80	4.81	.79	4.75*	.004
Ethnic identity	4.51	.93	3.98	.85	95.27***	.079
Interethnic attitudes	4.77	.91	4.68	1.04	2.60	.002
Perceived discrimination	2.43	1.39	1.86	1.18	49.80***	.043
Perceived ingroup status	3.89	1.14	4.56	1.08	93.05***	.077
Interethnic contact	3.17	.59	2.90	.65	44.64***	.039

Note: High scores indicate high levels in each construct.

$*p < 0.05; **p < 0.01; ***p < 0.001$.

Table 6.3
Bivariate Correlations among All Variables

	Esteem	Ident.	Attit.	Discr.	Status	Contact	City	SES	Gender	Age
Esteem		.28***	.10	.18***	.18***	.10	.00	.04	-.00	.08
Identity	.19***		-.00	.14**	-.01	.21***	-.01	.08	-.01	.03
Attit.	.12**	.11**		.31***	.10	.42***	-.08	.04	-.16**	-.01
Discr.	.19***	.02	-.20***		-.32***	.12	.08	.06	.13**	-.01
Status	.25***	.19***	.13***	.27***		.07	-.13**	.09	-.01	-.14**
Contact	.07	.24***	.51***	.07	.10**		.04	.03	-.12	.09
City	.03	.12**	.06	.01	-.09	.26***		.18***	-.13**	.17**
SES	.10**	.01	-.01	.05	.03	.02	-.16***		.04	.03
Gender	.16***	.01	-.06	.13***	-.01	.02	-.05	.05		.07
Age	.04	.03	.05	.06	-.03	.13***	.19***	.03	.00	

Note: Correlations for the Afro-Caribbean group are showed above the diagonal. *N*s vary from 375 to 408 and from 749 to 766 for Blacks and Whites, respectively, because of missing values (max. missing values < 8%). City of residence: San José = 1, Limón = 2; gender: female = 1, male = 2.

**$p < 0.01$; ***$p < 0.001$.

For Blacks, self-esteem was positively correlated with ethnic identity ($r = 0.28, p < 0.001$) and perceived in-group status ($r = 0.17, p < 0.001$) and negatively correlated with perceived ethnic discrimination ($r = -0.18, p < 0.001$). Ethnic identity correlated positively with interethnic contact ($r = 0.21, p < 0.001$) and ethnic discrimination ($r = 0.14, p < 0.01$). Finally, interethnic attitudes showed significant positive correlations with interethnic contact ($r = 0.42, p < 0.001$) and negative correlations with perceived ethnic discrimination ($r = -0.31, p < 0.001$). Demographic variables had a modest impact on the focal variables for Black participants. Only interethnic attitudes were associated with gender in this group ($r = -0.16, p < 0.01$) with females showing more positive interethnic attitudes than males.

For White participants, self-esteem was positively related to ethnic identity ($r = 0.19, p < 0.001$), interethnic attitudes ($r = 0.11, p < 0.01$), and perceived in-group status ($r = 0.25, p < 0.001$), and negatively correlated with perceived ethnic discrimination ($r = -0.19, p < 0.001$). Ethnic identity was positively related to interethnic contact ($r = 0.21, p < 0.001$) and in-group status ($r = 0.19, p < 0.001$). Finally, interethnic attitudes showed positive correlations with interethnic contact ($r = 0.51, p < 0.01$) and in-group status ($r = 0.12, p < 0.01$) and were negatively correlated with perceived ethnic discrimination ($r = -0.20, p < 0.01$). Demographic variables seem to have more impact on the focal variables in this group. Self-esteem was related to SES ($r = 0.10$, $p <$ 0.01) and gender ($r = 16$, $p < 0.001$). Here, participants from lower socioeconomic backgrounds and females reported lower levels of self-esteem than participants from higher SES and males. On the other hand, ethnic identity was related to city of residence ($r = 0.12$, $p < 0.01$), indicating that Whites from Limón reported higher levels of ethnic identity than Whites from San José.

Overall, the pattern of correlations among predictors of self-esteem (i.e., control and focal independent variables) suggests that multicolinearity is not a problem in this study (Maruyama, 1998).[5] Therefore, the analyses were continued within a regression approach. Table 6.4 presents the results of the simultaneous multiple regression analyses for the control variables predicting self-esteem, ethnic identity, and interethnic attitudes for each ethnic group.

Control Variables and Self-Esteem

For Black participants, the overall model for predicting self-esteem was significant, $F(7,339) = 3.03$, $p < 0.01$, but the amount of variance accounted for was low (6%). In this model, perceived ethnic discrimination ($\beta = -0.12$, $p < 0.05$) and in-group status ($\beta = 0.14$, $p < 0.05$) emerged as significant predictors of self-esteem when controlling for the remaining predictors. In concordance with Hypotheses 1 and 2, the perception of discrimination and low in-group status were associated with lower levels of self-esteem. Neither city of residence nor demographic variables were found to significantly contribute to predicting self-esteem. For White participants, the overall model for predicting self-esteem was significant, $F(7,691) = 14.02$, $p < 0.001$, with 12% of the variance accounted for. Self-esteem was predicted by perceived discrimination ($\beta = -0.14$, $p < 0.001$) and perceived in-group status ($\beta = 0.20$, $p < 0.001$) in the expected way. Among the demographic variables, SES ($\beta = 0.09$, $p < 0.01$) and gender ($\beta = 0.19$, $p < 0.001$) were significant predictors of self-esteem, with males and participants of higher socioeconomic status reporting higher levels of self-esteem than females and participants of lower socioeconomic status.

Control Variables and Ethnic Identity

For Black participants, interethnic contact and perceived ethnic discrimination remained significant predictors of ethnic identity when controlling for other variables in a significant model that accounts for 9% of the variance, $F(7,339) = 4.98$, $p < 0.001$. The data suggest that having interethnic contact is associated with higher levels of ethnic identity ($\beta = 0.25$, $p < 0.001$). On the other hand, higher levels of perceived ethnic discrimination were associated with stronger (not weaker) ethnic identity ($\beta = 21$, $p < 0.001$). Regional and demographic variables did not significantly contribute to the prediction of ethnic identity in this group. For White participants, interethnic contact ($\beta = 0.20$, $p < 0.01$), in-group status ($\beta = 0.19$, $p < 0.01$), and city of residence ($\beta = 0.09$,

Table 6.4

Simultaneous Multiple Regressions for the Control Variables Predicting Self-Esteem, Ethnic Identity, and Interethnic Attitudes among Black ($N = 406$) and White ($N = 698$) Participants

	Criterion											
	Self-esteem				Ethnic Identity				Interethnic Attitudes			
	Blacks		Whites		Blacks		Whites		Blacks		Whites	
Predictors	β	t	β	t	β	t	β	t	β	t	β	t
Discrimination	-.12	-2.15*	-.14	-3.85***	.21	3.76***	.07	1.89	-.23	-4.60***	-.13	-3.85***
Status	.14	2.52*	.20	5.28***	.09	1.74	.19	5.02**	.01	.36	.04	1.28
Contact	.09	1.84	.04	1.20	.25	4.77***	.20	5.30**	.41	8.88***	.52	15.62***
City of residence	.04	.65	.03	.76	.00	-.08	.09	2.40*	-.04	-.86	-.07	-2.18*
SES	.03	.54	.09	2.64**	.04	.74	.01	.33	.01	.23	-.01	-.53
Gender	.03	.46	.19	5.33***	-.02	-.43	-.02	-.61	-.11	-2.34*	-.05	-1.73
Age	.05	.88	.05	1.28	.00	.08	.00	.06	-.04	-.94	-.01	-.35
Summary statistics												
Multiple R	.24		.35		.30		.31		.53		.55	
R^2	.06		.12		.09		.10		.28		.30	
Model	$F_{(7,339)} =$		$F_{(7,691)} =$		$F_{(7,339)} =$		$F_{(7,691)} =$		$F_{(7,339)} =$		$F_{(7,691)} =$	
	3.03**		4.02***		4.90***		10.36***		19,03***		42.11***	

$*p < 0.05; **p < 0.01; ***p < 0.001.$

$p < 0.05$) remained significant predictors of ethnic identity, accounting for 10% of the variance in ethnic identity, $F(7,691) = 10.36, p < 0.001$). Specifically, high commitment to the ethnic group of reference was predicted by residing in Limón, having frequent interethnic contact, and the perception of secure in-group status.

Note that age was unrelated to ethnic identity across groups. This might be due to the fact that the variance on this variable is very small among high school students. Thus, the expected developmental pattern tested by Hypothesis 4 found no support in these samples.

Control Variables and Interethnic Attitudes

For Black participants, the overall model for predicting interethnic attitudes accounted for 28% of the variance, $F(7,339) = 4.90, p < 0.001$. Interethnic attitudes were primarily predicted by interethnic contact ($\beta = 0.42, p < 0.001$), followed by perceived discrimination ($\beta = -0.23, p < 0.001$), and gender ($\beta = -0.11, p < 0.05$). In line with Hypothesis 9, participants with experience of interethnic contact are more likely to express positive interethnic attitudes. By contrast, participants perceiving more discrimination are less likely to express positive attitudes toward ethnic out-group members, as expected by Hypothesis 7. Finally, in concordance with Hypothesis 6, females elicit more positive attitudes toward other ethnic groups than males.

For White participants, interethnic contact, perceived discrimination, and city of residence emerged as significant predictors of interethnic attitudes in a significant model that accounts for 30% of the variance, $F(7,691) = 42.11, p < 0.001$. As expected, having interethnic contact is associated with more positive interethnic attitudes ($\beta = 52, p < 0.001$), while the perception of discrimination is associated with less positive attitudes toward other ethnic groups ($\beta = -13, p < 0.001$). When controlling for these variables, the positive relationship between in-group status and interethnic attitudes was no longer significant ($\beta = 0.04$, n.s).

On the other hand, city of residence turned out to reach statistical significance, but note that its partial regression weight is opposite in sign to its zero-order correlation to interethnic attitudes (see Table 6.4). The inspection of the data suggests that this inconsistency is due to the overlap between city of residence and the measure of interethnic contact. As such, city of residence is only marginally related to interethnic attitudes ($r = 0.06, p = 0.08$). However, given the sample characteristics, city of residence is related to interethnic contact ($r = 0.26, p < 0.001$), which in turn emerges as the most important predictor of interethnic attitudes. More specifically, living in Limón increased the opportunities of interethnic contact for White participants, because the Black community is overrepresented in this province. Yet increasing opportunities for contact (i.e., residing in Limón) do not assure per se the conditions of positive contact (e.g., having interethnic friends). Thus, when city of residence and interethnic contact are included in the equation, the negative weight "subtracts out" the components of interethnic contact that are not directly related to interethnic attitudes and increases the predictive value of those components of interethnic contact that meet optimal conditions. These results are consistent with the idea that interethnic proximity is necessary but not sufficient to contribute positively to interethnic attitudes (cf. Allport, 1954; Pettigrew, 1997, 1998; Pettigrew et al., 1998; Wagner, Hewstone, & Machleit, 1989).

In sum, the correlates of interethnic attitudes were highly consistent with Hypotheses 7 and 9 across ethnic groups, while Hypothesis 6 was supported only among ethnic-minority members. In both groups, interethnic attitudes were unrelated to in-group status and SES, providing no support for Hypotheses 5 and 8.

Control Variables and Acculturation Strategies

Since the explanation of acculturation strategies is of central interest in this study, a discriminant function analysis was carried out for each ethnic group to identify those control variables that optimally differentiate between integrated, assimilated, separated, and marginalized participants. Table 6.5 presents the results of the discriminant function analyses for each ethnic group.

For Black participants, two of the three possible discriminant functions were significant, $\chi^2_{(21)} = 99.34$, $p < 0.01$ and $\chi^2_{(12)} = 25.68$, $p < 0.01$. The first function accounted for 76% of the variance, while the second for 18%. As indicated by the standardized discriminant coefficients, both functions are primarily constituted by interethnic contact and perceived discrimination, contact being the best discriminant variable in the first function and discrimination the best predictor for separating acculturation strategies in the second function. Since both variables are related to the perceived characteristics of interethnic contact, the first function can be labeled "optimal contact," while the second can be thought to represent "threat" and "negative contact."

As shown by the group centroids, the "optimal contact" function discriminates integrated and assimilated participants from separated and marginalized participants. The "threat" function discriminates between the separated participants from the assimilated groups, with integrated and marginalized groups falling in between. For a better interpretation of the data, Table 6.6 shows means and standard deviations for these variables by acculturation modes for Black participants.

The inspection of the mean scores reveals that individuals who adopt integration and assimilation strategies constitute the groups with most experience of interethnic contact, but the assimilation strategy is primarily characterized by a low perception of ethnic discrimination. On the other hand, the adoption of separation and marginalization is indicated by low contact and high perceived discrimination, but participants in the separation modus are particularly aware of ethnic discrimination.

Table 6.5
Results of the Discriminant Function Analysis among Black and White Participants

| | Blacks | | Whites | |
| | (N = 347) | | (N = 699) | |
Discriminant functions	Function 1	Function 2	Function 1	Function 2
Eigenvalue	.24	.06	.33	.04
% of Variance	75.75%	18.67%	86.18%	10.95%
Canonical Correlation	.44	.24	.50	.20
Wilks' Lambda	.75	.93	.72	.95
Df	21	12	21	12
χ^2	99.34***	25.68*	231.62***	35.68***
Standardized discriminant coefficients				
Discrimination	-.54	.80	-.32	.68
Status	.03	.07	.16	.80
Contact	.77	.55	.93	-.04
City of residence	-.08	-.23	-.11	.27
SES	.02	.28	-.05	.15
Gender	-.18	-.04	-.11	.17
Age	-.02	.08	.03	.16
Group Centroides				
Integration	.47	.18	.63	.02
Assimilation	.44	-.26	.35	-.13
Separation	-.46	.32	-.44	.33
Marginalization	-.57	-.22	-.75	-.22

$*p < 0.05; **p < 0.01; ***p < 0.001.$

Overall, 42% of the cases can be correctly classified with both functions (compared to 25% by chance alone). More specifically, the greatest accuracy in the classification was achieved for assimilated participants, with 44% correctly classified. The poorest accuracy was achieved by the integrated group, with approximately 40% correct classified and almost 30% misclassified as assimilated.

For White participants, two discriminant functions were also isolated, $\chi^2_{(21)}$ = 231.62, $p < 0.01$ and $\chi^2_{(12)}$ = 35.68, $p < 0.01$. The amount of variance accounted for by these functions was 86.18% and 10.95%, respectively. The standardized discriminant coefficients indicated that interethnic contact was the best predictor variable for the first function. The second function was primarily based on perceived in-group status and ethnic discrimination, with in-group status as the variable that distinguished most between the acculturation

Table 6.6
Means and Standard Deviations for Interethnic Contact and Perceived Discrimination by Acculturation Mode for Black Participants

Acculturation Strategy	Interethnic contact		Perceived discrimination	
	M	SD	M	SD
Integration	3.43	.52	2.20	1.42
Assimilation	3.29	.52	1.81	1.45
Separation	3.05	.52	3.08	1.02
Marginalization	2.86	.64	2.63	1.36

Note: High scores indicate frequent and positive contact and more perception of discrimination; $N = 347$.

strategies in this dimension. Therefore, the first dimension can be labeled "optimal contact" and the second "in-group prestige." The group centroids reveal that the first function separated integrated and assimilated participants from separated and marginalized groups. The dimension of in-group prestige was especially successful in discriminating separated from marginalized individuals, with the integration and assimilation modes falling between. Mean scores and standard deviations for the variables involved in this function are presented in Table 6.7.

These data suggest that White participants with an integration or assimilation strategy have frequent interethnic contact and perceive less ethnic dis-

Table 6.7
Means and Standard Deviations for Interethnic Contact, Perceived Discrimination, and Perceived In-Group Status by Acculturation Mode for White Participants

Acculturation Strategy	Interethnic contact		Perceived discrimination		Perceived in-group status	
	M	SD	M	SD	M	SD
Integration	3.23	.54	1.60	.98	4.75	1.11
Assimilation	3.06	.59	1.58	.99	4.61	1.06
Separation	2.69	.58	2.17	1.39	4.63	1.00
Marginalization	2.49	.60	2.04	1.14	4.19	1.07

Note: High scores indicate frequent and positive interethnic contact, more perception of discrimination, and high (perceived) in-group status; $N = 699$.

crimination. The separation and integration strategies showed a reverse pattern. Individuals adopting these modes have less interethnic contact and perceive more discrimination than the former. The major difference between the latter groups is that marginalized individuals perceive that their ethnic in-group has low social prestige.

Based on these two functions, 45% of the cases can be correctly classified. Greater accuracy was reached by the classification of the integration and marginalization strategy, with a hit ratio of 54% and 56.6%, respectively. By contrast, the classification of assimilated participants was around chance level, with only 29.5% of cases correctly classified and almost 40% misclassified as integrated.

PRIMARY ANALYSES

Primary analyses concentrated on the effects of ethnic identity and interethnic attitudes on self-esteem when including the control variables in the same model. According to the central hypotheses, a strong identification with the ethnic group of reference (H10) and positive attitudes toward out-groups (H11) will be associated with higher self-esteem. The goal of these analyses is not only to examine the independent effect of acculturation dimensions on adolescents feelings of self-regard, but also their combined effect on self-esteem in the form of four acculturation modes. Specifically, it is expected that respondents who adopt an integration strategy will show higher levels of self-esteem than those who adopt the assimilation, separation, and marginalization strategies (H12). Adolescents who adopt the marginalization mode will have lower levels of self-esteem than those classified in the other three groups (H13).

Acculturation Dimensions, Strategies, and Self-Esteem

To test these hypotheses, self-esteem was first subjected to a 2×2 analyses of variances with ethnic identity (high versus low) and interethnic attitudes (high versus low) as factors. The effects were then examined with perceived discrimination, in-group status, interethnic contact, city of residence, socioeconomic status, gender, and age entered as covariates in a 2×2 analysis of covariance.

In both analyses, t-tests for a priori comparisons were performed to test for differences on self-esteem across the four cell means; that is, across the acculturation strategies. Specifically, the mean score on self-esteem of the integration cell (i.e., the high ethnic identity–high interethnic attitudes cell) was compared to the mean of the remaining cells. Similarly, the mean score on self-esteem of the marginalization cell (i.e., the low ethnic identity–low interethnic attitudes cell) was contrasted to the mean of the remaining cells. An additional contrast was finally performed to test for differences on self-esteem between separation (i.e., the high ethnic identity–low interethnic attitudes cell) and assimilation (i.e., the low ethnic identity–high interethnic attitudes cell).

Results of the 2 (high versus low ethnic identity) x 2 (high versus low interethnic attitudes) are presented in Table 6.8.

Results of the ANOVA provide initial evidence supporting Hypotheses 10 and 11. For Black participants, the ANOVA revealed a significant effect for ethnic identity, $F(1,398) = 16.153, p < 0.001$, and interethnic attitudes, $F(1,754) = 5.61, p < 0.05$. Inspection of the means shows that participants with a strong ethnic identity elicit higher levels of self-esteem than participants low in ethnic identity ($M_{high} = 4.86$ versus $M_{low} = 4.54$). Also, participants scoring high in interethnic attitudes show higher levels of self-esteem than those low in interethnic attitudes ($M_{high} = 4.80$ versus $M_{low} = 4.59$). There was no significant interaction between the factors suggesting that the effects of the dimensions of acculturation are largely additive. For White participants, the ANOVA also showed a significant effect for ethnic identity, $F(1,754) = 12.89, p < 0.001$, and interethnic attitudes, $F(1,754) = 9.40, p < 0.01$. The means indicate that participants with a strong ethnic identity show higher levels of self-esteem than participants low in ethnic identity ($M_{high} = 4.91$ versus $M_{low} = 4.69$). Similarly, participants showing more positive interethnic attitudes elicit higher levels of self-esteem than those low in interethnic attitudes ($M_{high} = 4.89$ versus $M_{low} = 4.71$). Again, there was no significant effect for the interaction in this ethnic group.

In terms of the acculturation strategies, t-tests for a priori comparisons provide strong support for Hypotheses 12 and 13 across ethnic groups.[6] Mean scores on self-esteem for each acculturation strategy are presented in Table 6.9 for each ethnic group.

Table 6.8
Results of the Analyses of Variance among Black and White Participants

	Blacks ($N = 401$)		Whites ($N = 757$)	
Means	High	Low	High	Low
Ethnic Identity	4.86	4.54	4.91	4.69
Interethnic Attitudes	4.80	4.59	4.89	4.71
Source of Variation	$F(1,398)$	η^2	$F(1,754)$	η^2
Ethnic Identity	16.13***	.039	12.89***	.017
Interethnic Attitudes	5.61*	.014	9.40**	.012
Ethnic Identity x Interethnic attitudes	.07	.000	.13	.000

Note: High scores indicate high self-esteem.
*$p < 0.05$; **$p < 0.01$; ***$p < 0.001$.

Table 6.9
Mean Scores for Self-Esteem as a Function of Ethnic Identity and
Interethnic Attitudes among Black and White Participants

	Blacks ($N = 401$)		Whites ($N = 757$)	
	Ethnic identity			
Interethnic attitudes	High	Low	High	Low
High	4.93	4.64	4.97	4.78
	Integration	Assimilation	Integration	Assimilation
Low	4.77	4.44	4.81	4.59
	Separation	Marginalization	Separation	Marginalization

Note: High scores indicate high self-esteem.

Overall, results reveal that integrated participants show significantly higher self-esteem than the separated, assimilated, and marginalized groups combined, $t(398) = 3.69$, $p < 0.001$ and $t(754) = 3.89$, $p < 0.001$ for Blacks and Whites, respectively. Also, participants in the marginalization mode reported lower levels of self-esteem compared with the other groups, $t(398) = 3.85$, $p < 0.001$ for Blacks and $t(754) = 3.92$, $p < 0.001$ for Whites. Finally, data show that assimilated and separated groups do not differ significantly in their levels of self-esteem, $t(398) = 1.28$, and $t(754) = 0.36$ for Blacks and Whites, respectively.

However, the pattern of means suggests that acculturation strategies can be ranged in terms of their contribution to self-esteem, with integration linked to the highest levels of self-esteem, followed by separation over assimilation, and marginalization associated with the lowest levels of personal regard. Linear contrast analyses confirmed a significant linear trend toward higher levels of self-esteem from marginalization, through assimilation and separation, to integration across ethnic groups, $F(1,398) = 22.88$, $p < 0.001$ for Blacks and $F(1,754) = 21.77$, $p < 0.001$ for Whites. Neither the quadratic [$F(1,398) = 0.07$ for Blacks and $F(1,754) = 0.13$ for Whites] nor the cubic trend [$F(1,398) = 0.10$ for Blacks and $F(1,754) = 1.25$ for Whites] were statistically significant.

Looking at these effects when including the control variables as covariates, results of the 2 (high versus low ethnic identity) x 2 (high versus low interethnic attitudes) present the picture shown in Table 6.10.

For Black participants, the ANCOVA revealed a significant effect for ethnic identity, $F(1,336) = 17.15$, $p < 0.001$, after adjustment by the covariates. Inspection of the adjusted means shows, in concordance with the ANOVA results, that participants with a strong ethnic identity elicit higher levels of

Table 6.10
Results of the Analyses of Covariance among Black and White Participants

	Blacks ($N = 347$)		Whites ($N = 699$)	
Adjusted means	High	Low	High	Low
Ethnic Identity	4.87	4.52	4.89	4.73
Interethnic Attitudes	4.75	4.64	4.86	4.75
Covariates	$F(1,336)$	η^2	$F(1,688)$	η^2
Discrimination	5.84*	.017	13.56***	.019
Status	6.25*	.018	23.06***	.032
Contact	.41	.001	.01	.000
City of residence	.86	.002	.45	.001
SES	.07	.000	7.38**	.001
Gender	.43	.001	30.16***	.042
Age	.73	.002	1.70	.002
Source of Variation				
Ethnic Identity	17.15***	.049	7.98**	.011
Interethnic Attitudes	1.36	.004	2.78	.004
Ethnic Identity x Interethnic attitudes	.55	.002	.29	.000

Note: High scores indicate high self-esteem. Covariates were entered first.

$*p < 0.05; **p < 0.01; ***p < 0.001$.

self-esteem than participants low in ethnic identity (M_{high} = 4.87 versus M_{low} = 4.52). However, there was no significant main effect for interethnic attitudes on self-esteem, nor was the interaction effect significant. In other words, the effects of interethnic attitudes on self-esteem were no longer significant when controlling for other important predictors of self-esteem. Here, results revealed a significant effect for two of the seven covariates; namely, perceived ethnic discrimination and in-group status.

For White participants, the ANCOVA revealed a significant effect for ethnic identity, $F(1,688) = 7.98, p < 0.01$. In line with the ANOVA results, the adjusted means show that participants with a strong ethnic identity elicit higher levels of self-esteem than participants low in ethnic identity (M_{high} = 4.89 versus M_{low} = 4.73). Interethnic attitudes did not significantly affect self-esteem, nor was the interaction significant. In addition, results revealed a significant effect for perceived ethnic discrimination, perceived in-group status, SES, and gender.

In terms of the acculturation strategies, data show that the pattern of relations between acculturation strategies and self-esteem holds true after adjustment for the covariates across ethnic groups (see Table 6.11).

Table 6.11
Adjusted Mean Scores for Self-Esteem as a Function of Ethnic Identity and Interethnic Attitudes among Black and White Participants

	Blacks ($N = 401$)		Whites ($N = 757$)	
	Ethnic identity			
Interethnic attitudes	High	Low	High	Low
	4.90	4.60	4.95	4.76
	Integration	Assimilation	Integration	Assimilation
	4.85	4.43	4.82	4.69
	Separation	Marginalization	Separation	Marginalization

Note: High scores indicate high self-esteem. Means are adjusted for perceived discrimination, perceived in-group status, interethnic contact, city of residence, socioeconomic status, gender, and age.

Overall, *t*-tests for a priori comparisons reveal that integrated participants show significantly higher self-esteem than the separated, assimilated, and marginalized groups combined, $t(336) = 2.77$, $p < 0.01$ and $t(688) = 3.02$, $p < 0.01$ for Blacks and Whites, respectively. Also, participants in the marginalization mode reported lower levels of self-esteem compared with the other groups, $t(336) = 3.47$, $p < 0.001$ for Blacks and $t(688) = 2.20$, $p < 0.05$ for Whites, respectively. Assimilated and separated groups do not differ significantly in their level of self-esteem, $t(336) = 1.89$, n.s. for Blacks and $t(688) = 0.65$, n.s. for Whites. It should be noted, however, that among Black participants the difference in self-esteem between these groups was marginally significant ($p = 0.06$), with participants in the separation model scoring higher in self-esteem than those in the assimilation mode.

The linear trend toward higher levels of self-esteem from marginalization, through assimilation and separation, to integration was also confirmed after adjustment for differences in the covariates across groups, $F(1,336) = 18.73$, $p < 0.001$ for Blacks and $F(1,688) = 10.52$, $p < 0.01$ for Whites. Once more, neither the quadratic [$F(1,336) = 0.55$ for Blacks and $F(1,688) = 0.29$ for Whites] nor the cubic trend [$F(1,336) = 0.44$ for Blacks and $F(1,688) = 0.13$ for Whites] were statistically significant.

In sum, the data show that even when controlling for several social–psychological and demographic variables, ethnic identity remains an important source of self-esteem, giving strong support to Hypotheses 10. But the expected link between interethnic attitudes and self-esteem was no longer significant when including the control variables in the analyses. There was also no evidence of an interaction between interethnic attitudes and ethnic identity. As such, Hypothesis 11 received no support in these samples. Rather, the impact of interethnic attitudes on self-esteem was only evident in terms of the acculturation strategies. As expected by Hypothesis 12 and 13, those participants who identify with the ethnic group of reference and elicit more positive interethnic attitudes show the highest level of self-esteem. On the contrary, participants who distance themselves from their ethnic group of references and elicit less positive attitudes toward other ethnic groups showed the lowest level of self-regard. The separation and assimilation modes seem to be linked with intermediate levels of self-esteem. A more detailed inspection of the data suggests an increase in self-esteem from marginalization, through assimilation and separation, to integration. These trends hold true across ethnic groups and after adjustment for differences that can be accounted for by seven covariates.

Taken together, preliminary and primary analyses reveal two major opposite influences on psychological adaptation, which are partially mediated by the acculturation dimensions and strategies, in particular by ethnic identity. On the one hand, perceived threats such as discrimination or low in-group status affect self-esteem directly, but they also seem to have an indirect impact on individuals' feelings of self-regard via ethnic identity. On the other hand, interethnic contact has no direct impact on self-esteem, but due to its effects on ethnic identity, interethnic attitudes, and acculturation strategies it contributes indirectly to a positive adjustment. It is interesting to note that these trends generalize across groups, suggesting the presence of a common mechanism fundamental to both ethnic-minority and ethnic-majority members.

However, these data also suggest ethnically differentiated patterns in the multivariate impact on self-esteem. Ethnic differences emerge principally on the predictors of self-esteem and ethnic identity. The results show that gender is predictive of self-esteem for White participants but not for Black participants, but the central difference across ethnic groups is the impact of ethnic discrimination and in-group status on ethnic identity. More specifically, for ethnic-minority members, in-group affirmation and commitment appears to be a response to systematic discrimination. For ethnic-majority members, ethnic discrimination seems to be unrelated to their in-group commitment. On the other hand, White participants base their in-group commitment from the secure status of their group in the society, while this seems to be irrelevant for ethnic-minority members. According to these results, there are specific factors that contribute differentially to adaptation in plural societies, which depend on the ethnic group in question and its relative status in the society. The next section provides an overall test of these trends.

Modeling Personal Outcomes of Acculturation

Structural equation modeling (SEM) techniques were used for a final test of the multivariate relationship between the variables under study. Like multiple regression techniques, SEM provides information on the strength of the relationship between the variables of interest, but it has several advantages over traditional multiple regression. Two of them are particularly relevant for the purposes of the present study (see Maruyama, 1998, for a more detailed account of the advantages of this approach). First, SEM allows researchers to articulate the impact of the variables, including both direct and indirect effects. This is especially helpful here, because ethnic identity is expected to be the central mediating variable of the effects of the control variables on self-esteem. Second, with the incorporation of latent variables, SEM allows one to separate error variance from the more meaningful covariation between the measures. This is particularly useful when testing the measures of the constructs in new samples, as in the present study. The question here is whether the proposed relationships between the variables hold when the measured error is separated and controlled.

Model estimation was conducted separately for each ethnic group and included the following steps: First, those variables that emerged as significant predictors of focal independent and dependent variables in previous analyses were included in a baseline model, which was calculated on a half of each sample (random split). Second, the respective initial models were improved on the basis of modification indices and cross-validated with the other half of each sample. In these phases the analyses were carried out with observed variables; that is, with single measures of each variable of interest. The rationale for proceeding in this way is that the high number of indicators used for measuring each construct produced highly restrictive models, in which even small cross-loadings led to significant departures from the data. Therefore, after model fitting, a final test of the models was carried out on the basis of latent variables. As pointed out before, the primary concern here is to test whether the hypothesized relationship among the variables can be observed after controlling measurement error.

The covariance matrix of the variables was estimated using the structural equation program EQS 5.7 (Bentler, 1992). Parameter estimates were calculated using the maximum likelihood method. Model fit was evaluated using the conventional criteria: the chi-square goodness of fit statistic (χ^2), the chi-square/degrees of freedom ratio (χ^2/d.f.), the comparative fit index (CFI), and the root mean square error of approximation (RMSEA). Although there is some disagreement among researchers about the interpretation of these indices (see Maruyama, 1998), a model is generally said to fit the data well if

1. the χ^2/d.f. is small (with values below 3.0 being desirable)
2. the CFI values are above 0.90

3. the RMSEA values are below to 0.10 (see van Dick, 1999, for a review).

The χ^2 divided by the degrees of freedom can be seen as a less biased index of fit than the χ^2 statistic itself, because the latter is highly influenced by sample size. With large samples, as in the present study, a significant value is likely to be obtained even with small departures from the data. Therefore, χ^2 will be used here more as a guide and less as a rule. For a more compressive assessment of the relations between the variables, the interpretation of the fit indices should be complemented with an inspection of the parameter estimates, the variances accounted for, and the modification indices. The latter can be especially helpful for the improvement of model fit, but should be carefully tested on the basis of theoretical considerations.

Modeling Acculturation Outcomes among Ethnic-Minority Members

For Black participants, the baseline model included perceived in-group status, perceived ethnic discrimination, interethnic contact, and gender as independent variables (given their significant association with the focal variables), and ethnic identity, interethnic attitudes, and self-esteem as dependent variables. Figure 6.2 presents a model that articulates the empirical evidence presented in previous analyses.[7]

As Figure 6.2 shows, perceived threats (particularly ethnic discrimination) have a negative direct effect on self-esteem, while a strong commitment to the ethnic group of reference shows the opposite effect. In addition, ethnic identity is assumed to have a "bolstering" function, mediating the negative effect of perceived discrimination on self-esteem. Interethnic contact shows a positive effect on ethnic identity, and therefore contributes indirectly to a positive self-esteem. Finally, interethnic attitudes are strongly influenced by gender, perceived discrimination, and particularly by interethnic contact. As pointed out before, the path from interethnic attitudes to self-esteem was included for a better description of the multivariate influences of self-esteem. Since previous analyses indicated that this linkage is not significant, the baseline model was calculated without this path.

The fit indices in the first subgroup of Black participants ($N = 197$) show that the model provides a relative good fit with the data, $\chi^2 = 24.67$, d.f. = 13, $p = 0.03$, $\chi^2/\text{d.f.} = 1.90$, CFI = 0.92, RMSEA = 0.07. However, the Lagrange multiplier test (LM) indicated that the model fit could be improved by allowing in-group status and discrimination to correlate with each other, which would lead to an approximate drop in χ^2 value of 13.8 (d.f. = 1, $p < 0.001$). This empirical relationship is highly concordant with the theoretical linkage between the two constructs. Both perceived in-group status and discrimination are considered here as part of the subjective perception of the actual characteristics of intergroup relations, where low perceived in-group status is assumed

Figure 6.2
Baseline Model of Factors Influencing Acculturation and Psychological Adaptation among Black Participants

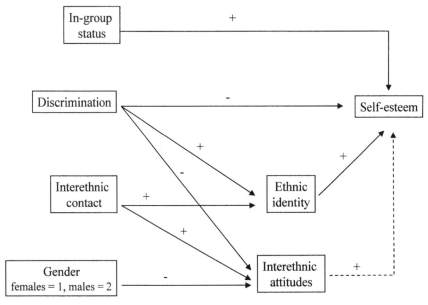

Note: Developed on the basis of preliminary regression analyses. Dashed lines indicate that the expected path was not significant in the regression analyses.

to be related to higher levels of ethnic discrimination. Therefore, the model was reestimated with this adjustment. The standardized solution for the final model is presented in Figure 6.3.

As indicated by the fit indices, the final model can be successfully used to represent the relations between the variables under study: $\chi^2 = 10.41$, d.f. = 12, $p = 0.58$, χ^2/d.f. = 0.87, CFI = 1.00, RMSEA = 0.00. The path coefficients (all significant at $p < 0.05$) confirm the correlational and regression analyses presented earlier. Self-esteem was predicted by perceived in-group status (ß = 0.16), perceived ethnic discrimination (ß = –0.22), and particularly by ethnic identity (ß = 0.28). The more perceived discrimination the adolescents reported, the lower self-esteem they had. By contrast, the higher in-group status they perceived and the higher their commitment to the ethnic group of reference, the higher their self-esteem. These variables accounted for 15% of the variance on self-esteem. Perceived ethnic discrimination (ß = 0.16) and interethnic contact (ß = 0.27) were also significant predictors of ethnic identity, accounting for 10% of its variance. Both variables, but interethnic contact in particular, appeared to reinforce commitment to the in-group, which in turn reinforced the self-esteem of the adolescents. Interethnic attitudes were pri-

Figure 6.3

Factors Influencing Acculturation and Psychological Adaptation in the First Subsample of Black Participants ($N = 197$).

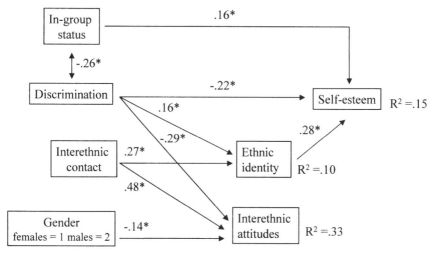

$*p < 0.05.$

marily predicted by interethnic contact ($\beta = 0.48$), followed by perceived discrimination ($\beta = -0.29$) and gender ($\beta = -0.14$). These variables accounted for 33% of the variance in interethnic attitudes. As in previous results, interethnic contact leads to more positive interethnic attitudes, while perceived ethnic discrimination is associated with less positive interethnic attitudes. Finally, females display more positive interethnic attitudes than males.

In sum, this model confirms the presence of two opposite influences on psychological adaptation that are totally and/or partially mediated by individuals' commitment to their ethnic groups of reference. Ethnic discrimination, on the one hand, and optimal interethnic contact, on the other, appear as central factors affecting adolescents' self-esteem. However, ethnic identity is shown to be the most important predictor of their feelings of self-regard, mediating both the negative influences of perceived threats and the positive effects of optimal contact on self-esteem.

For purposes of cross-validation, the final model was estimated in the second subsample of Black participants ($N = 182$). The model also shows a good fit with the data in this sample, $\chi^2 = 20.47$, d.f. $= 12$, $p = 0.06$, $\chi^2/$d.f. $= 1.71$, CFI $= 0.91$, RMSEA $= 0.06$. The models were then tested simultaneously with all parameters across them constrained to be equal. The goodness of fit for the constrained two-group model turned out to be good, $\chi^2 = 39.15$, d.f. $= 33$, $p = 0.21$, $\chi^2/$df $= 1.18$, CFI $= 0.97$. This clearly indicates that the model can be successfully replicated across the second group.

Given findings of adequate fit across subsamples, the final test of the latent variables model was carried out for the whole sample ($N = 362$). Preliminary analyses using a total of fifty-one indicators of the latent variables produced a highly restrictive covariance matrix that did not fit the data well, $\chi^2 = 2887.40$, d.f. $= 1266$, $p = 0.001$, χ^2/d.f. $= 2.28$, CFI $= 0.71$, RMSEA $= 0.06$. Attempts to fit the model would lead to considering more than fifty parameter modifications, mainly referred to minor cross-loadings (to mention only the major modifications suggested by the LM multivariate statistics). Such modifications would not lead to a substantial improvement in the overall fit of the model, but to an overfitted solution. In the interest of parsimony, the model was reestimated using subsets of the measures as indicators of the respective latent constructs. More specifically, half of the items of each scale were randomly selected to be combined in a subscale, so that each latent variable was operationalized by two indicators (identified with the letters a and b). Table 6.12 shows the items corresponding to each subscale.

This allows the conceptual variables to be defined in terms of the commonalties among the subscales, and so separates the measurement error from the constructs, which is in line with the principles of full latent structures equation modeling. Figure 6.4 shows the parameter estimates of the latent variables model for Black participants.

The model shows a very good fit with the data, $\chi^2 = 107.79$, d.f. $= 57$, $p = 0.01$, χ^2/d.f. $= 1.89$, CFI $= 0.97$, RMSEA $= 0.05$. Looking first at the measurement model, results show that all of the indicators were significantly related to the constructs they were assumed to tap. In addition, the proportion of the variance in the measures accounted for by their respective factors (R^2) suggest

Table 6.12
Operationalization of the Latent Constructs

Scale	Subscale	Items
Self-esteem	Esteem(a)	$1 - 6 - 7 - 8 - 11 - 13 - 15 - 16$
	Esteem(b)	$2 - 3 - 4 - 5 - 9 - 10 - 12 - 14$
Ethnic identity	Identity(a)	$2 - 4 - 8 - 10 - 11 - 12$
	Identity(b)	$1 - 3 - 5 - 6 - 7 - 9$
Interethnic attitudes	Attit.(a)	$1 - 2 - 4$
	Attit.(b)	$3 - 5 - 6$
Perceived ingroup status	Status(a)	$1 - 4$
	Status(b)	$2 - 3$
Perceived discrimination	Discr.(a)	$3 - 4$
	Discr.(b)	$1 - 2$
Interethnic contact	Contact(a)	$2 - 3 - 6 - 8 - 9$
	Contact(b)	$1 - 4 - 5 - 7$

Note: Item numbers correspond to those presented in Appendices D and E.

Figure 6.4

Latent-Variables Model of Factors Influencing Acculturation and Psychological Adaptation among Black Participants (N = 362).

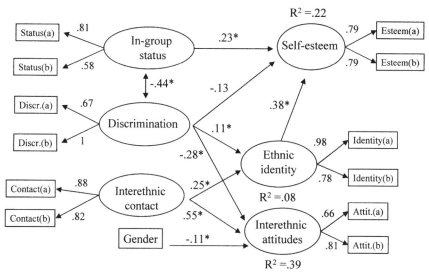

$*p < 0.05.$

that with the exception of the measure of in-group status, all indicators seem to measure adequately their respective constructs. With respect to the structural model, the path coefficients indicate that the relationships among the latent variables are highly consistent with previous results with observed variables. Note, however, that the path from perceived discrimination to self-esteem is no longer significant, while the effects of perceived in-group status and particularly of ethnic identity become larger. Similarly, the relative contribution of discrimination on ethnic identity and interethnic attitudes decreases. Here, positive interethnic contact emerges as the most important predictor of these variables. Finally, there was a notable increase in the variance accounted for: 22%, 8%, and 39% for self-esteem, ethnic identity, and interethnic attitudes, respectively.

Modeling Acculturation Outcomes among Ethnic-Majority Members

As in the case of Black participants, the baseline model in this group included perceived in-group status, perceived ethnic discrimination, interethnic contact, gender, and SES as independent variables, and ethnic identity, interethnic attitudes, and self-esteem as dependent variables. However, the relationship among the variables is somewhat different. Figure 6.5 articulates the results of the regression analyses.[8]

Figure 6.5
Baseline Model of Factors Influencing Acculturation and Psychological Adaptation among White Participants

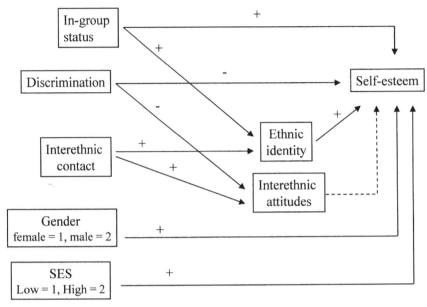

Note: Developed on the basis of preliminary regression analyses. Dashed lines indicate the expected path was not significant in the regression analyses.

For White participants, perceived threats also have a negative direct effect on self-esteem, and ethnic identity also shows the opposite effect. Contrary to Black participants, however, gender and socioeconomic status contribute to predict self-esteem in this group. A further difference across groups is observed in the predictors of ethnic identity. Here, perceived in-group status (but not ethnic discrimination) directly affects ethnic identity. Together with interethnic contact, a relative secure in-group status increases ethnic identification, which in turn contributes positively to self-esteem. Finally, interethnic attitudes are strongly influenced by perceived discrimination, and particularly by interethnic contact, but not by gender.

The standardized solution of the initial model in the first subsample ($N = 322$) showed that the hypothesized covariance matrix did not provide an adequate fit to the data, $\chi^2 = 57.04$, d.f. = 19, $p < 0.01$, χ^2/d.f. = 3, CFI = 0.80, RMSEA = 0.08. The LM and Wald tests indicated that the model fit could be improved by some parameter modifications. First, more parsimony could be reached by the removal of the regression path from SES to self-esteem, which did not significantly contribute to predict self-esteem. The Wald test showed that the exclusion of this variable did not produce a significant decrement in the model's fit ($\Delta\chi^2_{(1)}$ = 3.05, d.f. = 1, p = 0.08). Second, the LM test suggested the addition of the correlation between in-group status and discrimination, which would lead to a significant drop in χ^2 value of 22.15 (d.f. = 1, $p <$ 0.01). Finally, the test showed that allowing a relation between gender and discrimination would contribute significantly to the model fit, with a drop in χ^2 value of 20.1 (d.f. = 1, $p < 0.01$). However, the latter adjustment was not included, given that this relation is (theoretically speaking) much less meaningful than the former. It rather appears to be dependent on the characteristics of this sample, with White males reporting higher perceived discrimination than White females. Therefore, only the first two adjustments were tested. Parameter estimates of the final model are presented in Figure 6.6.

As can be seen, the final model provides a relative good fit to the data, χ^2 = 32.47, d.f. = 12, p = 0.01, χ^2/d.f. = 2.70, CFI = 0.90, RMSEA = 0.07. The path coefficients (all significant at $p < 0.05$) are consistent with previous analyses. Perceived in-group status (β = 0.12) and ethnic identity (β = 0.18) were predictive of higher self-esteem, while perceived discrimination predicted lower levels of self-esteem (β = –0.12). In this ethnic group, self-esteem was more strongly predicted by gender (β = 0.23), with females scoring lower in self-esteem than males. These variables accounted for 14% of the variance on self-esteem. In-group status (β = 0.17) and interethnic contact (β= 0.15) were significant predictors of ethnic identity, but the variance accounted for by them

Figure 6.6
Factors Influencing Acculturation and Psychological Adaptation in the First Subsample of White Participants (N = 322)

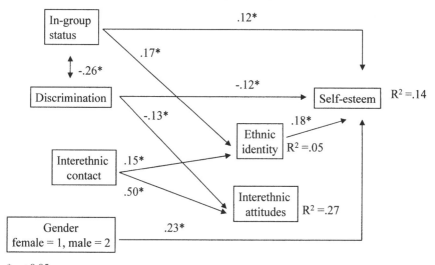

*$p < 0.05$.

was only 5%. Both in-group status and interethnic contact led to stronger commitment to the in-group, which in turn led to higher levels of self-esteem. Perceived discrimination ($\beta = -0.13$) and interethnic contact ($\beta = 0.50$) significantly predicted interethnic attitudes, accounting for 27% of its variance. Optimal interethnic contact predicts positive interethnic attitudes. By contrast, participants who perceive more discrimination are less likely to express positive attitudes toward ethnic out-groups.

On the whole, the model for White participants also shows two opposite influences on acculturation and adaptation represented by ethnic discrimination and positive interethnic contact, respectively. The model also shows the role of ethnic identity as a mediating variable of effects of the control variables on self-esteem. In this group, however, ethnic discrimination has no impact of participants' commitment to their in-group. Not surprising, for members of the ethnic majority it is the relative prestige of the in-group in the society that contributes to reinforce their ethnic identity and in turn to reinforce their self-esteem.

In the cross-validation sample ($N = 380$), the model also shows a good fit to the data, $\chi^2 = 24.04$, d.f. $= 12$, $p = 0.02$, $\chi^2/\text{d.f.} = 2.00$, CFI $= 0.96$, RMSEA $= 0.05$. The goodness of fit for the constrained two-group model was $\chi^2 = 45.50$, d.f. $= 31$, $p = 0.05$, $\chi^2/\text{d.f.} = 1.47$, CFI $= 0.97$. Thus, the correspondence between the subsamples is sufficient to speak of a successful replication of the model across them.

The test of the latent variables model with all fifty-one indicators also produced a highly restricted covariance structure, not fitting the data, $\chi^2 = 3839.05$, d.f. $= 1266$, $p = 0.01$, $\chi^2/\text{d.f.} = 3.03$, CFI $= 0.71$, RMSEA $= 0.06$. Therefore, subscales were constructed (as described earlier) and were used as indicators of each latent construct. The standardized solution of the latent variables model for the whole sample of White participants ($N = 710$) is presented in Figure 6.7.

As indicated by the fit indices, the model fit was good, $\chi^2 = 171.76$, d.f. $= 57$, $p = 0.001$, $\chi^2/\text{df} = 3.00$, CFI $= 0.96$, RMSEA $= 0.05$. All the paths from the constructs to their respective indicators were significant. The variances in the measures accounted for indicate that they assess adequately the respective constructs, with the noted exception of CSES(b). With all paths significant at $p < 0.05$, the structural model confirms the results reported before, but it also provides a better representation of the data, since the measurement error is separated. Also, ethnic identity emerges as the most important predictor of self-esteem, while interethnic contact turned out to be the major determinant of ethnic identity and interethnic attitudes. The variance accounted for also increased. The model accounts for 20%, 12%, and 41% of the variance in self-esteem, ethnic identity, and interethnic relations, respectively.

Causality Issues

Cross-sectional studies always raise the question of the causal order. Although the proposed model for predicting psychological adaptation is logi-

Figure 6.7
**Latent-Variables Model of Factors Influencing Acculturation and
Psychological Adaptation among White Participants (N = 710)**

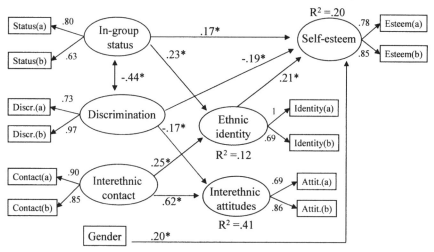

*p < 0.05.

cally and theoretically sound and the analytic strategy used here is highly conservative by including eight control variables, alternative causal explanations for these patterns can be anticipated. One might argue that people high in self-esteem are more likely to be proud of their ethnic background, and further, that people higher in ethnic identity are more likely to be aware of ethnic discrimination cues. Thus, a rival causal explanation will posit that high self-esteem will increase ethnic pride, which in turn will increase the perception of discrimination. This alternative explanation has an important problem: Recall that ethnic identity and interethnic contact are also positively intercorrelated across ethnic groups. If the causal order is reversed, one should accept that people who are strongly committed to their ethnic group of reference will perceive more ethnic discrimination and, at the same time, will be more likely to seek interethnic contact, which is somewhat illogical. Nevertheless, the causal impact from self-esteem to ethnic identity is plausible. Also, the link between interethnic contact and interethnic attitudes raises an alternative causal explanation. It could be possible that people who have positive attitudes toward other ethnic groups tend to seek more interethnic contact. In other words, instead of contact promoting favorable attitudes, it is plausible that people holding less favorable attitudes tend to avoid interethnic contact.

The best way to address reciprocal causation is longitudinally. However, when only cross-sectional data are available, structural equation modeling can be used to test reciprocal causation by means of nonrecursive models. Models examining bidirectional paths can be estimated if each of the two variables that are reciprocally related has an *instrumental* variable or *instrument*. An instrument is an exogenous latent variable that is related (i.e., has a direct causal path) to one of the constructs in the reciprocal relation but not to the other. According to Maruyama (1998, p. 212), the critical issues when testing nonrecursive models are that (1) each of the latent variables in the reciprocal relationship has its own separate instrument and (2) the predictors acting as instruments are not highly intercorrelated.

Unfortunately, the present data do not meet the conditions for testing causal direction between interethnic contact and attitudes. Note that perceived discrimination has a direct path to interethnic attitudes and is unrelated to interethnic contact, but note also that there is no exogenous latent variable in the data set that is associated with interethnic contact. However, the conditions for testing causal direction between ethnic identity and self-esteem can be met with some model modifications. Specifically, for Black participants, intergroup status and interethnic contact can serve as instrumental variables. Perceived intergroup status has a direct causal path to self-esteem but not to ethnic identity. By contrast, interethnic contact is related to ethnic identity but not to self-esteem. Finally, intergroup status and interethnic contact are not intercorrelated ($r = 0.07$, n.s.). Since perceived intergroup status and perceived discrimination share much common variance and perceived discrimination relates to both ethnic identity and self-esteem, this construct is excluded from the model to assure that the instrumental variables have independent effects. The results of the nonrecursive model for testing of reciprocal paths between ethnic identity and self-esteem for Black participants ($N = 362$) are presented in Figure 6.8.

The model fits the data adequately, $\chi^2 = 171.75$, d.f. $= 39$, $p = 0.01$, χ^2/d.f. $= 1.96$, CFI $= 0.97$, RMSEA $= 0.05$. Looking at the paths of interest, the model clearly shows that ethnic identity has a significant effect on increasing self-esteem (ß $= 0.41$, $p < 0.05$), while self-esteem does not contribute significantly to increased ethnic identity (ß $= -0.06$, n.s.). In other words, the data are consistent with the causal sequence assumed by the model for predicting personal outcomes of acculturation.[9]

For White participants, perceived discrimination and interethnic contact were specified as instruments for testing the reciprocal paths between ethnic identity and self-esteem. In this group, perceived discrimination is related to self-esteem but not to ethnic identity, while interethnic contact relates directly to ethnic identity but not to self-esteem. These instrumental variables are essentially independent ($r = 10$, $p < 0.01$). Finally, perceived in-group status was dropped from the model to guarantee that the instrumental variables had independent effects. The standardized solution for the nonrecursive model among White participants ($N = 710$) is presented in Figure 6.9.

This model also fits the data adequately, $\chi^2 = 119.14$, d.f. $= 38$, $p = 0.01$, χ^2/d.f. $= 3.13$, CFI $= 0.97$, RMSEA $= 0.05$, and provides further support for the causal order proposed here by showing that the path from ethnic identity to self-

Figure 6.8
Nonrecursive Model Testing Reciprocal Paths between Ethnic Identity and Self-Esteem for Black Participants (*N* = 362)

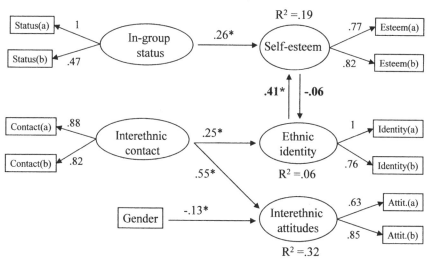

*$p < 0.05$.

esteem is statistically significant ($\beta = -0.28$, $p < 0.05$), while the reverse path not ($\beta = -0.02$, n.s.).

SUMMARY

This chapter is devoted to presenting the central results of the research. Psychometric data in the main study corroborate findings from the pilot study, indicating that all scales represent undimensional measures of the theoretical constructs under study. Results also show that the structures of the scales are substantially similar across different ethnic groups. A close inspection of the scale structures indicates the presence of a valence-sensitive response bias in some scales (particularly in the self-esteem measure), which have been widely reported in research using psychological rating scales (see Marsh, 1996; Robinson et al., 1991). The evidence presented here draws attention to the need to approach these method effects for what they are; namely, as bias due to responses to negatively worded items, and not as meaningful content.

Most scales yielded satisfactory Cronbach's alphas across ethnic groups. The reliability coefficients are also consistent with psychometric data reported in previous studies in which these scales have been employed in adolescent samples (see Phinney, 1992; Phinney et al., 1997; Verkuyten & Lay, 1998). Furthermore, the internal consistency of the scales confirms the decision to combine their respective items into a single scale. An important exception is

Figure 6.9
Nonrecursive Model Testing Reciprocal Paths between Ethnic Identity and Self-Esteem for White Participants ($N = 710$)

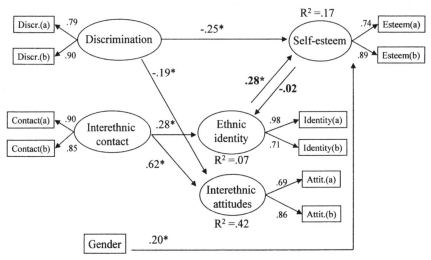

*$p < 0.05$.

the collective self-esteem scale, which, contrary to previous results, yielded only poor reliability coefficients. It was shown that the scale tends to be susceptible to education-level effects.

A further feature of the scales is the presence of small deviations from normality. Specifically, the measures of self-esteem, interethnic attitudes, interethnic contact, and perceived in-group status tend to be negatively skewed, while the measure of ethnic discrimination is skewed toward the low end of the scale.

Preliminary results indicate that there are complex relations between the variables under study, which are largely dependent on the ethnic group in question. In effect, ethnicity turns out to have a consistent impact on all variables under study. This reinforces the importance of testing the research hypotheses separately for each ethnic group. Although complex, the pattern of associations is relatively consistent with several predictions advanced from research on interethnic relations, providing important insights for the subsequent analyses. Results show that ethnic-minority members perceive higher ethnic discrimination, report lower in-group status, have more interethnic contact, and attribute more importance to the role of their ethnicity in their lives than members of the White majority.

Sources of threat such as perceived discrimination and low in-group status are associated with low self-esteem, a weak commitment to the ethnic group of reference, and less favorable attitudes toward members of other ethnic groups.

By contrast, optimal interethnic contact is associated with positive interethnic attitudes and positive ethnic identity. This, indeed, varies across ethnic groups. For instance, the commitment to their own group among White participants seems to be more determined by relative in-group status and less by perceived discrimination. For Black participants, on the contrary, perceived discrimination (and not in-group status) emerges as one of the most important predictors of ethnic identity. Here, higher levels of perceived ethnic discrimination were associated with high scores on ethnic identity for Black participants, suggesting that exposure to discrimination makes ethnicity more salient, resulting in stronger ethnic identification and affirmation.

Not surprising, interethnic contact, perceived discrimination, and perceived in-group status also emerge as the most important determinants of the adoption of acculturation strategies. Once more, this depends on the acculturating group in question. Under conditions of optimal contact, Black participants are more likely to adopt integration or assimilation strategies, while perceived discrimination is particularly associated with the endorsement of separation attitudes. For members of the ethnic majority, interethnic contact is also associated with the adoption of the integration or assimilation strategies. Under conditions of threat but secure in-group status, individuals tend to endorse the separation strategy, while threat combined with insecure in-group status is associated with the marginalization mode.

Age, socioeconomic status, gender, and ethnic density have a modest impact on the focal variables for Black participants. Only gender was associated with interethnic attitudes in this group, with females showing more positive interethnic attitudes than males, as reported in previous research. For White participants, the impact of regional and demographic variables was much clearer, which might be related to the fact that this group was more heterogenous on these variables than Black participants. Regional differences on ethnic identity suggest that ethnic issues become more important for self-definition as the presence of other ethnic groups increases. Finally, gender and socioeconomic status affect feelings of self-regard in this group, with females and participants of lower socioeconomic status tending to elicit lower levels of self-esteem than males and participants from higher socioeconomic backgrounds.

Primary analyses focused on the role of ethnic identity and interethnic attitudes on self-esteem when controlling for several variables that were found to be related to them. Consistent with the central hypotheses under study, the data show that a positive sense of ethnic identity is strongly related to feelings of self-regard. By contrast, interethnic attitudes seem to be unrelated to self-esteem. The effect of the second dimension of acculturation on self-esteem is only evident in terms of the acculturation strategies. Here, the data are highly concordant with the hypotheses of this study. Integration seems to afford the best psychological outcomes, followed by separation and assimilation, while marginalization was associated with the worst psychological outcomes. These trends hold across ethnic groups, and even when controlling for important determinants of self-esteem such as perceived discrimination, in-group status, and participants' demographic characteristics.

A general test of the multivariate relationship among the variables using the SEM approach suggests that the process of acculturation and adaptation in ethnically plural societies is shaped by two opposite influences; namely, sources of threat and optimal interethnic contact. The results also show that ethnic identity has an important role as a mediating variable of the effects of these factors on psychological adaptation. In addition, the present data reveal the existence of both general aspects of the acculturation processes that apply across groups and specific outcomes, depending on the particular characteristics of the ethnic groups, specifically on their relative status in the society. Finally, the present analyses address the question of causality, using nonrecursive models to test for reciprocal paths between ethnic identity and self-esteem. The data are highly concordant with the proposed causal link by showing that the effect of ethnic identity on self-esteem is much stronger than the reverse effect.

NOTES

1. Fluctuations in Ns reported here are due to missing values (max. missing < 8%).

2. Confirmatory factor analyses (EQS; see Bentler, 1992) were used for a further test of this decision. Two competing models were tested for each ethnic group separately. Model 1 argues, as expected here, that the sixteen items are best represented as measuring the general construct of self-esteem with a negative-item method effect. In this model, the covariation of the negative items is assumed to be explained by their regression on both the general self-esteem factor and the factor labeled method (cross-loadings). Model 2 argues that the data are best represented by two different but correlated latent factors representing self-esteem and self-derogation. Here, the covariation of each set of items should be fully and exclusively explained by their regression on their respective factors. Neither model 1 nor model 2 fit the data well. For Black participants, fit indices were $\chi^2 = 309.16$, d.f. = 96, $p = 0.001$, χ^2/d.f. = 3.22, CFI = 0.87, RMSEA = 0.08 for model 1 and $\chi^2 = 331.94$, d.f. = 103, $p = 0.001$, χ^2/d.f. = 3.22, CFI = 0.86, RMSEA = 0.08 for model 2. For White participants, the CFA results were $\chi^2 = 531.74$, d.f. = 96, $p = 0.001$, χ^2/d.f. = 5.54, CFI = 0.88, RMSEA = 0.08 for model 1 and $\chi^2 = 589.71$, d.f. = 103, $p = 0.001$, χ^2/d.f. = 5.72, CFI = 0.87, RMSEA = 0.07 for model 2. However, the χ^2-difference test indicated that model 1 was significantly superior in fit than model 2 in both groups, providing further support for the use of this scale as a single measure of global self-esteem ($\Delta\chi^2_{(7)} = 22.78$ and 59.97, $p < 0.01$ for Blacks and Whites, respectively).

3. To avoid confounding grade level with age, Cronbach's alphas were also computed separately for "younger" and "older" students using the median split procedure. Among Blacks, Cronbach's alphas were 0.51 and 0.57 for younger and older students, respectively. Among Whites, alphas were 0.55 and 0.62 for younger and older students, respectively. These results show that the measure is largely sensible to education-level (not age) effects.

4. As a general rule of thumb, multicollinearity problems are expected when the simple correlations among the predictors are greater than 0.80 (see Maruyama, 1998).

5. Another way to detect collinearity problems requires inspecting the "variance inflation factors" (i.e., the diagonal elements of the inverse of the correlation matrix among predictors), where variance inflation factors greater than 6 or 7 are indicative of multicollinearity problems (see Maruyama, 1998). In this study, none of the variance inflation factors of the variables in question was greater than 1.54.

6. Note that because comparisons were planned, the analyses proceed in spite of the absence of a significant interaction. Also, since the comparisons do not exceed the number of cells minus one, the analysis was conducted without correcting the significance level.

7. Preliminary analyses showed that any attempt to include the acculturation strategies in addition to ethnic identity and interethnic attitudes led to collinearity problems. In a first attempt, acculturation strategies were included in the models as product terms of ethnic identity and interethnic attitudes. In a second attempt, they were included after transforming them into an ordered categorical variable with four levels, as indicated by the linear trend toward higher levels of self-esteem from 1 = marginalization to 4 = integration. In both cases, however, model estimation became unstable and the results unreliable. Therefore, they were excluded from the analyses. The reader might also be concerned about the inclusion of interethnic attitudes in the models. Theoretically, interethnic attitudes are assumed to contribute positively to self-esteem, but the analyses showed that the expected relationship was not significant. Yet the path was included in Figure 6.2 for a better account of the relationships among the variables. Recall that the central aim of this overall test was to examine the structural relations of all components of the acculturation processes.

8. As in the case of Black participants, acculturation strategies were dropped for the analyses to avoid multicollinearity problems. Recall that for White participants, city of residence emerged as a significant predictor of interethnic attitudes. However, this variable was also excluded for the SEM analyses to avoid the suppressor effects associated with it.

9. The χ^2-difference test indicated, however, that this model is not of superior fit to an alternative model in which these two paths are constrained to be equal ($\Delta\chi^2_{(1)} =$ 1.20, n.s.). Yet the fact that the path from ethnic identity to self-esteem differs significantly from zero and the reverse path does not provides strong evidence for the causal order proposed here.

7

Conclusions

This chapter summarizes the central results of the present research and provides some concluding remarks on relevant theoretical and methodological issues. The first section provides an integrative overview of the findings. Special attention will be paid to two aspects: (1) the presence of a common mechanism of acculturation fundamental to both ethnic-majority and ethnic-minority groups and (2) the emergence of ethnic-differentiated patterns of acculturation. The second section focuses on methodological issues concerning the assessment of the two dimensions and four strategies of acculturation. Finally, the third section examines the limitations of the present research and provides some suggestions for future research.

AN INTEGRATIVE OVERVIEW

The broader goal of the present research was to increase the understanding of the effects of intercultural contact and acculturation on individuals' feelings of self-regard in Latin American settings. The more specific interest was to test the particular contribution of acculturation dimensions and strategies to self-esteem. Results show, however, that these effects can only be understood when including the potential effects of other important factors that deeply shape the way in which individuals acculturate. The first part of this section focuses on the specific impact of acculturation dimensions and strategies on self-esteem. The second part provides a more differentiated picture of the multiple causation of psychological adaptation, while incorporating the relative impact of control variables on the focal variables of interest.

The Role of Acculturation Dimensions and Strategies in Shaping Individuals' Self-Esteem

Results show some differences in acculturation dimensions and self-esteem between Black and White adolescents. Black adolescents report higher levels of ethnic identity and lower levels of self-esteem than their White classmates. As hypothesized, members of ethnic-minority groups tend to attribute more importance to the role of their ethnicity in their lives than members of the White majority. Similar results have been found in different cultural settings (e.g., Martinez & Dukes, 1997; Phinney & Alpuria, 1990; Phinney & Tarver, 1988; Verkuyten, 1990). These differences can be interpreted in terms of the impact of the social structure on self-perception. For ethnic-majority members, ethnicity might have relatively lower importance compared with other social categories. In effect, previous research has shown that members of ethnic majorities (e.g., Whites) tend to think of other ascribed categories (e.g., gender) when responding to measures of ethnic identification (see Luhtanen & Crocker, 1992), and sometimes they do not understand very well what is meant by "ethnic group" when responding to the scales (see Phinney, 1992). By contrast, for clearly identifiable ethnic-minority members, issues such as prejudice and discrimination might reinforce the concern with their own ethnicity.

On the other hand, differences on self-esteem should be seen with caution. In terms of the percentage of variance accounted for, differences were rather low. This confirms Crocker and Major's (1989) contention that members of stigmatized and privileged groups elicit comparable levels of self-esteem. In other words, the traditional assumption that members of "marked" groups tend to be unsatisfied with their social categories and tend to elicit more psychological distress than members of privileged groups was clearly disconfirmed in this research.

When examining the impact of acculturation dimensions on self-esteem, the present data show strong similarities across ethnic groups. More specifically, predictions regarding the positive impact of ethnic identity on self-esteem were supported for both ethnic-minority and ethnic-majority members. Participants scoring high in ethnic identity show higher levels of self-esteem than those low in ethnic identification. In addition, structural equation models show that ethnic identity is one of the strongest predictors of self-esteem. These results are highly consistent with the social identity theory, indicating that ethnic categories are important sources of self-definition and self-satisfaction for both ethnic-majority and ethnic-minority members (Tajfel & Turner, 1979). Findings also show, as predicted by two-dimensional models of acculturation, that the maintenance (not the relinquishing) of cultural distinctiveness is predictive of positive adaptation to ethnically plural settings (Doná & Berry, 1994; Ward & Rana-Deuba, 1999; Lorenzo-Hernández & Ouellette, 1998).

By contrast, the expected positive effect of interethnic attitudes on self-esteem was rather weak and no longer significant when controlling for other important determinants of self-esteem. It seems that, at least for Whites and Blacks in Costa Rica, adaptation depends more on in-group identification than on out-group orientation. This might be due to the particular experiences of the type of acculturating groups investigated in this research. Blacks and Whites in Costa Rica are members of ethnic groups with a secure status of residence. These groups represent structured ethnic subcommunities within the larger national state. They have a long experience of interethnic contact; there are no "new" cultural patterns that they must acquire; there is no "host" culture to which they have to adapt. For them, hence, orientation toward other groups might be less relevant for their psychological adaptation.

A further explanation for the lack of association between ethnic attitudes and self-esteem is that attitudes toward out-groups might be related to some but not all domains of adaptation. According to recent conceptualizations, the adjustment to ethnically plural settings can take different forms, including psychological, sociocultural, and economic adaptation (Berry, 1997). The first is particularly related to psychological well-being (i.e., positive sense of personal identity, life satisfaction, good mental health), while the latter two are related to the ability to interact effectively in multicultural settings (i.e., the ability to deal with daily problems in areas such as family life, work, school, etc.). In effect, previous research has shown that in-group identification is predictive of psychological adjustment, but not of sociocultural adaptation, whereas other-group orientation is related to sociocultural adjustment, but not to psychological outcomes (Ward & Rana-Deuba, 1999). Similar mechanisms might operate in this case. More research is needed to further test the relative impact of each acculturation strategy on different domains of acculturation and adaptation.

The fact that ethnic identity and interethnic attitudes are differentially related to self-esteem reinforces the idea that they represent two independent dimensions of acculturation. Moreover, these results point to the need to investigate acculturation dimensions separately from acculturation strategies, as suggested by Ward and colleagues (see Ward & Kennedy, 1993; Ward & Rana-Deuba, 1999).

With regard to the distribution of acculturation strategies, the data also show remarkable similarities across groups. For Black participants, the categorization resulted in 322 (78.9%) participants classified as integrated, 41 (10%) as assimilated, 28 (6.9%) as separated, and only 3 (0.7%) as marginalized. Similarly, 493 (64.4%) White participants were classified as integrated, 150 (19.6%) as assimilated, 60 (7.8%) as separated, and 32 (4.2%) as marginalized. As in previous research conducted in different countries, the data show that integration is the most preferred strategy, while marginalization is the least endorsed (Berry, Kim, Power, Young, & Bujaki, 1989; Doná & Berry, 1994; Phinney, Chavira, & Williamson, 1992; Piontkowski, Florack, Hoelker, & Obdrzálek, 2000; Roccas, Horenczyk, & Schwartz, 2000). Interestingly, while most research shows that separation is preferred over assimilation, in the present case assimilation was preferred over separation.

The question remains whether this distribution is partly due to response style; that is, to participants' tendency to agree or disagree with the items of the scales. For instance, the overwhelming preference for integration might be due to the tendency to agree with both ethnic-identity and interethnic-attitudes scales. However, recall that these scales were found to be essentially orthogonal (as indicated by the simple correlation between them). In addition, the fact that some participants tend to agree with the items of one scale and disagree with those of the other scale (and therefore were classified in the separation or assimilation strategies) suggests that this distribution reflects something more than pure acquiescence tendencies.

The present findings can rather be interpreted in terms of the "climate" in the larger society concerning the integration of ethnic groups, as well as the specific characteristics of the acculturating groups. As pointed out before, there are several indicators suggesting that the Costa Rican state tends to recognize and value ethnic diversity as one important characteristic of the country. Thus, the preference for integration might reflect these trends in the recent policies of integration in the country. On the other hand, following the idea that Blacks and Whites belong to communities that form an integral part of the larger society, the preference for assimilation over separation might reflect the sense of belonging to the national community.

In terms of the impact of acculturation strategies on self-esteem, these data provide strong support for the central hypotheses of this research. As expected, participants who identify higher with the ethnic group of reference and, at the same time, elicit more positive interethnic attitudes (i.e., integration) show the highest level of self-esteem. On the contrary, participants who distance themselves from their ethnic groups of reference and elicit less positive attitudes toward other ethnic groups (i.e., marginalization) show the lowest level of self-regard. The separation and assimilation modes fall in-between regarding their contribution to self-esteem. A more detailed inspection of the data suggests an increase in self-esteem from marginalization through assimilation and separation to integration.

These results clearly support Berry's (1997) contention that integration is the most adaptive strategy. Not surprising, integration provides individuals with the benefits of membership in two social support systems, represents the absence of interethnic conflict, and reflects individuals' achievement of social and cultural competencies providing them with a sense of self-efficacy. Separation and assimilation are both linked with intermediate levels of adjustment. The pattern of means on self-esteem across ethnic groups suggests, however, that in-group identification affords more positive outcomes than an exclusive out-group orientation. Finally, marginalization clearly appears as the least adaptive acculturation strategy, which is in line with the idea that psychological distance from both the ethnic group of reference and other relevant groups is associated with acculturative stress.

Two features of these trends deserve special comment. First, this pattern holds true across ethnic groups and after adjustment for differences in relevant predictors of self-esteem, suggesting that the link between acculturation strategies and self-esteem is not simply an artifact of preexisting psychological or demographic variables. Second, these results show that integration represents an important requirement, not only for ethnic-minority members but also for members of the dominant group. This shows that effects of interethnic contact can be observed among members of all groups involved in the intercultural contact, and more specifically, that both majority- and minority-group members respond to the demands of interacting in social settings that are increasingly ethnically and racially diverse.

In sum, the present research presents strong evidence that the development of positive ties with both one's own and other relevant groups provides a more solid basis for self-esteem than relinquishing ties to the ethnic group of reference. These results generalize to both ethnic-minority and ethnic-majority members, which has important implications for research on acculturation. Due to the structural inequalities that characterize modern ethnically plural societies, acculturation processes are more evident among immigrant and ethnic-minority members. Therefore, much research has focused on these groups, leading to the impression that host or majority groups remain unchangeable during acculturation. By contrast, these data suggest that psychological changes occur in all groups involved in the contact. This reinforces the idea that acculturation is a special case of mutual influence between all cultural groups involved in the contact.

Factors Affecting Acculturation and Psychological Adaptation

To say that the acculturation dimensions and strategies have an unambiguous effect on self-esteem is not to say that they explain the total variation on psychological adjustment to ethnically plural societies. On the contrary, these data clearly show that there are many other factors influencing all components of acculturation.

In the attempt to detect these relevant variables, a general framework for research on acculturation with ethnic groups was outlined for the present research (see Figure 1.5). The framework selects those variables assumed to deeply shape the way in which individuals come into interethnic contact and acculturate. These are (1) perceived ethnic discrimination, which provides information about how the attitudes toward the individual's own ethnic group prevailing in the larger society contribute to the definition of the self; (2) perceived in-group status, which is the subjective reflection of the prestige of the in-group in the society; (3) ethnic density, as an indicator of the ethnic composition of the immediate environment, which might regulate the opportunities of interethnic contact; (4) individuals' experience of interethnic contact; and demographic variables such as (5) ethnicity, (6) socioeconomic status, (7) gender, and (8) age. Recall that the first three variables are conceptualized here as group-level factors affecting acculturation. They represent the characteristics of the social context (ethnic density) and the subjective experience of the intergroup context (perceived discrimination and in-group status). The remaining five variables are considered as individual-level factors affecting acculturation. These refer to the subjective and objective experiences that individuals bring into the interethnic contact (interethnic contact and demographic variables).

When taking into account the potential effect of the control variables, the data reveal two opposite influences on acculturation and psychological adaptation that are partially or totally mediated by the acculturation dimensions and strategies. The former are composed of sources of threat, such as perceived discrimination or low in-group status, while the positive effects of interethnic contact represent the latter force. In addition, the inclusion of these variables makes the presence of ethnic-differentiated patterns in the processes of acculturation more patent. The following paragraphs discuss the impact of these variables on self-esteem, ethnic identity, interethnic attitudes, and acculturation strategies. The effects of demographic variables will be briefly discussed in the last part of this section.

The Features of the Intergroup Context: Perceived Threats versus Optimal Contact

As expected, perceived discrimination and low in-group status predicted lower levels of self-esteem. These results are highly consistent with previous research among other acculturating groups, and provide strong evidence of a "reflected-appraisals processes" in the definition of the self (see Berry, 1997; R. Clark, Anderson, Clark, & Williams, 1999; Cross, 1991; Helms, 1990; Jasinskaja-Lahti & Liebkind, 2001; Liebkind, 1996; Luhtanen & Crocker, 1992; Mead, 1934; Phinney, 1991).

Research has commonly focused on the impact of perceived discrimination on psychological well-being among minority groups. This reflects the concern with the psychological consequences of the objective situation of minorities in societies stratified by power, wealth, and status. In effect, this research replicates the findings of previous research by showing that ethnic-minority members report more ethnic discrimination and lower in-group status than ethnic-majority members (see Luhtanen & Crocker, 1992). However, the negative effects of perceived threats to self-esteem were also observed among ethnic-majority members, raising a question about the meaning of discrimination among members of privileged groups.

Although this cannot be fully answered by the data presented here, two possible explanations can be offered. First, it might be the case that the perception of discrimination among White participants is partially due to their tendency to think of other group memberships that are perhaps more important for their self-definition than ethnicity. For instance, White females might tend to think more about gender discrimination than ethnic discrimination when responding to items assessing these issues. Yet the data show that White males report more perceived discrimination than White females. Thus, the observed link between perceived discrimination and self-esteem is not simply due to a confusion of social categories when responding to the scales.

The second (and more) plausible interpretation is that the perception of discrimination among members of privileged groups results from intragroup comparisons rather than intergroup comparisons (e.g., across the temporal dimension). In effect, the present results show that Whites' perception of discrimination was related to personal self-esteem but unrelated to ethnic-group identification. This suggests that members of dominant groups perceive discrimination less as an intergroup phenomenon and more as a matter of personal discrimination. Similar results were recently reported by Schmitt, Branscombe, Kobrynowicz, and Owen (2002). In their study, women's perception of discrimination was related to both group identification and self-esteem exactly in the same manner as reported here for ethnic-minority members. Men's perception of discrimination, however, had no effect on in-group identification or self-esteem in their study. Thus, as suggested by Branscombe (2001), these results seem to indicate that perceived discrimination has a general negative effect on self-esteem across groups, but its meaning differs depending on their position in the social hierarchy.

Of particular interest for this research is the fact that both perceived discrimination and low in-group status have an overall consistent negative effect on self-esteem, but relate differently to ethnic identity depending on the ethnic group in question. For White participants, in-group status but not perceived discrimination was predictive of high levels of ethnic identity. For Black participants, on the contrary, perceived discrimination (and not in-group status) emerged as an important predictor of ethnic identity, with higher levels of perceived ethnic discrimination associated with higher scores on ethnic identity. One might have some concern about these patterns given the low reliability of the measure of in-group status. However, by forming latent factors out of subsets of the measures, it was possible to define the constructs in terms of the shared commonalties among the subscales, and therefore to control for the measurement error. In other words, measurement issues cannot fully account for the pattern of associations observed here.

Rather, these results can be interpreted in light of predictions made by the social identity theory (Tajfel & Turner, 1979). These data are highly concordant with the idea that under certain conditions group members cope with the negative consequences of threats by increasing identification with the in-group. Structural equation models clearly show that ethnic identity has a "bolstering" function, mediating the negative effect of perceived discrimination on self-esteem. The fact that these effects were found for ethnic-minority members but not for ethnic-majority members provides further support for the assumption that the management of social-identity threats depends on both the structural characteristics of the intergroup relations (note that Blacks report lower in-group status than Whites) and the degree of identification with the relevant in-group (note also that Blacks elicit higher levels of ethnic identity than Whites). Given the correlational nature of this research, these effects represent only a limited test of the central principles of the social identity theory. At the same time, however, these results are impressive in that they were found in natural settings among natural groups (as opposed to artificially created group memberships), enhancing their ecological validity.

In addition, these findings provide some evidence of Crocker's (2001) argument that ethnic-minority and ethnic-majority members base their feelings of self-worth on different contingencies. Using data from a recent longitudinal study, she and her colleagues show that African-American students are less likely to base their self-esteem on other's approval than White students, and are more likely to base their feelings of personal worth on moral and spiritual aspects such as "God's love" (see Crocker, Luhtanen, & Bouvrette, 2001). In a similar vein, the results of the present research show that Whites' feelings of attachment and pride toward their ethnic in-group are based on the social prestige attributed to it in the society. By contrast, ethnic-minority members' feelings of attachment to the in-group and ethnic pride are unrelated to the negative evaluations of others. This is not surprising: Why should one base one's feelings of worth on the prestige of the social group of reference when other's attitudes toward the own group are the reflection of discrimination and prejudice? Although Crocker's ideas are limited to personal self-esteem, the present results show that these assumptions could be extended to individuals' feelings of worth as group members.

In sum, results appear to contradict the idea that perceived threats to social identity are always reflected in low levels of identification with the ethnic in-group. Rather, these data are supportive of the assumption that under certain conditions ethnic-group members manage identity threats through more collective strategies, maintaining or reinforcing their ethnic identification. These strategies result from the interaction between the structural characteristics of the intergroup relations and individuals' commitment with the groups involved in the interaction.

Sources of threat, in particular perceived ethnic discrimination, were also found to have an important impact on interethnic attitudes across ethnic groups. As expected, perceived discrimination was predictive of less positive attitudes toward other groups. These results clearly indicate that the perception of discrimination is an important source of threat that is reflected in negative responses to out-groups, as predicted by several group-conflict models (Bobo, 1983; W. S. Stephan & Stephan, 2000). However, it is not clear what kind of feeling of threat is involved in the perception of discrimination. One might argue that respondents interpret discrimination as the result of an objective conflict between ethnic groups; that is, as a realistic threat. Yet given that perceived discrimination was operationalized in terms of personal experiences of discrimination, one can rather infer that feelings of discrimination represent a kind of intergroup anxiety. That is, the perception of discrimination might be related to the anticipation of negative personal outcomes during interethnic contact, which in turn operate as important inhibitors on the positive effects of interethnic contact (see Pettigrew, 2000). Further research should analyze more deeply what kind of threat is involved in the perception of discrimination. The relevance of a better understanding of these issues lays in their practical consequences. As indicated by W. G. Stephan, Ybarra, and Bachman (1999), perceived threats (symbolic and realistic) can be reduced by changing cognitions about ethnic groups (e.g., by stressing that the supposed conflicts are unrealistic and overblown). By contrast, attempts to reduce intergroup anxiety might rather focus on the affect, by reinforcing individuals' cultural and social competencies to interact effectively in bicultural settings (see also LaFromboise, Coleman, & Gerton, 1993).

In terms of the impact of perceived threats on acculturation strategies, results provide important insights into how the adoption of a specific strategy is largely defined by characteristics of the intergroup situation and how they are experienced by the participants in the interaction. When individuals perceive high discrimination, they tend to choose (or are forced to choose) the separation or marginalization strategies. By contrast, when the perception of discrimination is rather low, individuals tend to adopt the integration and particularly the assimilation strategies. These results are highly consistent with previous research on acculturation strategies in European settings. Piontkowski and colleagues (2000) also found that members of nondominant groups tended to adopt the separation or marginalization mode when they perceived the intergroup situation as negative (i.e., when the group boundaries were impermeable). These findings are also congruent with predictions derived from Bourhis's interactive acculturation model by showing that separation and marginalization (or anomie) are associated with problematic and conflictual outcomes (Bourhis, Moise, Perreault, & Senéca, 1997). However, given the low accuracy in correct classifications reached by the predictors of acculturation strategies, these trends should be taken with caution. With a hit ratio of approximately 43% across ethnic groups, results suggest that the discriminant functions were less successful in discriminating between groups, in particular between integrated and assimilated individuals. Further research should try to detect other potential predictors of the acculturation strategies. Given that demographic and regional variables had virtually no effect on the adoption of acculturation strategies, special attention should be paid to social-psychological variables, in particular intergroup variables such as the perceived permeability of the group boundaries, the stability of group status, and the legitimacy of the status hierarchy (see Piontkowski et al., 2000, for a promising research strategy on theses issues).

Turning now to the effects of interethnic contact, the present data nicely illustrate the central principles of the intergroup contact theory (Allport, 1954; Pettigrew, 1998). Interethnic contact was found to be the strongest predictor of interethnic attitudes for both ethnic-minority and ethnic-majority members, improving the evaluative responses toward members of other ethnic groups. In addition, findings show that in conditions of optimal contact, ethnic-group members tend to endorse integration and assimilation strategies, which are associated with more positive relational outcomes (Bourhis et al., 1997). Finally, the positive effects of interethnic contact were extended to ethnic identity and, in turn, to self-esteem.

The results are impressive in two ways. First, the data reinforce the importance of the distinction between "facilitating" and "critical" conditions of optimal contact (see Pettigrew, 1997, 1998). In the present research, this was clearly observed in the case of ethnic-majority members. For Whites, city of residence was an important precondition of contact, as it regulated the opportunities for interethnic contact. Recall that living in Limón increases the opportunities of interethnic contact for White participants, because the Black community is overrepresented in this province. However, regression analyses showed that it was the "real" use of contact (and not the sole interethnic proximity) that contributed to improve their interethnic attitudes (see also van Dick et al., 2001; Wagner, van Dick, Pettigrew, & Christ, 2001).

Second, these results highlight the importance of further research on the mediation of contact effects, especially on the processes of in-group reappraisal and its consequences for interethnic attitudes. These data show that having interethnic contact reinforces the commitment with the ethnic group of references and, at the same time, promotes positive interethnic attitudes. In addition, the data clearly show that in-group commitment and interethnic attitudes represent orthogonal dimensions (as indicated by interscale correlations of $r = 0.00$ and $r = 0.10$ for Blacks and Whites, respectively). This evidence clearly challenges the idea that evaluative responses toward the own group and out-groups are "competitively interdependent" (i.e., gains in ethnic identity result in loss of out-group attitudes). In-group preference does not always imply less positive out-group attitudes, and contact effects are not always mediated by in-group reappraisals in terms of decategorization. Clearly, cross-sectional data are not adequate to examine predictions of models that are intrinsically longitudinal. However, given the strong impact of interethnic contact on both ethnic identity and interethnic attitudes, these findings represent a "snapshot" that is congruent with the idea that the best outcomes of contact emerge from an intergroup situation in which mutual differentiation is promoted, as assumed by recent conceptualizations (Dovidio, Kawakami, & Gaertner, 2000; Hewstone & Brown, 1986; Pettigrew, 1998).

Demographic and Regional Influences

Besides the strong moderating effects of ethnicity, demographic factors showed a weak and unsystematic impact on the focal variables. For Black participants, demographic and regional variables were virtually unrelated with the focal variables under study. Only interethnic attitudes were associated with gender in this group, with females showing more positive interethnic attitudes than males, as reported in previous research (e.g., Phinney, Ferguson, & Tate, 1997; Masson & Verkuyten, 1993; Qualls, Cox, & Schehr, 1992; Wagner, 1983; Watts, 1996). These results can be interpreted in terms of the existence of gender-differentiated patterns of socialization that reinforce men's tendency to competitiveness and women's communal and emotional concerns (see Verkuyten, 1997b, for a similar interpretation of his data). In effect, there is evidence that males tend to base their self-concept on personal achievements, whereas women derive their self-perceptions from attachment to others (see Banaji & Prentice, 1994). These tendencies might affect not only the perception of the self, but also responses toward out-group members. However, it is important to mention that the unique contribution of gender in predicting interethnic attitudes was rather low compared to the strong effects of social-psychological variables such as perceived discrimination and interethnic contact.

For White participants, the impact of regional and demographic variables was more apparent. White participants residing in Limón (high ethnic density in terms of the presence of the Black community) showed higher levels of ethnic identity than those residing in San José (low ethnic density). This suggests that the ethnic composition of the immediate context has a certain impact on ethnic identity, probably by increasing the salience of ethnicity. Previous research has also shown that ethnic issues become more important for self-definition among ethnic-majority members as the presence of other ethnic groups increases (see Phinney, 1992). Finally, gender was found to affect feelings of self-regard, with females reporting lower levels of self-esteem than males. These results are similar to those reported by Phinney, Cantu, and Kurtz (1997), who found that gender was predictive of self-esteem among Latino and White adolescents (with females showing lower self-esteem than males), but not among African-American adolescents. Similar results have been reported by Martinez and Dukes (1991) in a study involving White- Asian-, Hispanic-, Native-, and Black-American adolescents. Within all these ethnic groups (with the exception of Blacks), females scored lower on self-satisfaction than males. The present data cannot give a satisfactory answer to these differences. It is only clear here that these findings concur with the assumption that institutional racism and sexism have an additive negative effect on self-esteem, suggesting that different forms of institutional discrimination interact with the specific characteristics of ethnic groups.

In summary, the small and inconsistent contribution of demographic and regional variables on the focal variables under study suggests that acculturation and psychological adaptation is largely defined by social-psychological variables such as the subjective perception of the characteristics of the intergroup situation. Among these variables, acculturation dimensions and strategies were found to have a particular contribution to psychological adaptation. More specifically, they serve as mediators of both the negative influences of perceived threat and the positive effects of interethnic contact.

THE MEASUREMENT OF ACCULTURATION DIMENSIONS AND STRATEGIES

In addition to the central empirical goals, this research addressed methodological issues by exploring an alternative way to assess acculturation strategies. Here, participants were classified into one of the four acculturation strategies on the basis of their scores on measures of ethnic identity and interethnic attitudes. Two criteria were defined to test the adequacy of this categorical approach: (1) the measures employed to tap both dimensions should be reliable, and (2) the scales should be relatively independent or at least not strongly correlated. These criteria were met across ethnic groups. The second criterion is of special relevance because it provides strong support to one of the central contentions of acculturation research; namely, the orthogonality of the dimensions of acculturation. Somewhat surprisingly, this premise has been accepted in the past without empirical test. Only in recent publications have researchers devoted time to the examination of such basic assumptions, which has led to a reexamination of the operationalization of the theoretical constructs.

In addition, the categorical approach used here has several advantages compared to the traditional use of four independent measures of acculturation strategies. First, this approach allowed testing of both the main effects of acculturation dimensions on self-esteem and their combined effects in the form of the four acculturation strategies. By means of the overall analyses of variance in conjunction with planned comparisons, it was possible to make the relative impact of each acculturation dimension and each acculturation strategy on self-esteem more evident. In effect, these data show that dimensions and strategies are related differently with psychological adaptation.

Second, this approach contributes to a better operationalization of the second dimension of acculturation. Recall that Berry's research program exclusively focused on how acculturating group members accept and practice the customs, values, and traditions of the host society, but not on how they relate to out-groups in specific terms of contact and participation. Recent approaches attempt to overcome this limitation with a reformulation in terms of identification with the host society (e.g., Ward & Kennedy, 1994; Ward & Rana-Deuba, 2000), but they still ignore the specific issue of intergroup attitudes and behaviors. By contrast, the use of independent measures of in-group commitment and evaluative responses toward members of other ethnic groups is clearly more congruent with the conceptualization of the acculturation dimensions as individuals' decisions concerning maintaining their cultural identity and engaging in positive intergroup contact.

Third, the problem of item content is also addressed with this approach. One should also recall that acculturation strategies have been commonly assessed by combining (in a single statement) attitudes toward both in-groups and out-groups. The measures used here are clearly "user-friendlier" by focusing each scale on one attitudinal object, reducing the number of items and reducing the complexity of the statements. Finally, this technique is characterized by its high flexibility. Measures require no modification for cross-group or cross-cultural application, which facilitates data comparison. If it is required, the measures can be complemented with specific items, depending on the areas or domains and the type of acculturating groups under study.

Despite the number of advantages, this approach is also associated with some limitations, especially with regard to the dichotomization procedure. In general terms, any technique that implies dichotomization is inevitably associated with loss of sensibility. In most cases this results in the loss of considerable variance. In the case of this research, this technique had consequences in structural equation modeling. Here, the inclusion of the interaction term in the models was inevitably associated with collinearity, given its strong association to the variables whose interaction is included in the analyses (see Maruyama, 1998).

In addition, this approach raises some questions related to its accuracy in reflecting participants' actual acculturation strategies. In particular, Doná and Berry (1994), have criticized the use of median split procedures. According to them, these approaches "force" participants into one of the four categories independently of "where" they score in the scale. Therefore, they argue in favor of using the scale midpoint as the cutoff for the classification of participants, which allows a more direct approximation of participants' preferences. In effect, in their study with Central American refugees in Canada, this approach resulted in no respondents being classified in the marginalization mode, four (4%) in the assimilation mode, seventeen (18%) in the separation model, and seventy-two (78%) in the integration strategy.

Contrary to these authors, it is argued here that both scalar midpoint and median split procedures are equally useful and accurate, but they respond to two different research questions. Consequently, both approaches were used in this research. The scalar midpoint split was used for descriptive purposes. It was shown that this procedure was especially helpful in providing information about the distribution of the acculturation modes in the sample. However, given the low number of cases classified in the marginalization cell, this classification system was less appropriate to make comparisons with balanced groups, which was the central aim of this research. Therefore, the median split approach was used to test the specific predictions about the relative contribution of each acculturation strategy to self-esteem.

Besides the discussion about the adequacy of specific splits, other authors have criticized the use of any splitting procedures with the argument that analyses with continued data are more robust (e.g., Ryder, Alden, & Paulhus, 2000). Once more, the specific technique to be employed should respond to the specific research questions. For certain types of hypotheses it is not necessary to split the dimensions of acculturation into high and low. As observed here, acculturation dimensions are at least as important as the acculturation strategies in predicting acculturation outcomes. This relevant information can be captured without splits via regression techniques.

In sum, the present research demonstrated the usefulness of alternative approaches in the assessment of acculturation, contributing to a better understanding of the processes leading to psychological adaptation to ethnically plural societies. What is needed are systematic comparative studies to test the cross-group and cross-cultural adequacy of these techniques.

LIMITATIONS AND FUTURE DIRECTIONS

Although the present results are highly concordant with several predictions from research on intergroup phenomena, this research has several limitations that warrant consideration. First, as in any cross-sectional study, the question of causality cannot be fully addressed here. By means of structural nonrecursive models it was possible to restrict rival causal explanations, but only for some components of the model. Contrary to the idea that higher self-esteem leads to higher ethnic pride, nonrecursive models show that the path from ethnic identity to self-esteem is stronger than the reverse path, across ethnic groups. However, alternative explanations for other pieces of the model cannot be ruled out empirically.

Future research should attempt to disentangle such causal reciprocal effects by conducting laboratory studies, testing nonrecursive models more adequately, and—in particular—using longitudinal data. In effect, previous research has provided data consistent with the model proposed here. For instance, previous laboratory studies have shown that ethnic identification increases with the exposure to negative information toward the in-group (see Schmitt, Branscombe, Kobrynowicz, & Owen, 2002, for a review). Also, nonrecurisve models tested by van Dick et al. (in prep.), Pettigrew (1997), and Wagner et al. (2001) suggest a causal impact from contact to interethnic attitudes and not the reverse. Finally, Nesdale and Todd (2000) reported data congruent with the contact hypothesis from a longitudinal study in which the positive effects of contact on interethnic attitudes were observed while controlling for participants' initial interest in interethnic contact programs.

A further limitation of the present results is related to the measurement of the variables used to test the hypotheses. For instance, the low reliability of the measure of in-group status might have affected the pattern of multivariate relations observed here. Also, the observed ethnic-differentiated patterns might be due to the fact that the reliability of some scales was lower for Blacks than for Whites and vice versa. Although the measurement error was clearly reduced by means of latent-variables structural equation models, further efforts should be taken in order to develop measures that reliably tap these constructs. In addition, some of the measures were not balanced (i.e., all items were positively worded), introducing the problem of response bias. Once more, although such measurement issues cannot account for the systematic differences observed across ethnic groups, more research is needed in order to improve the assessment of these relevant constructs.

Finally, the variables under study accounted for a limited amount of the variance in self-esteem, indicating that other variables exist that contribute to individuals' feelings of self-regard. Future research could increase the understanding of the social-psychological basis for self-esteem by detecting other potential predictors of positive adjustment.

In spite of these limitations, this research provides important insights into the way in which people interact and acculturate in Latin American settings and has important implications for future research. First, given the impressive impact of intergroup variables on psychological adjustment, future research should pay special attention to the role of macro-level variables such as state integration ideologies on determining interethnic contact and its psychological outcomes. Together with the self-report measures of perceived discrimination and in-group status, it would be of interest to collect information about majority members' acculturation orientations, citizenship laws, and education policies as indicators of macro-structural factors affecting acculturation. Another way to address the issues is by comparing different acculturating groups in different Latin American countries with different integration policies.

Second, the inclusion of other acculturating groups in future research is central for a better understanding of acculturation processes within the same national framework. The present research focused on long-established ethnic groups. Consequently, the research strategy was designed to detect those variables that contribute to understanding the unique experience of these groups, and the specific effects observed here have been interpreted with attention to their particular characteristics. However, the validity of these interpretations can only be addressed by comparing different acculturating groups with different histories, social conditions, and cultural characteristics, such as indigenous people or immigrants.

Finally, future research might benefit from the theoretical distinction between psychological and sociocultural adaptation. This also has implications for the measures employed to assess these variables. In this study a general measure of global self-esteem was used. However, the results presented here suggest that the dimensions of acculturation relate differently to a global feeling of self-regard, which led to the hypothesis that different dimensions of acculturation might predict different psychological outcomes depending on the specific acculturation domains. Further, it is widely known that self-esteem is multidimensional, domain specific, and context dependent (Harter, 1996). This is especially relevant for understanding psychological adjustment among members of stigmatized groups, because certain dimensions, domains, and contexts might be more beneficial for their self-esteem than others (T. F. Pettigrew, personal communication, May 2001). This would also be helpful for understanding the variation on acculturation and adaptation within the same acculturating group.

In general, more research—especially outside North American contexts—is needed for a thorough understanding of the multiple causation of acculturation and adaptation to ethnically plural settings. A broader view that incorporates different research perspectives and different levels of explanation will be promising in this attempt.

Instructions for the Classification of Parents' Occupations

Estimado Juez:

Su tarea consiste en clasificar las profesiones dentro de las siguientes categorías:

1. EXTRACCION SOCIAL BAJA: El trabajo del padre no requiere una educación formal.
2. EXTRACCION SOCIAL MEDIA/ALTA: El trabajo del padre implica formación superior (técnica o universitaria).

Utilicen los números (1 y 2) para clasificar las profesiones y por favor clasifíquenlas TODAS (esto, aunque tengan dudas).

Dear Judge:

Your job is to classify the occupations into the following categories:

1. Low socioeconomic status: Father's occupation is an unskilled work not requiring formal education.

2. Middle/high socioeconomic status: Father's occupation requires formal (technical or university) education.

Use the numbers (1 and 2) to classify the occupations and please classify ALL of them (even if you have some doubts).

Results of the Classification of Parents' Occupations

Empleos (occupations)	Juez 1 (Judge 1)	Juez 2 (Judge 2)	Juez 3 (Judge 3)
Abogado (Lawyer)	2	2	—
Administrador de Empresas (Business administrator)	2	2	—
Agente vendedor (Salesman)	1	1	—
Agricultor (Farmer)	1	1	—
Albañil (Bricklayer)	1	1	—
Arquitecto (Architect)	2	2	—
Asistente ejecutivo (Executive assistant)	2	2	—
Auxiliar de contabilidad (Accounting assistant)	2	1	2
Auxiliar de proveduria (Supplier assistant)	2	1	2
Cajero de banco (Bank cashier)	2	1	2
Chofer (Chauffeur)	1	1	—
Comerciante (Trader)	1	1	––
Contador (Accountant)	2	2	—
Contador privado (Private accountant)	2	2	—
Director de cine (Film director)	2	2	—

Empleos (occupations)	Juez 1 (Judge 1)	Juez 2 (Judge 2)	Juez 3 (Judge 3)
Diseñador gráfico (Graphic designer)	2	2	—
Ebanista (Cabinetmaker)	1	1	—
Economista (Economist)	2	2	—
Filósofo (Philosopher)	2	2	—
Fontanero (Plumber)	1	1	—
Fotógrafo (Photographer)	2	1	2
Gerente público (Manager)	2	2	—
Guarda de seguridad (Watchman)	1	1	—
Hojalatero (Tinsmith)	1	1	—
Industrial (Industry owner)	1	2	2
Ingeniero (Engineer)	2	2	—
Maestro (Primary school teacher)	2	2	—
Marinero (Sailor)	1	1	—
Mecanico (Mechanic)	1	1	—
Médico (Medical doctor)	2	2	—
Notificador (Messenger)	2	1	1
Oficinista (Office worker)	2	2	—
Periodista (Journalist)	2	2	—
Pescador (Fisherman)	1	1	—
Profesor de colegio (High school teacher)	2	2	—
Profesor de la universidad (University professor)	2	2	—
Psicólogo (Psychologist)	2	2	—
Sociólogo (Sociologist)	2	2	—
Supervisor del muelle de Moín (Pier supervisor)	2	1	2
Taxista (Taxi driver)	1	1	—
Técnico electricista (Electrical technician)	2	2	—
Técnico en computación (Computer technician)	2	2	—
Técnico en comunicaciones (Telecommunications technician)	2	2	—
Topógrafo (Topographer)	2	2	—
Trabajador social (Social worker)	2	2	—
Transportista (Carrier)	1	1	—
Zapatero (Shoemaker)	1	1	—

Note: 1 = low class, 2 = middle/high class. Judges agreement was 85%. Interjudge agreement corrected for chance (Cohen's *kappa*) was 0.69. Disagreement was solved by the third judge.

Questionnaire

The questionnaire was presented in Spanish. For communicative purposes, the instructions and items are shown here in both Spanish and English.

¡Primero que todo muchas gracias por participar en esta Investigación!

El siguiente cuestionario tiene como objetivo conocer las experiencias y opiniones de jóvenes costarricenses en relación a varios aspectos de su vida cotidiana. Recuerde que esto no es un examen, no hay respuestas buenas o malas, todo depende de sus opiniones y eso es precisamante lo que nos interesa. Eso sí, asegúrese por favor de LLENAR TODO EL CUESTIONARIO. Por nuestra parte le aseguramos que su información será tratada de manera TOTALMENTE CONFIDENCIAL.

First of all, thank you very much for participating in this research!

The following questionnaire aims to know the experiences and opinions of Costa Rican youths about several aspects of their everyday life. Remember that this is not an examination, there are neither good answers nor bad answers, all depends on your opinions, and that is what we are interested in. But please, ANSWER ALL THE QUESTIONS. We ensure you that the information will be treated CONFIDENTIALLY.

A) Én la siguiente sección nos interesa conocer sus opiniones sobre USTED MISMO(A). Con el fin de conocer sus opiniones al respecto, se le presentan una serie de frases. Para cada frase existen seis posibles respuestas. Se trata de una escala en donde 1 significa "TOTALMENTE EN DESACUERDO" con la frase y 6 "TOTALMENTE DE ACUERDO" con ella. Encierre en un círculo la respuesta (es decir, el número) que más se acerque a su opinión o experiencia.

A) In the following section we are interested in your opinions about YOUR-SELF. To know your opinions about it, we present you a series of statements. For each statement there are six possible answers. It is a scale, in which 1 means "TOTALLY DISAGREE" and 6 "TOTALLY AGREE." Please circle the answer (i.e., the number) that is closest to your opinion or experience.

1. Siento que soy una persona tan valiosa como las demás.
   I feel that I am a person of worth, at least on an equal basis with others.
   Totalmente en desacuerdo 1 2 3 4 5 6 Totalmente de acuerdo
   Totally disagree 1 2 3 4 5 6 Totally agree

2. Siento que tengo un buen número de buenas cualidades.
   I feel that I have a number of good qualities.
   Totalmente en desacuerdo 1 2 3 4 5 6 Totalmente de acuerdo

3. En general, tendo a sentir que soy un fracaso.
   All in all, I am inclined to feel that I am a failure.
   Totalmente en desacuerdo 1 2 3 4 5 6 Totalmente de acuerdo

4. Tengo una opinión positiva sobre mí mismo(a).
   I take a positive attitude toward myself.
   Totalmente en desacuerdo 1 2 3 4 5 6 Totalmente de acuerdo

5. La verdad es que me gustaria tener mas respeto por mí mismo.
   I wish I could have more respect for myself.
   Totalmente en desacuerdo 1 2 3 4 5 6 Totalmente de acuerdo

6. Tengo la sensación de que no tengo mucho de lo que me pueda sentir orgulloso(a).
   I feel I do not have much to be proud of.
   Totalmente en desacuerdo 1 2 3 4 5 6 Totalmente de acuerdo

7. Soy capaz de hacer las cosas tan bien como los demás.
   I am able to do things as well as most other people.
   Totalmente en desacuerdo 1 2 3 4 5 6 Totalmente de acuerdo

8. En general estoy satisfecho(a) conmigo mismo(a).
   On the whole, I am satisfied with myself.
   Totalmente en desacuerdo 1 2 3 4 5 6 Totalmente de acuerdo

9. Algunas veces me siento inútil.
   I certainly feel useless at times.
   Totalmente en desacuerdo 1 2 3 4 5 6 Totalmente de acuerdo

10. De vez en cuando pienso que no soy bueno(a) para nada.
    At times I think I am no good at all.
    Totalmente en desacuerdo 1 2 3 4 5 6 Totalmente de acuerdo

11. Cambio mi opinión sobre mí mismo(a) costantemente.
    I change my opinion of myself a lot.
    Totalmente en desacuerdo 1 2 3 4 5 6 Totalmente de acuerdo

12. Tengo una idea muy clara de lo que quiero ser.
    I've got a clear idea of what I want to be.
    Totalmente en desacuerdo 1 2 3 4 5 6 Totalmente de acuerdo

13. Por lo general me siento muy confundido(a).
    I feel mixed up.
    Totalmente en desacuerdo   1   2   3   4   5   6   Totalmente de acuerdo

14. Tengo muy claro que tipo de persona soy.
    I know what kind of person I am.
    Totalmente en desacuerdo   1   2   3   4   5   6   Totalmente de acuerdo

15. No puedo decidirme sobre lo que quiero hacer con mi vida.
    I can't decide what I want to do with my life.
    Totalmente en desacuerdo   1   2   3   4   5   6   Totalmente de acuerdo

16. Me gusta como soy y estoy orgulloso(a) de mí mismo(a).
    I like myself and am proud of what I stand for.
    Totalmente en desacuerdo   1   2   3   4   5   6   Totalmente de acuerdo

17. Realmente no sé quién soy.
    I don't really know what I'm on about.
    Totalmente en desacuerdo   1   2   3   4   5   6   Totalmente de acuerdo

18. Tengo claro cuáles son las cosas importantes en la vida.
    The important things in life are clear to me.
    Totalmente en desacuerdo   1   2   3   4   5   6   Totalmente de acuerdo

B) La mayoría de las sociedades actuales están compuestas por diversos GRUPOS ETNICOS. Los grupos étnicos se diferencian los unos de los otros en aspectos culturales como por ejemplo en sus costumbres, tradiciones, idioma, religión, música, la forma de preparar las comidas y/o en sus características físicas. En Costa Rica viven por ejemplo los grupos INDÍGENAS, ASIÁTICOS (ej. descendientes de chinos, coreanos o japoneses), AFROCARIBEÑOS, MESTIZOS (mezcla entre blancos europeos e indígenas latinoamericanos), o BLANCOS (como buena parte de los descendientes de Italianos o Españoles). Todas las personas nacemos en uno o más grupos étnicos. La siguiente sección trata de sus opiniones respecto a este tema.

Específicamente, nos gustaría conocer sus experiencias en relación con SU grupo étnico, así como sus opiniones respecto a OTROS grupos étnicos que viven en Costa Rica. Para ello le presentamos varias frases. Para cada frase existen seis posibles respuestas. Encierre en un círculo por favor la respuesta que más se acerque a su opinión o experiencia.

B) Most societies are made up of diverse ETHNIC GROUPS. Ethnic groups differ from each other in aspects such as customs, traditions, language, religion, music, the way to prepare food, and/or in their physical characteristics. In Costa Rica there are diverse ethnic groups such as INDIGENOUS PEOPLE, ASIANS (e.g., Chinese, Korean, or Japanese descendants), AFRO-CARIBBEANS, MESTIZOS (mixture between White Europeans and Latin American indigenous people), or WHITES (such as people with Italian or Spanish ancestry). Everybody is a member of one or more ethnic groups. The following section deals with your opinions about this issue.

Specifically, we would like to know your opinions and experiencies about YOUR ethnic group, as well as your opinions about OTHER ethnic groups living in Costa Rica. For these purposes, we present you several sentences. For each sentence, there are six possible answers. Please circle the answer that is closest to your opinion or experience.

1. Me he dedicado a conocer más sobre la historia, tradiciones y costumbres de mi grupo étnico.
   I have spent time trying to find out more about my ethnic group, such as its traditions.
   Totalmente en desacuerdo 1   2   3   4   5   6   Totalmente de acuerdo

2. Asisto a grupos y organizaciones que están compuestas, en su mayoría, por personas de *mi* grupo étnico.
   I am active in organizations or social groups that include mostly members of my own ethnic group.
   Totalmente en desacuerdo 1   2   3   4   5   6   Totalmente de acuerdo

3. Me gusta conocer y relacionarme con personas de *otros* grupos étnicos.
   I like meeting and getting to know people from ethnic groups other than my own.
   Totalmente en desacuerdo 1   2   3   4   5   6   Totalmente de acuerdo

4. Estoy feliz de ser miembro de *mi* grupo étnico.
   I am happy that I am a member of the ethnic group I belong to.
   Totalmente en desacuerdo 1   2   3   4   5   6   Totalmente de acuerdo

5. Estoy consciente de mis "raíces étnicas" y de lo que éstas significan para mi.
   I have a clear sense of my ethnic background and what it means for me.
   Totalmente en desacuerdo 1   2   3   4   5   6   Totalmente de acuerdo

6. Participo en actividades donde hay personas de *otros* grupos étnicos.
   I am involved in activities with people from other ethnic groups.
   Totalmente en desacuerdo 1   2   3   4   5   6   Totalmente de acuerdo

7. A menudo paso el tiempo con personas de grupos étnicos *distintos* al mío.
   I often spend time with people from ethnic groups other than my own.
   Totalmente en desacuerdo 1   2   3   4   5   6   Totalmente de acuerdo

8. Me siento fuertemente ligado(a) a mi grupo étnico.
   I have a strong sense of belonging to my own ethnic group.
   Totalmente en desacuerdo 1   2   3   4   5   6   Totalmente de acuerdo

9. En general la gente muestra respeto hacia *mi* grupo étnico.
   In general, others respect the social groups that I am a member of.
   Totalmente en desacuerdo 1   2   3   4   5   6   Totalmente de acuerdo

10. Muchos consideran que *mi* grupo étnico no es tan valioso o digno como los otros.
    In general, others think that the social groups I am a member of are unworthy.
    Totalmente en desacuerdo 1   2   3   4   5   6   Totalmente de acuerdo

11. Pienso algunas veces que sería mejor si las personas de diferentes grupos étnicos no intentaran mezclarse entre sí.
    I sometimes feel it would be better if different ethnic groups didn't try to mix together.
    Totalmente en desacuerdo 1   2   3   4   5   6   Totalmente de acuerdo

12. Me siento muy comprometido(a) con *mi* grupo étnico.
    I feel a strong attachment toward my own ethnic group.
    Totalmente en desacuerdo 1   2   3   4   5   6   Totalmente de acuerdo

13. Con el fin de aprender más sobre *mi* tradición cultural, a menudo he conversado con otras personas acerca de mi grupo étnico.
    In order to learn more about my ethnic background, I have often talked to other people about my ethnic group.
    Totalmente en desacuerdo   1   2   3   4   5   6   Totalmente de acuerdo

14. Me gusta estar con gente de *otros* grupos étnicos.
    I enjoy being around people from ethnic groups other than my own.
    Totalmente en desacuerdo   1   2   3   4   5   6   Totalmente de acuerdo

15. Me siento muy bien con *mi* tradición étnica o cultural.
    I feel good about my cultural or ethnic background.
    Totalmente en desacuerdo   1   2   3   4   5   6   Totalmente de acuerdo

16. Entiendo bastante bien lo que significa para mí pertenecer a mi grupo étnico.
    I understand pretty well what my ethnic-group membership means to me.
    Totalmente en desacuerdo   1   2   3   4   5   6   Totalmente de acuerdo

17. Estoy muy orgulloso(a) de mi grupo étnico.
    I have a lot of pride in my ethnic group.
    Totalmente en desacuerdo   1   2   3   4   5   6   Totalmente de acuerdo

18. Por lo general *no* me siento inclinado(a) a buscar amigos de *otros* grupo étnicos.a
    I don't try to become friends with people from other ethnic groups.
    Totalmente en desacuerdo   1   2   3   4   5   6   Totalmente de acuerdo

19. Participo activamente de las tradiciones de *mi* grupo étnico como por ejemplo de su música, comida, idioma, etc.
    I participate in cultural practices of my own group, such as special food, music, or customs.
    Totalmente en desacuerdo   1   2   3   4   5   6   Totalmente de acuerdo

20. Generalmente *mi* grupo étnico es bien visto por los demás.
    Overall, my social groups are considered good by others.
    Totalmente en desacuerdo   1   2   3   4   5   6   Totalmente de acuerdo

21. Pienso mucho sobre cómo se podría ver afectada mi vida por el hecho de pertenener a *mi* grupo étnico.
    I think a lot about how my life will be affected by my ethnic-group membership.
    Totalmente en desacuerdo   1   2   3   4   5   6   Totalmente de acuerdo

22. Asisto a organizaciones y participo en actividades en donde se promueven las tradiciones de *mi* grupo étnico.
    I am active in organizations or social groups that promote the traditions of my ethnic group.
    Totalmente en desacuerdo   1   2   3   4   5   6   Totalmente de acuerdo

23. La mayoría de la gente considera que *mi* grupo étnico es improductivo comparado con los demás.
    Most people consider my social groups, on the average, to be more ineffective than other social groups.
    Totalmente en desacuerdo   1   2   3   4   5   6   Totalmente de acuerdo

C) Siguiendo con el tema de los grupos étnicos costarricenses, ahora indique por favor si usted ha tenido contacto personal con miembros de *otros* grupos étnicos en las siguiente áreas:

C) Continuing with the theme of Costa Rican ethnic groups, now please indicate whether you have personal contact with members of other ethnic groups in the following areas:

nunca   algunas veces   con frecuencia   muy frequentemente
never   sometimes   often   very often

1. En su familia cercana y lejana:
   Among family and relatives:
   1   2   3   4

2. En la escuela o trabajo:
   At school:
   1   2   3   4

3. En el barrio:
   In the neighborhood:
   1   2   3   4

4. En el grupo de amigos:
   Among your circle of friends:
   1   2   3   4

5. En organizaciones deportivas:
   In your sport organizations:
   1   2   3   4

6. En otras actividades:
   In other activities:
   1   2   3   4

7. ¿En general, con qué frecuencia tiene usted contacto con personas de otros grupos étnicos?
   How often do you have contact with people from other ethnic groups?
   1. Nunca   2. Algunas vees   3. Frecuentemente   4. Muy frecuentemente
   1. Never   2. Sometimes   3. Often   4. Very often

8. ¿Cuán importante es para usted tener contacto con personas de otros grupos étnicos?
   How important is it for you to have contact with people from other ethnic groups?
   1. Nada importante   2. Poco importante   3. Importante   4. Muy importante
   1. Not at all important 2. Few important   3. Important   4. Very important

9. ¿Cuán "fuerte" es su contacto con personas de otros grupos étnicos?
   How intensive is your contact with people from other ethnic groups?
   1. Nada fuerte   2. Poco fuerte   3. Fuerte   4. Muy fuerte
   1. Not intensive at all   2. Few intensive   3. Intensive   4. Very intensive

10. ¿Cree usted que el hecho de pertenecer a su grupo étnico le puede impedir conseguir *un buen trabajo*?
    To what extent do you believe that membership in your ethnic group hinders your opportunities to find a good job?
    Totalmente en desacuerdo 1   2   3   4   5   6   Totalmente de acuerdo

11. ¿Considera usted que el hecho de pertenecer a su grupo étnico le puede impedir *surgir economicamente*?
To what extent do you believe that membership in your ethnic group hinders your opportunities to do well economically?
Totalmente en desacuerdo 1   2   3   4   5   6   Totalmente de acuerdo

12. ¿Cree usted que el hecho de pertenencer a su grupo étnico le puede impedir a usted tener *éxito en los estudios*?
To what extent do you believe that membership in your ethnic group makes it difficult to do well in school?
Totalmente en desacuerdo 1   2   3   4   5   6   Totalmente de acuerdo

13. ¿Se ha sentido usted discriminado(a) por pertenecer a su grupo étnico?
Do you feel that you have been discriminated against because of membership in your ethnic group?
Totalmente en desacuerdo 1   2   3   4   5   6   Totalmente de acuerdo

D) Finalmente . . .
D) Finally . . .

Su grupo étnico es:

Your ethnic group is:

    Afrocaribeño   ( )

    Afro-Caribbean

    Blanco o Mestizo   ( )

    White or Mestizo

    Indígena   ( )

    Indigenous people

    Asiatico   ( )

    Asian

    Otros grupos (anotar) _____

    Other (indicate)

El grupo étnico de su padre es: _____

Your father's ethnic group is:

El grupo étnico de su madre es: _____

Your mother's ethnic group is:

Sexo: femenino ( )   masculino ( )

Gender: female ( )   male ( )

Edad:

Age:

Escolaridad: 7° ( ) 8° ( ) 9° ( ) 10° ( ) 11° ( )

Grade level:

Lugar de residencia (anotar sólo la provincia): _____

Place of residence (indicate the province):

Escolaridad de sus padres:	madre	padre
Parents' level of education:	mother	father
Primaria incompleta	( )	( )
Primary school uncompleted		
Primaria completa	( )	( )
Primary school concluded		
Secundaria incompleta	( )	( )
Secondary school uncompleted		
Secundaria completa	( )	( )
Secondary school concluded		
Formación técnica	( )	( )
Technical qualification		
Universidad incompleta	( )	( )
University studies uncompleted		
Universidad completa	( )	( )
University studies completed		

1. Profesión u oficio de su madre: _____
   Profession or occupation of your mother:

2. Profesión u oficio de su padre: _____
   Profession or occupation of your father:

Asegurese por favor de haber llenado todo el cuestionario.

Please be sure that you have filled in the questionnaire completely.

MUCHAS GRACIAS

THANK YOU VERY MUCH

Descriptive and Psychometric Data of All Measures in the Pilot Study

		Blacks		Whites		Total	
	Items	*M*	*SD*	*M*	*SD*	r_{it}	Factor 1
Self-Esteem Measure [a]							
1.	I feel that I am a person of worth, at least on an equal basis with others.	3.49	1.97	3.29	1.93	.41	.47
2.	I feel that I have a number of good qualities.	5.64	.61	5.44	.96	.44	.56
3.	I am able to do things as well as most other people.	5.91	.47	5.16	1.50	.34	.45
4.	I take a positive attitude toward myself.	5.73	.62	5.11	1.10	.63	.75
5.	One the whole, I am satisfied with myself.	5.51	.94	5.16	1.13	.66	.75

Note: Means and standard deviations are presented for each ethnic group for descriptive purposes. Item-total correlations and factor loadings are calculated for the whole sample. All items were answered on a 6-point scale from 1 (totally disagree) to 6 (totally agree), except for the interethnic-contact measure, which was answered on a 4-point scale from 1 (never/not at all intensive/not at all important) to 4 (very often/very intensive/very important). High scores indicate high levels in each construct. *N*s vary from 114 to 123 because of missing values (max. missing values < 9%). Perceived ethnic discrimination was not assessed in the pilot study.

[a]Self-esteem measure is derived from Rosenberg (1965) and Rosenthal, Gurney, and Moore (1981).

		Blacks		Whites			Total
	Items	M	SD	M	SD	r_{it}	Factor 1

Self-Esteem Measure [a] (continued)

		Blacks		Whites			Total
6.	I feel I do not have much to be proud of. *	3.11	1.61	2.90	1.44	.42	.45
7.	I certainly feel useless at times.*	4.04	.64	3.90	1.71	.63	.69
8.	At times I think I am no good at all.*	5.02	1.36	4.58	1.71	.61	.66
9.	I change my opinion of myself a lot.*	5.13	1.29	4.58	1.60	.46	.54
10.	I've got a clear idea of what I want to be.	4.71	1.38	4.75	1.53	.62	.67
11.	I feel mixed up.*	4.60	1.44	4.44	1.53	.57	.60
12.	I know what kind of person I am.	5.24	1.19	4.86	1.24	.55	.65
13.	I can't decide what I want to do with my life.*	4.44	1.82	4.60	1.75	.51	.54
14.	I like myself and am proud of what I stand for.	5.49	.94	5.16	1.15	.62	.74
15.	I don't really know what I'm on about.*	5.67	.74	5.37	1.18	.49	.56
16.	The important things in life are clear to me.	5.47	.89	5.21	1.07	.46	.53

Ethnic Identity Measure [b]

		Blacks		Whites			Total
1.	I have spent time trying to find out more about my ethnic group, such as its history, traditions, and customs.	3.98	1.32	3.08	1.73	.61	.69
2.	I feel good about my cultural or ethnic background.	4.67	1.79	3.72	1.81	.58	.67
3.	I have a clear sense of my ethnic background and what it means for me.	5.22	1.30	4.16	1.80	.68	.76
4.	In order to learn more about my ethnic background, I have often talked to other people about my ethnic group.	4.46	1.64	4.12	1.91	.61	.70
5.	I understand pretty well what my ethnic group membership means to me.	5.09	1.13	3.59	1.70	.76	.83
6.	I am happy that I am a member of the ethnic group I belong to.	5.87	1.50	5.19	1.21	.44	.52
7.	I participate in cultural practices of my own group, such as special food, music, or customs.	5.02	1.24	4.35	1.65	.51	.59
8.	I am active in organizations or social groups that promote the traditions of my ethnic group. †	3.87	1.64	3.31	1.58	.56	.62
9.	I have a strong sense of belonging to my own ethnic group.	4.70	1.43	3.55	1.65	.75	.82
10.	I have a lot of pride in my ethnic group.	5.54	.96	4.58	1.43	.44	.53
11.	I feel a strong attachment towards my own ethnic group.	4.39	1.36	3.31	1.71	.62	.70
12.	I am active in organizations or social groups that include mostly members of my own ethnic group.	3.35	1.69	3.19	.79	.34	.40

[a]Self-esteem measure is derived from Rosenberg (1965) and Rosenthal, Gurney, and Moore (1981).

[b]Ethnic-identity measure derived from the multigroup ethnic identity measure (Phinney, 1992).

*Item was reversed for scoring; †New item.

		Blacks		Whites		Total	
	Items	M	SD	M	SD	r_{it}	Factor 1

Interethnic Attitudes Measure [c]

		Blacks		Whites		Total	
1.	I like meeting and getting to know people from ethnic groups other than my own.	5.11	1.18	5.28	1.27	.56	.77
2.	I don't try to become friends with people from other ethnic groups. *	4.28	1.75	4.76	1.43	.33	.56
3.	I am involved in activities with people from other ethnic groups.	5.40	1.01	5.25	1.27	.48	.66
4.	I enjoy being around people from ethnic groups other than my own.	4.87	1.10	5.14	1.20	.58	.77
5.	I often spend time with people from ethnic groups other than my own.	5.34	1.09	4.04	1.70	.32	.55
6.	I sometimes feel it would be better if different ethnic groups didn't try to mix together. *	5.34	1.27	5.88	.54	.24	.41

Perceived Ingroup Status Measure [d]

		Blacks		Whites		Total	
1.	Overall, my ethnic group is considered good by others.	4.15	1.54	4.70	1.34	.63	.84
2.	Most people consider my ethnic group, on the average, to be more ineffective than other social groups. *	3.67	1.89	5.20	1.28	.53	.73
3.	In general, others respect the ethnic group that I am member.	4.15	1.57	4.61	1.31	.59	.81
4.	In general, others think that the ethnic group I am member of is unworthy. *	3.71	1.73	4.53	1.68	.48	.68

Interethnic Contact Measure [e]

		Blacks		Whites		Total	
1.	...Family and relatives?	2.88	.83	2.19	.88	.53	.63
2.	...Friends?	3.43	.83	2.94	.90	.72	.82
3.	...Neighborhood?	3.29	.92	2.42	1.02	.57	.66
4.	...School?	3.43	.80	3.28	.75	.63	.74
5.	...Sport?	3.17	.96	2.56	1.10	.54	.66
6.	...Other activities?	3.05	1.08	2.47	1.11	.46	.56
7.	How oft do you have contact with people from other ethnic groups?	3.33	.85	2.93	.74	.74	.83
8.	How important is for you to have contact with people from other ethnic groups?	2.93	.71	3.06	.77	.28	.41
9.	How intensive is your contact with people from other ethnic groups?	2.95	.79	2.53	.71	.55	.68

[c]Interethnic-attitudes measure is derived from other-group orientation measure (Phinney, 1992).

[d]Perceived in-group status measure is derived from public subscale from the collective self-esteem scale (Luhtanen & Crocker, 1992).

[e]Contact measure is derived from van Dick & Wagner (1995).

*Item was reversed for scoring.

Descriptive and Psychometric Data of the Measures in the Main Study

	Blacks				Whites			
Items	M	SD	r_{it}	Factor 1	M	SD	r_{it}	Factor 1
Self-Esteem Measure								
1. I feel that I am a person of worth, at least on an equal basis with others.	5.59	.95	.46	.61	5.63	.95	.42	.58
2. I feel that I have a number of good qualities.	5.26	.99	.49	.63	5.31	1.02	.55	.70
3. I am able to do things as well as most other people.	5.54	1.85	.30	.42	5.63	.85	.47	.62
4. I take a positive attitude toward myself.	5.23	1.20	.56	.71	5.33	1.08	.58	.73

Note: As in the pilot study, all items were answered on a 6-point scale from 1 (totally disagree) to 6 (totally agree), except for the interethnic-contact measure, which was answered on a 4-point scale from 1 (never/not at all intensive/not at all important) to 4 (very often/very intensive/very important). High scores indicate high levels in each construct. Ns vary from 368 to 408 and from 717 to 766 for Blacks and Whites, respectively, because of missing values (max. missing values < 8%).

	Blacks				Whites			
Items	M	SD	r_{it}	Factor 1	M	SD	r_{it}	Factor 1

Self-Esteem Measure (continued)

Items	M	SD	r_{it}	Factor 1	M	SD	r_{it}	Factor 1
5. One the whole, I am satisfied with myself.	5.13	1.31	.52	.67	5.27	1.12	.58	.72
6. I feel I do not have much to be proud of. *	2.74	1.89	.46	.53	2.60	1.81	.48	.54
7. I certainly feel useless at times. *	3.34	1.79	.39	.43	3.16	1.77	.43	.45
8. At times, I think I am no good at all. *	2.83	1.78	.50	.54	2.68	1.76	.53	.55
9. I change my opinion of myself a lot. *	3.15	1.79	.44	.47	3.01	1.81	.50	.52
10. I've got a clear idea of what I want to be.	4.73	1.55	.40	.48	4.73	1.52	.41	.48
11. I feel mixed up. *	3.58	1.70	.37	.39	3.38	1.74	.42	.44
12. I know what kind of person I am.	5.05	1.35	.38	.48	5.07	1.29	.50	.62
13. I can't decide what I want to do with my life. *	3.11	1.88	.39	.42	2.96	1.82	.41	.42
14. I like myself and am proud of what I stand for.	5.27	1.27	.57	.71	5.33	1.14	.61	.75
15. I don't really know what I'm on about.*	2.02	1.63	.53	.59	1.90	1.46	.54	.60
16. The important things in life are clear to me.	5.37	1.19	.45	.58	5.40	1.02	.34	.42

Ethnic Identity Measure

Items	M	SD	r_{it}	Factor 1	M	SD	r_{it}	Factor 1
1. I have spent time trying to find out more about my ethnic group, such as its history, traditions, and customs.	3.54	1.71	.44	.48	2.82	1.56	.37	.47
2. I fell good about my cultural or ethnic background.	5.41	1.06	.57	.71	5.15	1.18	.41	.56
3. I have a clear sense of my ethnic background and what it means for me.	4.72	1.46	.57	.69	4.16	1.64	.54	.68
4. In order to learn more about my ethnic background, I have often talked to other people about my ethnic group.	3.97	1.72	.48	.54	3.01	1.67	.45	.55
5. I understand pretty well what my ethnic group membership means to me.	5.26	1.19	.58	.71	4.64	1.48	.45	.59
6. I am happy that I am a member of the ethnic group I belong to.	5.42	1.23	.48	.62	5.39	1.16	.35	.49
7. I participate in cultural practices of my own group, such as special food, music, or customs.	4.98	1.43	.52	.61	4.41	1.68	.41	.52
8. I am active in organizations or social groups that promote the traditions of my ethnic group.	3.92	1.76	.54	.59	3.25	1.72	.45	.53

*Item was reversed for scoring.

| | Blacks | | | | Whites | | | |
Items	M	SD	r_{it}	Factor 1	M	SD	r_{it}	Factor 1
Ethnic Identity Measure (*continued*)								
9. I have a strong sense of belonging to my own ethnic group.	4.25	1.70	.59	.67	3.56	1.70.	.50	.61
10. I have a lot of pride in my ethnic group.	5.30	1.27	.60	.74	5.04	1.29	.39	.56
11. I feel a strong attachment towards my own ethnic group.	3.89	1.76	.58	.66	3.24	1.68	.49	.62
12. I am active in organizations or social groups that include mostly members of my own ethnic group. †	3.40	1.84	.42	.47	3.15	1.81	.28	.36
Interethnic Attitudes Measure								
1. I like meeting and getting to know people from ethnic groups other than my own.	5.17	1.34	.40	.65	5.06	.138	.56	.75
2. I don't try to become friends with people from other ethnic groups.*	3.61	1.86	.36	.52	3.07	1.82	.36	.51
3. I am involved in activities with people from other ethnic groups.	5.06	1.39	.38	.65	4.69	1.62	.50	.70
4. I enjoy being around people from ethnic groups other than my own.	5.17	1.24	.48	.71	5.01	1.38	.65	.82
5. I often spend time with people from ethnic groups other than my own.	4.76	1.53	.44	.69	4.35	1.67	.49	.68
6. I sometimes feel it would be better if different ethnic groups didn't try to mix together.*	1.91	1.54	.26	.39	1.97	1.62	.36	.52
Perceived Ethnic Discrimination Measure								
1. Do you feel that you have been discriminated because of the membership to your ethnic group?	2.80	1.83	.45	.64	1.97	1.59	.49	.68
2. To what extent do you believe that the membership to your ethnic group hinders your opportunities to find a good job?	2.52	1.81	.64	.82	1.80	1.44	.69	.82
3. To what extent do you believe that the membership to your ethnic group hinders your opportunities to do well economically?	2.33	1.70	.74	.89	1.65	1.31	.70	.85
4. To what extent do you believe that the membership to your ethnic group makes it difficult to do well in the school?	2.05	1.68	.64	.82	1.97	1.59	.49	.85

*Item was reversed for scoring; †new item.

	Blacks				Whites			
Items	M	SD	r_{it}	Factor 1	M	SD	r_{it}	Factor 1

Perceived Ingroup Status Measure

Items	M	SD	r_{it}	Factor 1	M	SD	r_{it}	Factor 1
1. Overall, my ethnic group is considered good by others.	4.01	1.70	.30	.64	4.52	1.57	.36	.69
2. Most people consider my ethnic group, on the average, to be more ineffective than other ethnic groups. *	3.53	1.94	.33	.63	2.72	1.82	.36	.63
3. In general, others respect the ethnic group that I am member.	4.30	1.52	.37	.71	4.79	1.33	.40	.71
4. In general, others think that the ethnic group I am member of is unworthy. *	3.19	1.80	.32	.62	2.33	1.68	.38	.66

Interethnic Contact Measure

Items	M	SD	r_{it}	Factor 1	M	SD	r_{it}	Factor 1
1. …Relatives	2.95	.98	.50	.62	2.42	.99	.42	.51
2. …Friends	3.33	.87	.64	.75	3.13	.94	.71	.80
3. …Neighborhood	3.35	.88	.51	.63	2.91	1.01	.63	.72
4. …School	3.49	.80	.59	.71	3.28	.86	.60	.70
5. …Sport	3.06	1.03	.57	.69	2.79	1.08	.59	.69
6. …Other activities	3.03	1.04	.43	.53	2.90	1.06	.54	.64
7. How often do you have contact with people from other ethnic groups?	3.30	.75	.67	.79	2.98	.82	.75	.84
8. How important is for you to have contact with people from other ethnic groups?	3.13	.83	.38	.48	3.05	.82	.51	.63
9. How intensive is your contact with people from other ethnic groups?	2.93	.87	.60	.70	2.62	.81	.65	.76

*Item was reversed for scoring.

Bibliography

Aberson, C. L., Healy, M., & Romero, V. (2000). Ingroup bias and self-esteem: A meta-analysis. *Personality and Social Psychology Review, 4*, 157–173.

Aboud, F. E. (1987). The development of ethnic self-identification and attitudes. In J. Phinney & M. Rotheram (Eds.), *Children's ethnic socialization: Pluralism and development* (pp. 32–55). London: Sage.

Aboud, F. E., & Doyle, A. B. (1995). The development of in-group pride in Black Canadians. *Journal of Cross-Cultural Psychology, 26*, 243–254.

Aboud, F. E, & Skerry, S. (1984). The development of ethnic attitudes: A critical review. *Journal of Cross-Cultural Psychology, 15*, 3–34.

Adorno, T., Frenkel-Brunswik, E., Levinson, D., & Sanford, R. (1950). *The authoritarian personality*. New York: Harper and Row.

Ajzen, I., & Fishbein, M. (1977). Attitude–behavior relations: A theoretical analysis and review of empirical research. *Psychological Bulletin, 84*, 888–918.

Allport, F. (1962). Individual and collective: I. Structural theory and the master problem of social psychology. *Journal of Abnormal and Social Psychology, 64*, 3–30.

Allport, G. (1954). *The nature of prejudice*. Reading, MA: Perseus.

Altemeyer, B. (1988). *Enemies of freedom*. San Francisco: Jossey-Bass.

Arroyo, C. G., & Zigler, E. (1995). Racial identity, academic achievement, and the psychological well-being of economically disadvantaged adolescents. *Journal of Personality and Social Psychology, 69*, 903–914.

Ashmore, R. D., & del Boca, F. K. (1981). Conceptual approaches to stereotypes and stereotyping. In D. Hamilton (Ed.), *Cognitive processes in stereotyping and intergroup behavior* (pp. 1–35). Hillsdale, NJ: Erlbaum.

Banaji, M. R., & Prentice, D. A. (1994). The self in social contexts. *Annual Review of Psychology, 45*, 297–332.

Banks, W. C. (1976). White preference in Blacks: A paradigm in search of a phenomenon. *Psychological Bulletin, 83*, 1179–1186.

Bentler, P. (1992). *EQS: Structural equations program manual*. Los Angeles: BMDP Statistical Software.

Berkowitz, L. (1962). *Aggression: A social psychological analysis*. New York: McGraw-Hill.

Berkowitz, L. (1972). Frustrations, comparisons, and other sources of emotion arousal as contributors to social unrest. *Journal of Social Issues, 28*, 77–91.

Berry, J. W. (1980). Acculturation as varieties of adaptation. In A. Padilla (Ed.), *Acculturation: Theory, models and some new findings* (pp. 9–25). Boulder, CO: Westview Press.

Berry, J. W. (1984). Cultural relations in plural societies: Alternatives to segregation and their sociopsychological implications. In B. Miller & M. Brewer (Eds.), *Groups in contact: The psychology of desegregation* (pp. 11–27). London: Academic Press.

Berry, J. W. (1995). Psychology of acculturation. In J. Bennet Veroff & N. Rule Goldberger (Eds.), *The culture and psychology reader* (pp. 457–488). New York: University Press.

Berry, J. W. (1997). Immigration, acculturation, and adaptation. *Applied Psychology: An International Review, 46*, 5–68.

Berry, J. W., Kim, U., Power, S., Young, M., & Bujaki, M. (1989). Acculturation attitudes in plural societies. *Applied Psychology: An International Review, 38*, 185–206.

Berry, J. W., Portinga, Y., Segall, M., & Dasen, P. (1992). *Cross-cultural psychology: Research and applications*. Cambridge: Cambridge University Press.

Berry, J. W., & Sam, D. (1997). Acculturation and adaptation. In J. W. Berry, M. H. Segall, & C. Kagitcibasi (Eds.), *Handbook of cross-cultural psychology* (vol. 3, pp. 291–326). Boston: Allyn and Bacon.

Bettencourt, B. A., & Hume, D. (1999). The cognitive contents of social-group identity: Values, emotions, and relationships. *European Journal of Social Psychology, 29*, 113–121.

Bobo, L. (1983). White's opposition to busing: Symbolic racism or realistic group conflict. *Journal of Personality and Social Psychology, 45*, 1196–1210.

Bogardus, E. S. (1933). A social distance scale. *Sociology and Social Science Research, 17*, 265–271.

Bourhis, R. Y., Moise, C., Perreault, S., & Senéca, S. (1997). Towards an interactive acculturation model: A social psychological approach. *International Journal of Psychology, 32*, 369–386.

Brand, E. S., Ruiz, R. A., & Padilla, A. M. (1974). Ethnic identification and preference: A review. *Psychological Bulletin, 81*, 860–890.

Branscombe, N. (2001, May). *Meanings and consequences of perceived discrimination in disadvantaged and privilieged groups*. Paper presented at the EAESP/SPSSI small meeting "Prejudice and Racism," Granada, Spain.

Branscombe, N. R., Ellemers, N., Spears, R., & Doosje, B. (1999). The context and content of social identity threat. In N. Ellemers, R. Spears, & B. Doosje (Eds.), *Social identity: Context, commitment, content* (pp. 35–58). Oxford: Blackwell.

Branscombe, N. R., & Wann, D. L. (1994). Collective self-esteem consequences of outgroup derogation when a valued social identity is on trial. *European Journal of Social Psychology, 24*, 641–657.

Brewer, M. B. (1996). When contact is not enough: Social identity and intergroup cooperation. *International Journal of Intercultural Relations, 20*, 291–303.

Brewer, M. B. (2000). Reducing prejudice through cross-categorization: Effects of multiple social identities. In S. Oskamp (Ed.), *Reducing prejudice and discrimination* (pp. 165–184). Mahwah, NJ: Lawrence Erlbaum.

Brewer, M. B., & Kramer, R. M. (1985). The psychology of intergroup attitudes and behavior. *Annual Review of Psychology, 36*, 219–243.

Brewer, M. B., & Miller, N. (1984). Beyond the contact hypothesis: Theoretical perspectives on desegregation. In N. Miller & M. B. Brewer (Eds.), *Groups in contact: The psychology of desegregation* (pp. 281–302). Orlando, FL: Academic Press.

Brigham, J. C. (1971). Ethnic stereotypes. *Psychological Bulletin, 76*, 15–38.

Brigham, J. C. (1973). Ethnic stereotypes and attitudes: A different mode of analysis. *Journal of Personality, 41*, 206–233.

Broman, C. L., Jackson, J. S., & Neighbors, H. W. (1989). Sociocultural context and racial group identification among black adults. *Review internationale de Psychologie Soziale, 2*, 367–378.

Broman, C. L., Neighbors, H. W., & Jackson, J. S. (1988). Racial group identification among Black adults. *Social Forces, 67*, 146–158.

Brookins, C. C., Anyabwille, T. M., & Nacoste, R. (1996). Exploring the links between racial identity attitudes and psychological feelings of closeness in African American college students. *Journal of Applied Social Psychology, 26*, 243–264.

Brown, R. (1984). The effects of intergroup similarity and cooperative vs. competitive orientation on intergroup discrimination. *British Journal of Experimental Social Psychology, 23*, 21–33.

Brown, R. (1995). *Prejudice: Its social psychology*. Oxford: Blackwell.

Brown, R. (2000). *Groups processes: Dynamics within and between groups*. Oxford: Blackwell.

Brown, R., Vivian, J., & Hewstone, M. (1999). Changing attitudes through intergroup contact: The effects of group membership salience. *European Journal of Social Psychology, 29*, 741–764.

Bruner, J. (1957). On perceptual readiness. *Psychological Review, 64*, 123–152.

Buriel, R. (1987). Ethnic labeling and identity among Mexican Americans. In J. Phinney & M. Rotheram (Eds.), *Children's ethnic socialization: Pluralism and development* (pp. 134–152). London: Sage.

Buriel, R., & Vasquez, R. (1982). Stereotypes of Mexican descent persons: Attitudes of three generations of Mexican Americans and Anglo-American adolescents. *Journal of Cross-Cultural Psychology, 13*, 59–70.

Cartwright, D., & Zander, A. (1968). Groups and group membership: Introduction. In D. Cartwright & A. Zander (Eds.), *Group dynamics: Research and theory* (pp. 45–62). New York: Harper and Row.

Chapman, L. J., & Chapman, J. P. (1967). Genesis of popular but erroneous psychodiagnostic observations. *Journal of Abnormal Psychology, 72*, 193–204.

Clark, K. B., & Clark, M. P. (1939). The development of consciousness of self and the emergence of racial identification in Negro preschool children. *Journal of Social Psychology, 10*, 591–599.

Clark, R., Anderson, N. B., Clark, V. R., & Williams, D. R. (1999). Racism as a stressor for African Americans: A biopsychosocial model. *American Psychology, 54*, 805–816.

Cook, S. W. (1978). Interpersonal and attitudinal outcomes in cooperating interracial groups. *Journal of Research and Development in Education, 12*, 97–113.

Cooley, C. H. (1956). *Human nature and social order.* New York: Free Press.

Coopersmith, S. (1967). *The antecedents of self-esteem.* San Francisco: W. H. Freeman.

Crocker, J. (2001, May). *Contingencies of self-worth among African-American and European-American college students: Implications for psychological well-being.* Paper presented at the EAESP/SPSSI small meeting "Prejudice and Racism," Granada, Spain.

Crocker, J., Blaine, B., & Luhtanen, R. (1993). Prejudice, intergroup behavior and self-esteem: Enhancement and protection motives. In M. A. Hogg & D. Abrams (Eds.), *Group motivation: Social psychological perspectives* (pp. 53–67). New York: Harvester Wheatsheaf.

Crocker, J., Luhtanen, R., Blaine, B., & Broadnax, S. (1994). Collective self-esteem and psychological well-being among White, Black, and Asian college students. *Personality and Social Psychology Bulletin, 20*, 503–513.

Crocker, J., Luhtanen, R., & Bouvrette, S. (2001). *The contingencies of self-worth in college students: I. The Contingencies of Self-Worth scale.* Unpublished manuscript, University of Michigan, Ann Arbor.

Crocker, J., & Major, B. (1989). Social stigma and self-esteem: The self-protective properties of stigma. *Psychological Review, 96*, 608–630.

Crocker, J., & Quinn, D. (1998). Racism and self-esteem. In J. Eberhardt & S. Fiske (Eds.), *Confronting racism: The problem and the response* (pp. 169–187). Beverly Hills, CA: Sage.

Crocker, J., Thompson, L., McGraw, K., & Ingerman, C. (1987). Downward comparison, prejudice, and evaluations of others: Effects of self-esteem and threat. *Journal of Personality and Social Psychology, 52*, 907–916.

Crosby, F. (1976). A model of egoistical relative deprivation. *Psychological Review, 83*, 85–113.

Crosby, F., Bromley, S., & Saxe, L. (1980). Recent unobtrusive studies of Black and White discrimination and prejudice: A literature review. *Psychological Bulletin, 87*, 546–563.

Cross, W. E. (1991). *Shades of black: Diversity in African-American identity.* Philadelphia: Temple University Press.

Dechamps, J. C., & Brown, R. (1983). Superordinate goals and intergroup conflict. *British Journal of Social Psychology, 22*, 189–195.

Deux, K., Reid, A., Mizrahi, K., & Ethier, K. A. (1995). Parameters of social identity. *Journal of Personality and Social Psychology, 68*, 280–291.

Dobles, I., Fournier, M., & Pérez, R. (1996). Representaciones sociales del quinto centenario del arribo de los Españoles a Améica y su relación con la identidad social. In R. Pérez, I. Dobles, & T. Cordero (Eds.), *Psicología social: Dominación social y subjetividad* (pp. 57–92). San José, C.R.: Editorial de la Universidad de Costa Rica.

Dollard, J., Doob, L. W., Miller, N. E., Mowrer, O. H., & Sears, R. R. (1939). *Frustration and aggression.* New Haven: Yale University Press.

Doná, G., & Berry, J. W. (1994). Acculturation attitudes and acculturative stress of Central American refugees. *International Journal of Psychology, 29* (1), 57–70.

Doosje, B., Ellemers, N., & Spears, R. (1999). Commitment and intergroup behavior. In N. Ellemers, R. Spears, & B. Doosje (Eds.), *Social identity: Context, commitment, content* (pp. 84–106). Oxford: Blackwell.

Dovidio, J. F., & Gaertner, S. L. (1986). Prejudice, discrimination and racism: Historical trends and contemporary approaches. In J. F. Dovidio & S. L. Gaertner (Eds.), *Prejudice, discrimination and racism*. Orlando, FL: Academic Press.

Dovidio, J. F., Kawakami, K., & Gaertner, S. L. (2000). Reducing contemporary prejudice: Combating explicit and implicit bias at the individual and intergroup level. In S. Oskamp (Ed.), *Reducing prejudice and discrimination* (pp. 137–164). Mahwah, NJ: Lawrence Erlbaum.

Duckitt, J. (1989). Authoritarianism and group identification: A new view of and old construct. *Political Psychology, 10*, 63–84.

Duckitt, J. (1992). *The social psychology of prejudice*. New York: Praeger.

Duckitt, J., & Mphuthing, T. (1998). Group identification and intergroup attitudes: A longitudinal analysis in South Africa. *Journal of Personality and Social Psychology, 74*, 80–85.

Duncan, Q., & Powel, P. (1988). *Teoría y práctica del racismo*. San José, C.R.: Editorial DEI.

Ellemers, N. (1993). The influence of socio-structural variables on identity management strategies. In W. Stroebe & M. Hewstone (Eds.), *European review of social psychology* (vol. 4, pp. 27–57). Chichester: Wiley.

Ellemers, N., Kortekaas, P., & Ouwerkerk, J. W. (1999). Self-categorization, commitment to the group and group self-esteem as related but distinct aspects of social identity. *European Journal of Social Psychology, 29*, 371–389.

Ellemers, N., van Knippenberg, A., de Vries, N., & Wilke, H. (1988). Social identification and permeability of group boundaries. *European Journal of Social Psychology, 18*, 497–513.

Ellemers, N., van Rijswijk, W., Roefs, M., & Simons, C. (1997). Bias in intergroup perceptions: Balancing group identity with social reality. *Personality and Social Psychology Bulletin, 23*, 186–198.

Ellemers, N., Wilke, H., & van Knippenberg, A. (1993). Effects of the legitimacy of low group or individual status on individual and collective identity enhancement strategies. *Journal of Personality and Social Psychology, 64*, 766–778.

Erikson, E. (1973). *Identität und Lebenszyklus: Drei Aufsätze*. Frankfurt am Main: Suhrkamp.

Ethier, K., A., & Deux, K. (1994). Negotiating social identity when contexts change: Maintaining identification and responding to threat. *Journal of Personality and Social Psychology, 67*, 243–251.

Fazio, R. H., Jackson, J. R., Dunton, B. C., & Williams, C. J. (1995). Variation in automatic activation as an unobtrusive measure of racial attitudes: A bona fide pipeline. *Journal of Personality and Social Psychology, 69*, 1013–1027.

Fernández, E. (1977). *La integración de la población negra a la política costarricense*. Tesis de Licenciatura, Universidad de Costa Rica.

Festinger, L. (1954). A theory of social comparison processes. *Human Relations, 7*, 117–140.

Fiske, S. (2000). Sterotyping, prejudice, and discrimination at the seam between the centuries: Evolution, culture, mind, and brain. *European Journal of Social Psychology, 30*, 299–322.

Fiske, S., & Taylor, S. E. (1991). *Social cognition*. New York: McGraw-Hill.

Gaertner, S. L., Dovidio, J. F., & Bachman, B. A. (1996). Revisiting the contact hypothesis: The induction of a common ingroup identity. *International Journal of Intercultural Relations, 20*, 271–290.

Ganter, S. (1997). *Stereotype und Vorurteile: Konzeptualisierung, Operationalisierung and Messung*. Manheim: Mannheimer Zentrum für Europäische Sozialforschung. Arbeitspapiere Arbeitsbereich III/22.

Giddens, A. (1993). *Sociology*. Oxford: Polity Press.

Gilbert, G. M. (1951). Stereotype persistence and change among college students. *Journal of Abnormal and Social Psychology, 46*, 245–254.

Gordon, M. (1978). *Human nature, class, and ethnicity*. New York: Oxford University Press.

Graves, T. D. (1967). Psychological acculturation in a tri-ethnic community. *Southwestern Journal of Anthropology, 23*, 336–350.

Greenwald, A. G., McGhee, D. E., & Schwartz, J. L. (1998). Measuring individual differences in implicit cognition: The implicit association test. *Journal of Personality and Social Identity, 74*, 1464–1480.

Grossman, B., Wirt, T., & Davids, A. (1985). Self-esteem, ethnic identity, and behavioral adjustment among Anglo and Chicano adolescents in West Texas. *Journal of Adolescence, 8*, 57–68.

Gudykunst, W. B., & Bond, M. H. (1997). Intergroup relations across cultures. In J. W. Berry, M. H. Segall, & C. Kagitcibasi (Eds.), *Handbook of cross-cultural psychology* (vol. 3, pp. 119–161). Boston: Allyn and Bacon.

Guglielmi, S. (1999). Psychophysiological assessment of prejudice: Past research, current status, and future directions. *Personality and Social Psychological Review, 3*, 123–157.

Gurin, P., Hurtado, A., & Peng, T. (1994). Group contacts and ethnicity in the social identities of Mexicanos and Chicanos. *Personality and Social Psychology Bulletin, 20*, 521–532.

Gurr, T. R. (1970). *Why men rebel*. Princeton, NJ: Princeton University Press.

Hafer, C., & Olson, J. M. (1993). Beliefs in a just world, discontent, and assertive actions by working women. *Personal and Social Psychology Bulletin, 19*, 30–38.

Hamberger, J., & Hewstone, M. (1997). Inter-ethnic contact as a predictor of blatant and subtle prejudice: Tests of a model in four West European nations. *British Journal of Social Psychology, 36*, 173–190.

Hamilton, D. L. (1981). Illusory correlation as a basis for stereotyping. In D. L. Hamilton (Ed.), *Cognitive processes in stereotyping and intergroup behavior* (pp. 115–144). Hillsdale, NJ: Erlbaum.

Hamilton, D. L., Stroessner, S. J., & Driscoll, D. M. (1994). Social cognition and the study of stereotyping. In P. C. Devine, D. L. Hamilton, & T. M. Ostrom (Eds.), *Social cognition: Impact on social psychology* (pp. 292–321). San Diego: Academic Press.

Harding, J., Kutner, B., Proshansky, H., & Chein, I. (1954). Prejudice and ethnic relations. In G. Lindzey (Ed.), *Handbook of social psychology* (vol. 2, pp. 1021–1061). Cambridge, MA: Addison-Wesley.

Harter, S. (1996). Historical roots of contemporary issues involving self-concept. In B. A. Bracken (Ed.), *Handbook of self-concept: Developmental, social, and clinical considerations* (pp. 1–37). New York: John Wiley and Sons.

Helms, J. E. (1990). *Black and White racial identity: Theory, research and practice*. Westport, CT: Greenwood.

Hewstone, M., & Brown, R. (1986). Contact is not enough: An intergroup perspective on the "contact hypothesis." In M. Hewstone & R. Brown (Eds.), *Contact & conflict in intergroup encounters* (pp. 1–44). Oxford: Basil Blackwell.

Hilton, J., & von Hippel, W. (1996). Stereotypes. *Annual Review of Psychology, 47,* 237–271.

Hinkle, S., & Brown, R. J. (1990). Intergroup comparisons and social identity: Some links and lacunae. In D. Abrams & M. A. Hogg (Eds.), *Social identity theory: Constructive and critical advances* (pp. 48–70). Hemel Hempstead: Harvester Wheatsheaf.

Hofstede, G. (1980). *Culture's consequences: International differences in work-related values.* Beverly Hills, CA: Sage.

Hogg, M. A., & Abrams, D. (1988). *Social identifications: A social psychology of intergroup relations and group processes.* London: Routledge.

Hogg, M. A., & Abrams, D. (1990). Social motivation, self-esteem, and social identity. In D. Abrams & M. A. Hogg (Eds.), *Social identity theory: Constructive and critical advances* (pp. 28–47). New York: Harvester Wheatsheaf.

Hogg, M. A., & Abrams, D. (1999). Social identity and social cognition. In D. Abrams & M. A. Hogg (Eds.), *Social identity and social cognition* (pp. 1–25). Oxford: Blackwell.

Hogg, M. A., & Mullin, B. (1999). Joining groups to reduce uncertainty: Subjective uncertainty reduction and group identification. In D. Abrams & M. A. Hogg (Eds.), *Social identity and social cognition* (pp. 249–279). Oxford: Blackwell.

Horowitz, R. E. (1939). Racial aspects of self-identification in nursery school children. *Journal of Psychology, 7,* 91–99.

Hovland, C. I., & Sears, R. R. (1940). Minor studies of aggression: VI. Correlation of lynching with economic indices. *Journal of Psychology, 9,* 301–310.

Hunter, J., Reid, J., Stokell, N., & Platow, M. (2000). Social attribution, self-esteem, and social identity. *Current Research in Social Psychology, 5,* 97–125.

Hutnik, N., & Sapru, S. (1996). The salience of ethnicity. *Journal of Social Psychology, 136,* 661–662.

Ichiyama, M., McQuarrie, E., & Ching, K. (1996). Contextual influences on ethnic identity among Hawaiian students in the mainland United States. *Journal of Cross-Cultural Psychology, 27,* 458–475.

Jasinskaja-Lahti, I., & Liebkind, K. (2001). Perceived discrimination and psychosocial adjustment among Russian-Speaking immigrant adolescents in Finland. *International Journal of Psychology, 36,* 174–186.

Jones, E. E., & Sigall, H. (1971). The bogus pipeline: A new paradigm for measuring affect and attitude. *Psychological Bulletin, 76,* 349–364.

Karlins, M., Coffman, T., & Walters, G. (1969). On the fading of social stereotypes: Studies in three generations of college students. *Journal of Personality and Social Psychology, 13,* 1–16.

Katz, D., & Braly, K. (1933). Racial stereotypes of one hundred college students. *Journal of Abnormal and Social Psychology, 28,* 280–290.

Katz, D., & Braly, K. (1935). Racial prejudice and racial stereotypes. *Journal of Abnormal and Social Psychology, 30,* 175–193.

Katz, P. (1987). Developmental and social process in ethnic attitudes and self-identification. In J. Phinney & M. J. Rotheram (Eds.), *Children's ethnic socialization: Pluralism and development* (pp. 92–99). London: Sage.

Keefe, S. E. (1980). Acculturation and the extended family among urban Mexican Americans. In A. Padilla (Ed.), *Acculturation: Theory, models and some new findings.* Boulder, CO: Westview Press.

Kinder, D. R., & Sears, D. O. (1981). Prejudice and politics: Symbolic racism versus racial threats to the good life. *Journal of Personality and Social Psychology, 40,* 414–431.

Kinket, B., & Verkuyten, M. (1997). Levels of ethnic self-identification and social context. *Social Psychology Quarterly, 60,* 338–354.

Klink, A., Mummendey, A., Mielke, R., & Blanz, M. (1997). *A multicomponent approach to group identification: Results from a field study in East Germany.* Jena: Unveröffentlichter Forschungsbericht des Lehrstuhls Sozialpsychologie, nr. 10.

Klink, A., & Wagner, U. (1999). Discrimination against ethnic minorities in Germany: Going back to the field. *Journal of Applied Social Psychology, 29,* 402–423.

Krause, N. (1983). The racial context of Black self-esteem. *Social Psychology Quarterly, 46,* 98–107.

Krueger, J. (1992). On the overestimation of between-group differences. In W. Stroebe & M. Hewstone (Eds.), *European review of social psychology* (vol. 3, pp. 31–56). Chichester: Wiley.

LaFromboise, T., Coleman, H., & Gerton, J. (1993). Psychological impact of biculturalism. *Psychological Bulletin, 114,* 395–412.

Lalonde, R., & Cameron, E. (1993). An intergroup perspective on immigrant acculturation with a focus on collective strategies. *International Journal of Psychology, 28* (1), 57–74.

Lambert, W. E., Mermigis, L., & Taylor, D. M. (1986). Greek Canadians' attitudes toward own group and other Canadian ethnic groups: A test of the multiculturalism hypothesis. *Canadian Journal of Behavioral Science, 18,* 35–51.

Lepore, L., & Brown, R. (1997). Category and stereotype activation: Is prejudice inevitable? *Journal of Personality and Social Psychology, 72,* 275–287.

Lewin, K. (1952). *Field theory in social science.* New York: Harper and Row.

Leyens, J. P., Yzerbyt, V., & Schadron, G. (1994). *Stereotypes and social cognition.* London: Sage.

Liebkind, K. (1996). Acculturation and stress: Vietnamese refugees in Finland. *Journal of Cross-Cultural Psychology, 27,* 161–180.

Lippmann, W. (1922). *Public opinion.* New York: Harcourt Brace.

Liu, J. H., Campbell, S. M., & Condie, H. (1995). Ethnocentrism in dating preferences for an American sample: The ingroup bias in social context. *European Journal of Social Psychology, 25,* 95–115.

Locke, V., & Walker, I. (1999). Stereotyping, processing goals, and social identity: Inveterate and fugacious characteristics of stereotypes. In D. Abrams & M. A. Hogg (Eds.), *Social identity and social cognition* (pp. 164–182). Oxford: Blackwell.

Lorenzi-Cioldi, F. (1998). Group status and perceptions of homogeneity. In W. Stroebe & M. Hewstone (Eds.), *European review of social psychology* (vol. 9, pp. 31–75). Chichester: Wiley.

Lorenzo-Hernández, J., & Ouellette, S. (1998). Ethnic identity, self-esteem, and values in Dominicans, Puerto Ricans, and African Americans. *Journal of Applied Social Psychology, 28,* 2007–2024.

Luhtanen, R., & Crocker, J. (1992). A collective self-esteem scale: Self evaluation of one's social identity. *Personality and Social Psychology Bulletin, 18,* 302–318.

Major, B., & Schmader, T. (1998). Coping with stigma trough psychological disengagement. In J. K. Swim & C. Stangor (Eds.), *Prejudice: The target's perspective* (pp. 219–241). San Diego: Academic Press.

Marcia, J. (1980). Identity in adolescence. In J. Adelson (Ed.), *Handbook of adolescent psychology* (pp. 159–187). New York: Wiley.

Marsh, H. W. (1996). Positive and negative global self-esteem: A substantively meaningful distinction or artifactors? *Journal of Personality and Social Psychology, 70*, 810–819.

Martinez, R., & Dukes, R. (1991). Ethnic and gender differences in self-esteem. *Youth & Society, 22*, 318–338.

Martinez, R., & Dukes, R. (1997). The effects of ethnic identity, ethnicity, and gender on adolescent well-being. *Journal of Youth and Adolescence, 26*, 503–516.

Maruyama, G. M. (1998). *Basics of structural equation modeling*. London: Sage.

Masson, C. N., & Verkuyten, M. (1993). Prejudice, ethnic identity, contact and ethnic group preferences among Dutch young adolescents. *Journal of Applied Social Psychology, 23*, 156–168.

McCauley, C., & Stitt, C. (1978). An individual and quantitative measure of stereotypes. *Journal of Personality and Social Psychology, 36*, 929–940.

McConahay, J. B. (1986). Modern racism, ambivalence, and the modern racism scale. In J. F. Dovidio & S. L. Gaertner (Eds.), *Prejudice, discrimination and racism* (pp. 91–126). Orlando, FL: Academic Press.

Mead, G. H. (1934). *Mind, self, and society*. Chicago: University of Chicago Press.

Meléndez, C. & Duncan, Q. (1981). *El negro en Costa Rica*. San José, C.R.: Editorial Costa Rica.

Meloen, J. (1993). The F Scale as predictor of fascism: An overview of 40 years of authoritarianism research. In W. Stone, G. Lederer, & R. Christie (Eds.), *Strength and weakness: The authoritarian personality today* (pp. 47–69). New York: Springer-Verlag.

Mielke, R. (1996, October). *Multidimensional models of acculturation attitudes: Testing the practicability in two different samples*. Paper presented at the third FIMO-Kolloquium, Florenz.

Milgram, S., Mann, L., & Harter, S. (1965). The lost-letter technique: A tool of social science research. *Public Opinion Quarterly, 29*, 437–438.

Mlicki, P., & Ellemers, N. (1996). Being different or being better? National stereotypes and identifications of Polish and Dutch students. *European Journal of Social Psychology, 26*, 97–114.

Mummendey, H., Bolten, H. G., & Isermann-Gerke, M. (1982). Experimentelle Überprüfung des Bogus-Pipeline-Paradigmas: Einstellungen gegenüber Türken, Deutschen and Holländern. *Zeitschrift für Sozialpsychologie, 13*, 300–311.

Nesdale, A. R., Dharmalingam, S., & Kerr, G. K. (1987). Effects of subgroup ratio on stereotyping. *European Journal of Social Psychology, 17*, 353–356.

Nesdale, D., Rooney, R., & Smith, L. (1997). Migrant ethnic identity and psychological distress. *Journal of Cross-Cultural Psychology, 28*, 569–588.

Nesdale, D., & Todd, P. (2000). Effect of contact on intercultural acceptance: A field study. *International Journal of Intercultural Relations, 24*, 341–360.

Neto, F. (1995). Predictors of satisfaction with life among second generation migrants. *Social Indicators Research, 35*, 93–116.

Oaks, P. J. (1996). The categorization process: Cognition and the group in the social psychology of stereotyping. In P. W. Robinson (Ed.), *Social groups & identities: Developing the legacy of Henri Tajfel* (pp. 95–120). Oxford: Butterworth-Heinemann.

Oaks, P. J., Haslam, A., & Reynolds, K. (1999). Social categorization and social context. In D. Abrams & M. A. Hogg (Eds.), *Social identity and social cognition* (pp. 55–79). Oxford: Blackwell.

Oaks, P. J., Haslam, A., & Turner, J. C. (1994). *Stereotyping and social reality*. Oxford: Blackwell.

Oskamp, S. (2000). Multiple paths to reducing prejudice and discrimination. In S. Oskamp (Ed.), *Reducing prejudice and discrimination* (pp. 1–19). Mahwah, NJ: Erlbaum.

Padilla, A. (1980). The role of cultural awareness and ethnic loyalty in acculturation. In A. Padilla (Ed.), *Acculturation: Theory, models and some new findings* (pp. 47–84). Boulder, CO: Westview Press.

Pettigrew, T. F. (1959). Regional differences in anti-Negro prejudice. *Journal of Abnormal and Social Psychology, 59*, 28–36.

Pettigrew, T. F. (1979). The ultimate attribution error: Extending Allport's cognitive analysis of prejudice. *Personality and Social Psychology Bulletin, 5*, 461–476.

Pettigrew, T. F. (1988). Integration and pluralism. In P. Katz & D. Taylor (Eds.), *Eliminating racism*. New York: Plenum.

Pettigrew. T. F. (1991). Discrimination. In E. Borgatta (Ed.), *Sociology* (vol. 3, pp. 498–503). New York: Macmillan.

Pettigrew, T. F. (1996). *How to think like a social scientist*. New York: HarperCollins.

Pettigrew, T. F. (1997). Generalized intergroup contact effects on prejudice. *Personality and Social Psychology Bulletin, 23*, 173–185.

Pettigrew, T. F. (1998). Intergroup contact theory. *Annual Review of Psychology, 49*, 65–85.

Pettigrew, T. F. (1999). Placing authoritarianism in social context. *Politics, Groups, and the Individual, 8*, 5–20.

Pettigrew, T. F. (2000, October). *Meta-analytic implications for a reformulation of intergroup contact theory*. Paper presented at the 2000 SESP Conference, Atlanta, GA.

Pettigrew, T. F., Jackson, J. S., Ben Brika, J., Lemaine, G., Meertens, R. W., Wagner, U., & Zick, A. (1998). Outgroup prejudice in Western Europe. In W. Stroebe & M. Hewstone (Eds.), *European review of social psychology* (vol. 8, pp. 241–273). Chichester: Wiley.

Pettigrew, T. F., & Meertens, R. W. (1995). Subtle and blatant prejudice in western Europe. *European Journal of Social Psychology, 25*, 57–75.

Pettigrew, T. F., & Meertens, R. W. (1996). The Verzuiling puzzle: Understanding Dutch intergroup relations. *Current Psychology: Developmental–Learning–Personality–Social, 15*, 3–13.

Pettigrew, T. F., & Tropp, L. R. (2000). Does intergroup contact reduce prejudice? Recent meta-analytic findings. In S. Oskamp (Ed.), *Reducing prejudice and discrimination* (pp. 93–115). Mahwah, NJ: Lawrence Erlbaum.

Phinney, J. (1989). Stage of ethnic identity development in minority group adolescents. *Journal of Early Adolescence, 9*, 34–49.

Phinney, J. (1990). Ethnic identity in adolescents and adults: Review of research. *Psychological Bulletin, 108*, 499–514.

Phinney, J. (1991). Ethnic identity and self-esteem: A review and integration. *Hispanic Journal of Behavioral Sciences, 13*, 193–208.

Phinney, J. (1992). The multi-group ethnic identity measure: A new scale for use with adolescents and young adults from diverse groups. *Journal of Adolescent Research, 7*, 156–176.

Phinney, J., & Alpuria, L. (1990). Ethnic identity in college students from four ethnic groups. *Journal of Adolescence, 13*, 171–183.

Phinney, J., & Alpuria, L. (1996). At the interface of cultures: Multiethnic/multiracial high school and college students. *Journal of Social Psychology, 136*, 139–158.

Phinney, J., Cantu, C. L., & Kurtz, D. A. (1997). Ethnic and American identity as predictors of self-esteem among African American, Latino and White adolescents. *Journal of Youth and Adolescence, 26*, 165–185.

Phinney, J., & Chavira, V. (1992). Ethnic identity and self-esteem: An exploratory longitudinal study. *Journal of Adolescence, 15*, 271–281.

Phinney, J., Chavira, V., & Tate, J. (1993). The effect of ethnic threat on ethnic self-concept and own-group ratings. *Journal of Social Psychology, 133*, 469–478.

Phinney, J., Chavira, V., & Williamson, L. (1992). Acculturation attitudes and self-esteem among high school and college students. *Youth and Society, 23* (3), 299–312.

Phinney, J., & Devich-Navarro, M. (1997). Variations in bicultural identification among African American and Mexican American adolescents. *Journal of Research on Adolescence, 7*, 3–32.

Phinney, J., Ferguson, D., & Tate, J. (1997). Intergroup attitudes among ethnic minority adolescents: A causal model. *Child-Development, 68*, 955–969.

Phinney, J., Madden, T., & Santos, L. (1998). Psychological variables as predictors of perceived ethnic discriminations among minority and immigrant adolescents. *Journal of Applied Social Psychology, 28*, 937–953.

Phinney, J., & Rosenthal, D. (1992). Ethnic identity in adolescence: Process, context, and outcomes. In G. Adams, T. Gullota, & R. Montemayor (Eds.), *Adolescent identity formation* (pp. 145–172). London: Sage.

Phinney, J., & Tarver, S. (1988). Ethnic identity search and commitment in Black and White eighth graders. *Journal of Early Adolescence, 8*, 265–277.

Piaget, J., & Inhelder, B. (1968). *The growth of logical thinking from childhood to adolescence: An essay on the construction of formal operational structures.* London: Routledge and Kegan Paul.

Piontkowski, U., Florack, A., Hoelker, P., & Obdrzálek, P. (2000). Predicting acculturation attitudes of dominant and non-dominant groups. *International Journal of Intercultural Relations, 24*, 1–26.

Polat, Ü. (1998). *Soziale und kulturelle Identität türkischer Migranten der zweiten Generation in Deutschland.* Hamburg: Kovac.

Porter, J. R., & Washington, R. E. (1982). Black identity and self-esteem: A review of studies of Black self-concept 1968–1978. In M. Rosenberg & H. B. Kaplan (Eds.), *Social psychology of the self-concept* (pp. 224–234). Arlington Heights, IL: Harlan Davidson.

Portera, A. (1985). Die kulturelle Identität italienischer Jugendlicher in Deuthscland. Empirische Untersuchung über psycho-soziale Situation und sozio-kulturelle Orientierung italienischer Jugendlicher in Freiburg. *Ausländerkinder: Forum für Schule & Sozialpädagogik, 21–24*, 4–22.

Projecto Estado de La Nación. (1998). *El estado de la nación.* San José: Editorial Costa Rica.

Qualls, R. C., Cox, M. B., & Schehr, T. L. (1992). Racial attitudes on campus: Are there gender differences? *Journal of College Student Development, 33*, 524–530.

Ramsey, P. (1987). Young children's thinking about ethnic differences. In J. Phinney & M. J. Rotheram (Eds.), *Children's ethnic socialization: Pluralism and development* (pp. 56–72). London: Sage.

Redfield, R., Linton, R., & Herskovits, M. J. (1936). Memorandum on the study of acculturation. *American Anthropologist, 38*, 149–152.

Rich, Y., Kedem, P., & Shlesinger, A. (1995). Enhancing intergroup relations among children: A field test of the Miller–Brewer model. *International Journal of Intercultural Relations, 19*, 539–553.

Rivera-Sinclair, E. (1997). Acculturation/biculturalism and its relationship to adjustment in Cuban-Americans. *International Journal of Intercultural Relations, 21*, 379–391.

Robinson, J., Shaver, P., & Wrightsman, L. (1991). *Measures of personality and social psychologial attitudes*. London: Academic Press.

Roccas, S., Horenczyk, G., & Schwartz, S. (2000). Acculturation discrepancies and well-being: The moderating role of conformity. *European Journal of Social Psychology, 30*, 323–334.

Rogler, L., Cortes, D., & Malgady, R. (1991). Acculturation and mental health status among Hispanics: Convergence and new directions for research. *American Psychologist, 46*, 585–597.

Rosenberg, M. (1965). *Society and the adolescent self-image*. Princeton, NJ: Princeton University Press.

Rosenberg, M., & Kaplan, H. B. (1982). *Social psychology of the self-concept*. Arlington Heights, IL: Harlan Davidson.

Rosenberg, M., & Pearlin, L. I. (1978). Social class and self-esteem among children and adults. *American Journal of Sociology, 84*, 53–77.

Rosenberg, M., & Simmons, R. (1972). *Black and White self-esteem: The urban school child*. Washington, DC: American Sociological Association.

Rosenthal, D. A., & Cichello, A. M. (1986). The meeting of two cultures: Ethnic identity and psychological adjustment of Italian-Australian adolescents. *International Journal of Psychology, 21*, 487–501.

Rosenthal, D. A., & Feldman, S. (1992). The nature and stability of ethnic identity in Chinese youths: Effects of length of residence in two cultural contexts. *Journal of Cross-Cultural Psychology, 23*, 214–227.

Rosenthal, D. A., Gurney, R., & Moore, S. (1981). From trust to intimacy: A new inventory for examining Erikson's stages of psychosocial development. *Journal of Youth and Adolescence, 10*, 525–537.

Rosenthal, D. A., & Hrynevich, C. (1985). Ethnicity and ethnic identity: A comparative study of Greek-, Italian-, and Anglo-Australian adolescents. *International Journal of Psychology, 20*, 723–742.

Rosenthal, D. A., Whittle, J., & Bell, R. (1989). The dynamic nature of ethnic identity among Greek-Australian adolescents. *Journal of Social Psychology, 129*, 249–258.

Rubin, M., & Hewstone, M. (1998). Social identity theory's self-esteem hypothesis: A review and some suggestions for clarification. *Personality and Social Psychology Review, 2*, 40–62.

Ruiz, A. (1988). *Racismo algo más que discriminación*. San José, C.R.: Editorial DEI.

Runciman, W. G. (1966). *Relative deprivation and social justice*. Berkeley and Los Angeles: University of California Press.

Ryder, A. G., Alden, L. E., & Paulhus, D. L. (2000). Is acculturation unidimensional or bidimensional? A head-to-head comparison in the prediction of personality, self-identity and adjustment. *Journal of Personality and Social Psychology, 79*, 49–65.

Sawyers, K., & Perry, F. (1996). Los Afrocentroamericanos: Redescubrimiento de la herencia africana. Costa Rica. In Minority Rights Group (MRG) (Ed.), *Los Afrocentroamericanos: El redescubrimiento de la herencia africana* (pp. 54–62). San José, C.R.: MRG.

Sayegh, L., & Lasry, J. C. (1993). Immigrants' adaptation in Canada: Assimilation, acculturation, and orthogonal cultural identification. *Canadian Psychology, 34*, 98–109.

Schmitt, M., Branscombe, N., Kobrynowicz, D., & Owen, S. (2002). Perceiving gender discrimination: Perceiving discrimination agains one's gender group has different implications for well-being in women and men. *Personality and Social Psychology Bulletin, 28*, 197–210.

Segall, M. H., Dasen, P. R., Berry, J. W., & Portinga, Y. H. (1990). *Human behavior in global perspective: An introduction to cross-cultural psychology*. New York: Pergamon.

Sellers, R. M., Smith, M. S., Shelton, J. N., Rowley, S. A., & Chavous, T. M. (1998). Multidimensional model of racial identity: A reconceptualization of African American identity. *Personality and Social Psychology Bulletin, 2*, 18–39.

Sherif, M. (1979). Superordinate goals in the reduction of intergroup conflict: An experimental evaluation. In S. Worchel & W. G. Austin (Eds.), *The social psychology of intergroup relations* (pp. 257–261). Monterrey, CA: Brooks/Cole.

Sherif, M., Harvey, O., White, B., Hood., W., & Sherif, C. (1961). *Intergroup conflict and cooperation: The Robbers' Cave experiment*. Norman: University of Oklahoma Press.

Sherif, M., & Sherif, C. (1979). Research on intergroup relations. In W. S. Austin & S. Worchel (Eds.), *The social psychology of intergroup relations* (pp. 7–18). Monterey, CA: Brooks/Cole.

Sigall, H., & Page, R. (1971). Current stereotypes: A little fading, a little faking. *Journal of Personality and Social Psychology, 18*, 247–255.

Simon, B. (1992). The perception of ingroup and outgroup homogeneity: Reintroducing the intergroup context. In W. Stroabe & M. Hewstone (Eds.), *European review of social psychology* (vol. 3, pp. 1–30). Chichester: Wiley.

Social Science Research Council Summer Seminar. (1954). Acculturation: An exploratory formulation. *American Anthropologist, 56*, 973–1002.

Sommerland, E., & Berry, J. W. (1970). The role of ethnic identification in distinguishing between attitudes towards assimilation and integration of a minority racial group. *Human Relations, 23*, 23–29.

Spears, R., Doojse, B., & Ellemers, N. (1997). Self-stereotyping in the face of threats to group status and distinctiveness. *Personality and Social Psychology Bulletin, 23*, 538–553.

Stangor, C., Sullivan, L., & Ford, T. (1991). Affective and cognitive determinants of prejudice. *Social Cognition, 9*, 359–380.

Stephan, W. G., & Stephan, C. W. (1984). The role of ignorance in intergroup relations. In N. Miller & N. B. Brewer (Eds.), *Groups in contact: The psychology of desegregation* (pp. 229–255). Orlando, FL: Academic Press.

Stephan, W. G., Ybarra, O., & Bachman, G. (1999). Prejudice toward immigrants. *Journal of Applied Social Psychology, 29*, 2221–2237.

Stephan, W. G., Ybarra, O., Martinez, C., Schwarzwald, J., & Tur-Kaspa, M. (1998). Prejudice toward immigrants to Spain and Israel: An integrated threat theory analysis. *Journal of Cross-Cultural Psychology, 29*, 559–576.

Stephan, W. S., & Stephan C. W. (2000). An integrated threat theory of prejudice. In S. Oskamp (Ed.), *Reducing prejudice and discrimination* (pp. 23–45). Mahwah, NJ: Lawrence Erlbaum.

Stone, W., Lederer, G., & Christie, R. (1993). Introduction: Strength and weakness. In W. Stone, G. Lederer, & R. Christie (Eds.), *Strength and weakness: The authoritarian personality today* (pp. 3–21). New York: Springer-Verlag.

Sumner, W. G. (1906). *Folkways: A study of the sociological importance of uses, manners, customs, more and morals.* Boston: Ginn.

Szapocznik, J., Kurtines, W. M., & Fernández, T. (1980). Bicultural involvement and adjustment in Hispanic-American youths. *International Journal of Intercultural Relations, 4*, 353–365.

Szapocznik, J., Scopetta, M., Kurtines, W., & Aranalde, M. (1978). Theory and measurement of acculturation. *Interamerican Journal of Psychology, 12*, 113–130.

Tajfel, H. (1978). Interindividual behavior and intergroup behavior. In H. Tajfel (Ed.), *Differentiation between social groups* (pp. 27–60). London: Academic Press.

Tajfel, H. (1981). *Human groups and social categories: Studies in social psychology.* Cambridge: Cambridge University Press.

Tajfel, H., & Turner, J. (1979). An integrative theory of intergroup conflict. In S. Worchel & W. G. Austin (Eds.), *The social psychology of intergroup relations* (pp. 33–47). Monterey, CA: Brooks/Cole.

Taylor, S. E. (1981). A categorization approach to stereotyping. In D. L. Hamilton (Ed.), *Cognitive processes in stereotyping and intergroup behavior* (pp. 88–114). Hillsdale, NJ: Erlbaum.

Taylor, S. E., Fiske, S. T., Etcoff, N. L., & Ruderman, A. J. (1978). Categorical and contextual bases of person memory and stereotyping. *Journal of Personality and Social Psychology, 36*, 778–793.

Triandis, H., Bontempo, K., Villareal, M., Asai, M., & Lucca, N. (1988). Individualism and collectivism: Cross-cultural perspectives on self-ingroup relationships. *Journal of Personality and Social Psychology, 54*, 232–338.

Triandis, H., Kashima, Y., Shimada, E., & Villareal, M. (1986). Acculturation indices as a means of confirming cultural differences. *International Journal of Psychology, 21*, 43–70.

Turner, J. C. (1975). Social comparison and social identity: Some prospects for intergroup behavior. *European Journal of Social Psychology, 5*, 5–34.

Turner, J. C. (1996). Hanri Tajfel: An introduction. In W. P. Robinson (Ed.), *Social groups & identities: Developing the legacy of Henri Tajfel* (pp. 1–24). Oxford: Butterworth-Heinemann.

Turner, J. C. (1999). Some current issues in research on social identity and self-categorization theories. In N. Ellemers, R. Spears, & B. Doosje (Eds.), *Social identity: Context, commitment, content* (pp. 6–34). Oxford: Blackwell.

Turner, J. C., Hogg, M. A., Oaks, P. J., Reicher, S. D., & Wetherell, M. S. (1987). *Rediscovering the social group: A self-categorization theory.* Oxford: Blackwell.

Turner, J. C., Oaks, P. J., Haslam, A., & McGarty, C. (1994). Self and collective: Cognition and social context. *Personality and Social Psychology Bulletin, 20,* 454–463.

Tzeng, O. C., & Jackson, J. W. (1994). Effects of contact, conflict and social identity on interethnic group hostilities. *International Journal of Intergroup Relations, 18,* 259–276.

van Dick, R. (1999). *Streß und Arbeitszufriedenheit im Lehrerberuf: Eine Analyse von Belastung und Beanspruchung im Kontext sozialpsychologischer, klinisch-psychologischer und organisationspsychologischer Konzepte.* Marburg: Tectum.

van Dick, R. (2001). *Identification in organizational contexts: Linking theory and research from social and organizational psychology.* Manuscript under review.

van Dick, R., & Wagner, U. (1995). *Ergebnisse einer Befragung von Zivildienstleistenden im Januar 1995.* Unveröffentlichtes Dokument. Philipps-Universität Marburg.

van Dick, R., & Wagner, U. (2001). *Group identification among school teachers: Dimensions, foci, and correlates.* Manuscript under review.

van Dick, R., Wagner, U., Adams, C., & Petzel, T. (1997). Einstellungen zur Akkulturation: Erste Evaluation eines Fragebogens an sechs deutschen Stichproben. *Gruppendynamik, 28,* 83–92.

van Dick, R., Wagner, U., Pettigrew, T. F., Christ, O., Petzel, T., Smith-Castro, V., & Jackson, J. S. (2001). *Contact hypothesis revisited: The role of perceived importance.* Manuscript under review.

van Knippenberg, A., & Ellemers, N. (1990). Social identity and differentiation processes. In W. Stroebe & M. Hewstone (Eds.), *European review of social psychology* (vol. 1, pp. 137–169). Chichester: Wiley.

van Oudenhoven, J. P., & Eisses, A. M. (1998). Integration and assimilation of Moroccan immigrants in Israel and The Netherlands. *International Journal of Intercultural Relations, 22,* 293–307.

Vanneman, R. D., & Pettigrew, T. F. (1972). Race and relative deprivation in the urban United States. *Race, 13,* 461–486.

Vaughan, G. (1987). A social psychological model of ethnic identity development. In J. Phinney & M. J. Rotheram (Eds.), *Children's ethnic socialization: Pluralism and development* (pp. 73–91). London: Sage.

Verkuyten, M. (1986). Impact of ethnic and sex differences on global self-esteem among adolescents in The Netherlands. *Psychological Reports, 59,* 446.

Verkuyten, M. (1990). Self-esteem and the evaluation of ethnic identity among Turkish and Dutch adolescents in The Netherlands. *Journal of Social Psychology, 130,* 285–297.

Verkuyten, M. (1992). Ethnic group preferences and the evaluation of ethnic identity among adolescents in The Netherlands. *Journal of Social Psychology, 132,* 741–750.

Verkuyten, M. (1995). Self-esteem, self-concept stability, and aspects of ethnic identity among minority and majority youth in The Netherlands. *Journal of Youth and Adolescence, 24,* 155–175.

Verkuyten, M. (1997a). Discourses of ethnic minority identity. *British Journal of Social Psychology, 36,* 565–586.

Verkuyten, M. (1997b). The structure of ethnic attitudes: The effects of target group, region, gender, and national identity. *Genetic, Social, and General Psychology Monographs, 123,* 261–284.

Verkuyten, M., & Lay, C. (1998). Ethnic minority identity and psychological well-being: The mediating role of collective self-esteem. *Journal of Applied Social Psychology, 28,* 1969–1986.

Wagner, U. (1983). *Soziale Schichtszugehörigkeit, formales Bildungsniveau und ethnische Vorurteile.* Berlin: EXpress.

Wagner, U. (1994). *Eine sozialpsychologische Analyse von Intergruppenbeziehungen.* Göttingen: Hogrefe.

Wagner, U., Hewstone, M., & Machleit, U. (1989). Contact and prejudice between Germans and Turks: A correlational study. *Human Relations, 42,* 561–574.

Wagner, U., Lampen, L., & Syllwasschy, J. (1986). In-group inferiority, social identity and outgroup devaluation in a modified minimal group study. *British Journal of Social Psychology, 25,* 15–23.

Wagner, U., van Dick, R., Pettigrew, T. F., & Christ, O. (2001). *Ethnic prejudice in East and West Germany: The explanatory power of intergroup contact.* Manuscript under review.

Wagner, U., & Zick, A. (1995). The relation of formal education to ethnic prejudice: Its realiability, validity, and explanation. *European Journal of Social Psychology, 25,* 41–56.

Walker, I., & Pettigrew, T. F. (1984). Relative deprivation theory: An overview and conceptual critique. *British Journal of Social Psychology, 23,* 301–310.

Ward, C., & Kennedy, A. (1993). Where's the "culture" in cross-cultural transition: Comparative studies of sojourner adjustment. *Journal of Cross-Cultural Psychology, 24,* 221–249.

Ward, C., & Kennedy, A. (1994). Acculturation strategies, psychological adjustment, and sociocultural competence during cross-cultural transitions. *International Journal of Intercultural Relations, 18,* 329–343.

Ward, C., & Rana-Deuba, A. (1999). Acculturation and adaptation revisited. *Journal of Cross-Cultural Psychology, 30,* 422–442.

Watts, M. W. (1996). Political xenophobia in the transition from socialism: Threat, racism and ideology among East German youth. *Political Psychology, 17,* 97–126.

Williams, C. L., & Berry, J. W. (1991). Primary prevention of acculturative stress among refugees: Application of psychological theory and practice. *American Psychologist, 46,* 632–641.

Woodmansee, J., & Cook, S. (1967). Dimensions of verbal racial attitudes: Their identification and measurement. *Journal of Personality and Social Psychology, 7,* 240–250.

Wylie, R. (1979). *The self-concept.* Lincoln: University of Nebraska Press.

Zick, A. (1997). *Vorurteile und Rassismus: Eine sozialpychologische Analyse.* Berlin: Waxmann.

Zirkel, P. A., & Moses, E. G. (1971). Self-concept and ethnic group membership among public school students. *American Educational Research Journal, 8,* 253–265.

Index

About the Author

VANESSA SMITH CASTRO is a researcher at the Institutes for Social and Psychological Research of the University of Costa Rica.